CW00376070

Hitler's Jihadis

HITLER'S
JIHADIS

MUSLIM VOLUNTEERS OF THE WAFFEN-SS

Jonathan Trigg

SPELLMOUNT

First published 2008
This edition published in 2012
By Spellmount, an imprint of
The History Press
The Mill, Brimscombe Port
Stroud, Gloucestershire, GL5 2QG
www.thehistorypress.co.uk

© Jonathan Trigg, 2008, 2012

The right of Jonathan Trigg to be identified as the Author
of this work has been asserted in accordance with the
Copyrights, Designs and Patents Act 1988.

All rights reserved. No part of this book may be reprinted
or reproduced or utilised in any form or by any electronic,
mechanical or other means, now known or hereafter invented,
including photocopying and recording, or in any information
storage or retrieval system, without the permission in writing
from the Publishers.

British Library Cataloguing in Publication Data.
A catalogue record for this book is available from the British Library.

ISBN 978 0 7524 6586 9

Typesetting and origination by The History Press
Printed in the EU for The History Press.

Contents

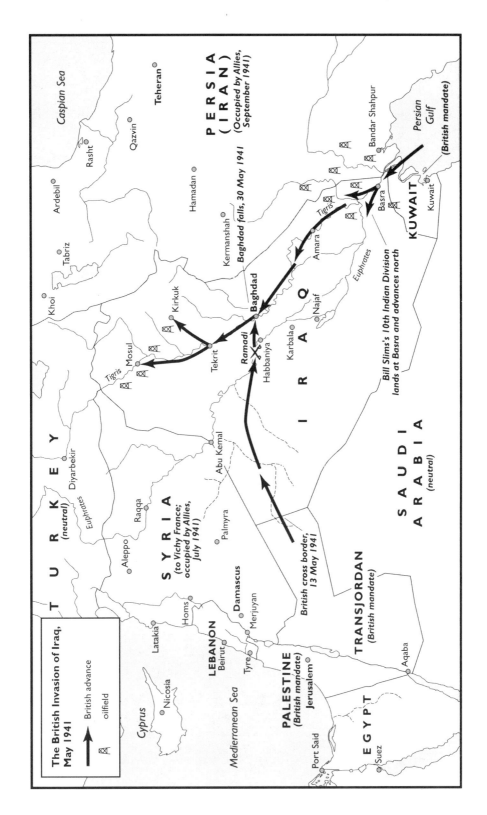

The British Invasion of Iraq, May 1941

→ British advance

⬣ oilfield

Caspian Sea

PERSIA (IRAN) (Occupied by Allies, September 1941)

Teheran

Qazvin

Rasht

Ardebil

Hamadan

Tabriz

Kermanshah

Baghdad falls, 30 May 1941

Khoi

Diyarbekir

TURKEY (neutral)

Kirkuk

Baghdad

Tigris

Mosul

Tekrit

Ramadi

Habbaniya

Karbala

Najaf

Amara

Euphrates

Tigris

Bandar Shahpur

Basra

KUWAIT

Kuwait

Persian Gulf (British mandate)

Bill Slims's 10th Indian Division lands at Basra and advances north

I R A Q

Euphrates

Raqqa

Aleppo

Abu Kemal

Palmyra

SYRIA (to Vichy France; occupied by Allies, July 1941)

S A U D I   A R A B I A (neutral)

British cross border, 13 May 1941

Damascus

Merjuyan

Homs

Latakia

LEBANON

Beirut

Tyre

TRANSJORDAN (British mandate)

Aqaba

Nicosia

Cyprus

Mediterranean Sea

PALESTINE (British mandate)

Jerusalem

EGYPT

Port Said

Suez

7

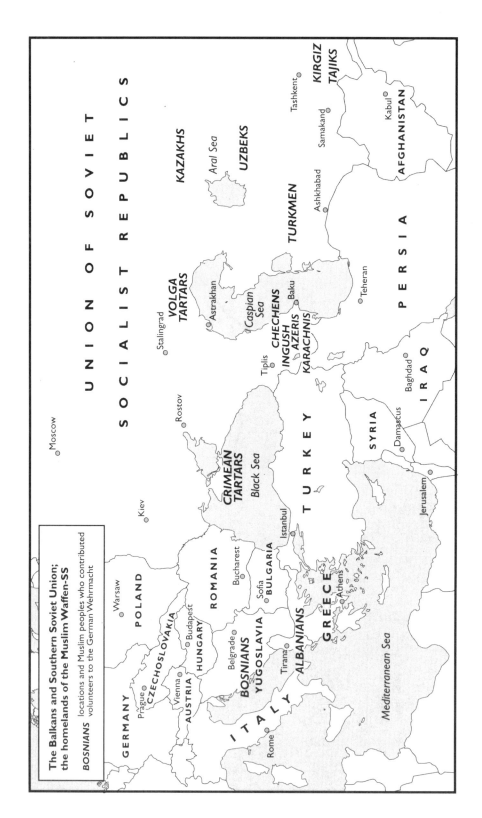

The Balkans and Southern Soviet Union; the homelands of the Muslim Waffen-SS

BOSNIANS locations and Muslim peoples who contributed volunteers to the German Wehrmacht

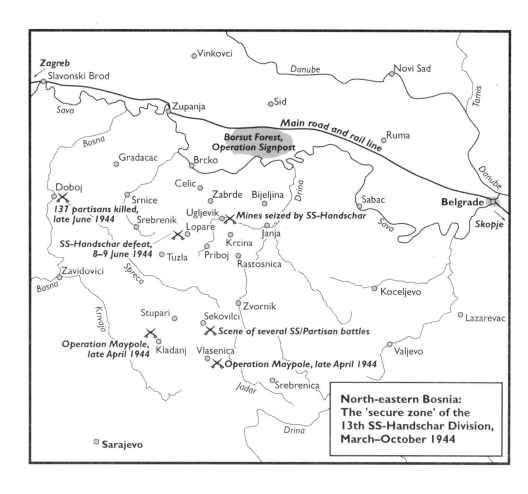

Vinkovci

Danube

Novi Sad

Zagreb
Slavonski Brod

Sava

Zupanja

Sid

Main road and rail line

Ruma

Bosna

Gradacac

Brcko

*Borsut Forest,
Operation Signpost*

Danube

Doboj

Celic

Zabrde   Bijeljina

Drina

Sabac

Belgrade

✗
*137 partisans killed,
late June 1944*

Srnice

Ugljevik

✗*Mines seized by SS-Handschar*

Sava

Skopje

Srebrenik

Lopare

Janja

*SS-Handschar defeat,
8–9 June 1944*

✗

Tuzla   Priboj

Krcina

Rastosnica

Zavidovici

Spreca

Koceljevo

Bosna

Krivaja

Stupari

Sekovilci

Zvornik

Lazarevac

✗

✗*Scene of several SS/Partisan battles*

*Operation Maypole,
late April 1944*

Kladanj

Vlasenica

Valjevo

✗*Operation Maypole, late April 1944*

Jadar

Srebrenica

Drina

North-eastern Bosnia:
The 'secure zone' of the
13th SS-Handschar Division,
March–October 1944

Sarajevo

Acknowledgements

I would like to express my thanks to a number of people, without whose help and support this book would never have been written. First to the surviving Muslim and non-Muslim veterans themselves from the huge array of formations covered in this book. The fate of many Waffen-SS survivors after the War was often harsh and sometimes arbitrary, but whereas in the West retribution most often came in the guise of judicial punishment such as imprisonment and loss of civil rights, in the East it was a different story. Put bluntly, most survivors of the fighting didn't survive the peace. Stalin and Tito did their level best to exterminate their fellow countrymen who had fought against them. As those familiar with the first two volumes in the series will know, in them I follow the lives and wartime careers of members of the units I cover from pre-War, through recruitment and training, to combat and the end of hostilities. This has not been possible in this volume, as no single formation is the theme of the book and post-War retribution so seriously denuded the ranks of men able and willing to talk about their experiences. For those that lived through the immediate post-War bloodbath it is a consequence of time that their numbers dwindle year by year, but as ever, without the help and patience of the veterans in answering endless questions on obscure details that happened more than 60 years ago this book would have been impossible to write. Thanks yet again to Frau Carina Notzke at the Bundesarchiv in Freiburg, and a new friend at the archive in Koblenz, Frau Martina Caspers. My pigeon German is not improving but they still humour me and have been enormously helpful.

To Shaun at The History Press for never stopping pushing, and a massive thanks to the printing version of Gandalf the Wizard, my best friend

Tim at County Print on the photographic side, you can make magic out of mud, it really does make all the difference. My research was made much more interesting and easier by the internet. There is a vast community online that is all networked together, and there is almost always 'someone who knows someone' who can help with any topic. Some of the best resources out there are military history websites and their users, two of the finest being Troy Tempest's www.feldpost.tv/forum and Jason Pipes's team at www.feldgrau.net, to them a heartfelt thanks. One of an author's greatest challenges in military history is the issue of finding photographs that are both interesting and illustrative of the text, and maybe even to find the ever elusive but always worthwhile goal of pictures that haven't been published before. As always people have been very kind with both their time and treasured possessions, so my thanks to the ever informative and knowledgeable James Mcleod in particular, to Mr R. P. Croston and Bruno Beger PhD, as well as Ostbataillon 43, Sandtrooper and Rene Chavez.

Special thanks goes to George Lepre, whose book on the SS-Handschar Division is by far the most definitive text on that misunderstood and little regarded formation, and who in my opinion has set new standards in writing objectively on such a controversial topic.

Several people helped me with proof reading and have helped with the text, made suggestions and amendments and corrected mistakes to improve the writing and flow, for that I thank them, and whilst I have of course made every effort to achieve accuracy if there are any mistakes then they are entirely my own.

Thank you as well to everyone who has bought and read *Hitler's Gauls* and *Hitler's Flemish Lions*, I hope that this third instalment does not disappoint. This has been without a doubt the hardest volume to research and write but that in itself has been hugely rewarding.

As ever I must pay tribute to the amazing resilience of my beautiful wife who I am trying desperately to convert into a fan of military history … one day darling! And specifically for school 'show and tell' in Lydgate here is a big mention for our two incredible children, Maddy and Jack, they have even started to read my books and are on page 5 of *Hitler's Gauls*, bless them! But as Maddy always says, 'It's alright dad but it's not as good as Paul Jennings!'

Notes on the Text

Military ranks: Waffen-SS ranks are used throughout for Waffen-SS personnel. A conversion chart to comparative British Army ranks has been provided as Appendix B. For officers and soldiers of the German Army (*Heer*) their ranks are given in firstly their original German and then the British Army equivalents in brackets. Red Army and Partisan ranks are given directly in British Army terms.

Military terminology: As far as possible the military terminology used is that of the time and the army involved, on occasion an attempt has been made to 'translate' that terminology into modern British Army parlance in order to aid understanding.

Unit designation: All German orders of battle use the original unit designation of the time and then an English translation e.g. *Gebirgs Korps* is followed by Mountain Corps in brackets, and this is continued throughout except in certain circumstances where it is further simplified to improve the flow of the text or to establish authenticity, as in the relevant chapter titles. Again, to remain true to the time, Russian and Yugoslav Partisan formations are numbered, while German formations at corps or army level are either written or use the original Roman numerals. Smaller units such as divisions and regiments are numbered.

Foreign words: Where non-English words are used they are italicised unless in common usage and English translations are either given before or immediately afterwards. If then used often in the text they are no longer italicised.

Measurements: Distances are given in miles but weapon calibres are given in their usual metric form.

Place names: Particularly as regards places in the Balkans and the Soviet Union I have stuck with one spelling if there are several, mostly the one in common usage at the time, but have also tried initially to include other derivations in brackets to aid the reader following the ebb and flow of campaigns on any modern maps they may have.

Serbo-Croat: German has its umlauts, French has its accents, and Serbo-Croat has its own inflections as well, however as they are less well known than their western European counterparts I have not used them but have instead used English spelling to indicate the correct pronunciation when appropriate, e.g. the royalist Serb resistance movement led by Draza Mihailovic were the 'cetniks', the pronunciation of the 'c' is a 'ch', so I have spelt it as 'chetniks'. I apologise to any Serbo-Croat speakers who balks at my simplicity or litany of linguistic mistakes!

Names of peoples: Particularly as regards the names of the Muslim peoples of the former Soviet Union I have tried to use the most commonly accepted name, so I have used the Crimean Tartars, for instance, instead of the other form, 'Tatars'.

Introduction

This book, the third in the 'Hitler's Legions' series, is a significant departure from its predecessors which dealt firstly with a single nationality, the French volunteers of the SS-Charlemagne in *Hitler's Gauls*, and secondly with the ethnic Flemings of the the SS-Langemarck in *Hitler's Flemish Lions*. This book, in contrast, seeks not to document a single nation or ethnic group and its contribution to the uniformed German war effort and the Waffen-SS in particular, but to bring together in one volume the entire panoply of different formations and units fighting on a plethora of fronts who shared one common, defining bond: adherence to Islam.

I have done this for several compelling reasons, not least of which is that it was the religion of the different people involved that was key to their recruitment in the first place. The men involved weren't recruited despite their religion, but primarily *because* of it. The story of how Nazism, a political ideology entirely based on the absurd belief in north-western European racial superiority, could enthusiastically open its arms to tens of thousands of men from Muslim communities scattered across the Balkans, the southern Soviet Union and through to the Indian sub-continent, is one of the strangest episodes to emerge from the Second World War.

My interest in the Muslims who served in the Waffen-SS was first stirred when reading Rupert Butler's history of the Waffen-SS, *The Black Angels*. In it Butler quickly glossed over the Muslims in the Waffen-SS but in a few lines he did write, he made one comment that stood out from the rest: 'Himmler was later to admit that the only solid achievement of the SS training [in this case referring to the Bosnian Muslim SS-Handschar Divison] was to stop the Muslims from stealing from one another.'

This assertion simultaneously repelled and intrigued me, and has done ever since. As a serving British Army officer, several years after reading this book, I had the good fortune to be posted to a country in the Middle East on what is termed by the British Army, 'loan service'. For those unfamiliar with this long standing practice it is where officers and senior NCOs are sent to train and support the armies of allied foreign governments. My appointment was initially to head up their NCO Training School, but this soon widened to include the Skill-at-Arms School and various other functions. In this command appointment I was lucky enough to be ably assisted by five incredibly competent British senior NCOs from both the Army and the Royal Marines (one of them, an ex-Household Division Regimental Sergeant-Major, had even converted to Islam) and also by over 80 Muslim instructors from the home nation and from countries across the region. The students of course were all Muslims, mostly Bedouin descendants barely two generations away from their desert-dwelling forebears. Throughout my time working with these soldiers I found them to display certain general flaws, especially as regards lack of discipline, but also to exhibit a strong willingness to learn and be led. Poor native officers were however in the majority. The soldiers we turned out of the training schools may not have been world beaters but neither were they somehow pathologically inclined to military ineptitude or the commission of war crimes.

However the basic tenet of Butler's commentary on Heinrich Himmler's attempts to recruit Muslim troops to fight the Nazis' enemies was that it was a conspicuous and miserable failure. Significantly, not only was it a failure, but more precisely it was a military failure. This clarification is important because the Waffen-SS prided itself first and foremost on its ability and reputation as an élite fighting force. Hitler's Black Guards were, without a shred of doubt, completely devoted to the pursuit of excellence in arms. Therefore, for them to expend such a significant amount of effort – and make the effort of will – that would be necessary to overturn their own cherished theories of supposed Nordic racial superiority and follow through with the recruiting, training, equipping and leading of more than four entire divisions of Muslim troops for nil military return is simply incredible.

After all, the hard bitten officer and NCO veterans of the Waffen-SS had taken tens of thousands of young men from almost every corner of Europe and forged them into formations such as the SS Divisions Wiking, Nordland and Nederland, all famed for their bravery and superior fighting skills. If Butler is to be believed why then was this not the case for the Muslims in the Waffen-SS? Further to that, why did Himmler and his henchmen not learn from their initial experience if it was a disaster?

Those four Muslim SS divisions, as well as several smaller formations, were not all raised at once. The only reasonable answer has to be that the story of Muslims in the Waffen-SS is of far greater complexity than has been previously been acknowledged.

But trying to come to grips with the real story is extremely difficult, to say the least. Any reading of an anthology of the Waffen-SS during the War rarely does anything more than touch on its Muslim formations, and details are scarce, as most works simply parrot the same old tired comments. The picture painted is almost always one of near universal contempt, not only for the idea itself but overwhelmingly for the Muslim combat record, or rather the lack of it. The Muslim SS units are derided not only for their lack of military prowess but also their seemingly appalling record of war crimes. Butler again: 'When the Division [SS-Handschar] was sent to France, its first action was a flat refusal to fight. Instead, it fell with dreadful glee on defenceless Christians and massacred scores of them.' If true, this would be a shocking indictment both of Himmler's policy and the behaviour of the volunteers themselves. But then why would Bosnian Muslims commit mass murder against French Catholics? If Christianity itself were a good enough reason for murder then why did the Muslims volunteer to serve with the ostensibly Christian Germans? Himmler may well have tried to make the Waffen-SS a pseudo-pagan organisation but the reality was that a significant minority of Waffen-SS men stubbornly clung onto their Christianity regardless of Himmler's ramblings about mystical oak groves. Leaving that baffling inconsistency aside it would seem from most writers that as soon as a Muslim SS formation was given arms they used them not to fight an armed enemy but to butcher the nearest helpless civilians, and that they in fact represented the very worst excesses of the Waffen-SS.

The second, and more controversial, reason I have been drawn to chronicling the Muslim Waffen-SS is that there are some parallels, though by no means are they universal, with the rise of militant Islam in recent years. Al-Quaeda did not spring from the same well as the volunteers in the Handschar, Skanderbeg or any other Waffen-SS formation, but it is probably fair to say that it has tapped into some of the same motivations of real or perceived community persecution, religious suppression, and pan-Islamic solidarity that saw thousands of young Muslim men don Nazi Germany's field grey in the dark days of the early 1940s.

A third more prosaic and practical reason that played a part is the fact that while there were a large number of Muslim formations both in the Waffen-SS and the German Heer the vast majority were either formed very late in the War, like the Caucasian Osttürkischer Waffen-Verbände der SS, and so have relatively little history to write about, or the units themselves were disbanded soon after establishment, such as the Bosnian Muslim SS-Kama Division. To write about any one such unit in isolation would be wholly unsatisfactory, and the ability to bring them together enables the full context of the situation to be given.

I believe that this book is a first and that there is probably no other text in the English language that covers all of the Muslim Waffen-SS formations and their German Heer predecessors and counterparts, I only hope that the readers believe, as I do, that it was a task worth undertaking.

I

Nazism and Islam

Nazism and religion

At first sight there would seem to be no common ground at all between Nazism and any of the world's great monotheistic religions; Christianity, Islam and Judaism. The latter was, of course, identified by Adolf Hitler as his movement's mortal enemy and a scourge that had to be exterminated. Therein lay the reason for the infamy of the Holocaust and the butchery of over six million innocents. As for Christianity, it is a religion that preaches peace, tolerance and forgiveness and these are not traits that are associated with the Nazis. Islam is also a religion of peace and benevolence, and one that has taken root mainly in the Middle East, Africa and Asia. As the Nazis were essentially 'white supremacists' it would be too big a leap to think that they would look with anything but contempt on a religion that was overwhelmingly practised by those whom they deemed to be 'racially inferior'. But throughout its mercifully short lifespan Nazism had something of a schrizophrenic relationship with both Christianity and Islam. Perhaps the answer to the paradox lies in the idea that Nazism itself had many of the characteristics of the extremist fringes of organised religions through the ages, including a hatred of non-believers and the celebration of violence, and many of its adherents were just as fanatical in their beliefs.

Before the outbreak of war, the Nazis' feelings towards Christianity were characterised by the hostility that dominated their thinking at this time, but were quietly shelved as an impediment to its wider goals once hostilities began. It was Hitler who made this accommodation, and it was entirely in keeping with his modus operandi once he achieved power, as he quietly went about making peace with the establishment in Germany, including the military, big business and of course, organised religion. During their street brawling days Hitler and his party had ranted and raved about remaking Germany in their own image, and the likes of Himmler were allowed to dream about a return to a pre-Christian pagan era. While the strutting and bombastic Ernst Röhm planned the replacement of Germany's professional army, the *Reichswehr*, with a 'people's army' based on his brown-shirted stormtroopers of the *Sturmabteilung*, the SA. On Hitler's ascension to the position of Chancellor in 1933 Himmler took his master's hint and did not seriously challenge the churches; Röhm however did not read the runes and his journey ended on 1 July 1934 in a cell in Munich's Stadelheim prison with a bullet in the head from his old Party comrade Theodor Eicke. Outside the cell door was Eicke's Adjutant, SS-Hauptsturmführer Michael Lippert, who would go on to be the first commander of the Flemish SS-Legion Flandern in 1941 (see *Hitler's Flemish Lions* for more information).

Keeping both the Protestant and Catholic churches on side was an essential policy for Hitler as Germany itself was still a strongly Christian country in the 1930s and '40s with large and devout populations of Catholics in southern Germany and Austria, and Protestants in the north of the country. A strident anti-Christian policy would have given the Nazis huge problems domestically. The general rule tended to be that as long as the various Christian churches left the Nazis alone to do what they wanted then they in turn would leave the churches in peace. Principled Christian opposition, as exemplified by the likes of the courageous pastor Dietrich Bonhoffer, and the retribution that followed, was rare.

Islam by contrast was a religion that barely figured in Nazi Germany. Modern-day Germany is home to a large Muslim, predominantly Turkish, community but prior to the War there were only a tiny number of Muslims calling Germany home and they were usually foreign diplomats, academics, professionals and their families. Islam was not an issue on the Nazi radar. There was no official stance on Islam and no real references to it in Nazi racial thinking. This was to change radically with the advent of the Second World War. Aggressive war brought the Nazis into contact with large Muslim populations, both in the Balkans, the Soviet Union and in North Africa, and the exigencies of the fighting would see the Nazis hurriedly develop their thinking on Islam. However, to say that the Nazis' links to Islam and their willingness to use it for their own ends only began with the advent of *blitzkrieg* would be wrong. The answer to the conundrum of the Nazis' interest in Islam lay in Germany's past, and especially in the First World War.

Imperial Ambition

Germany came incredibly late to the business of establishing an over-seas empire. By the time Germany was unified under the Kaiser in 1871 most of Africa and Asia had already been taken as colonies by other European Powers. The Portuguese were in southern Africa, the Dutch had the East Indies and even Belgium had the massive African Congo. As for the imperial giants of France and Britain it would be fair to say that the tricolor and the Union Jack held sway over empires that would have made Rome's Caesars blush. This did not stop Germany from join-ing in though, however belatedly, and she managed to secure colonies in Africa: German South-West and East Africa (modern-day Namibia and Tanzania) as well as the Cameroons, were far larger in size than the Fatherland itself. In comparison to Britain's African possessions these lands were relatively small and poor, but German policymakers were content to play second fiddle to Britain in the quest for overseas prestige and power.

World War One and Jihad

Unsurprisingly this delicate balancing act fell apart with the onset of war in 1914. Ottoman Turkey declared for the Central Powers and on 2 November 1914 the Sultan proclaimed jihad (holy war) against the Entente Powers. This announcement sent a shiver through the capitals of Imperial Russia, France and above all, Great Britain. All had significant Muslim populations under their control, but none more so than Britain in India and its Suez Canal lifeline through the Middle East. Germany's intent was clear; if indigenous Muslim populations could be stirred up to rebellion it would severely hamper the Entente Powers' ability to wage war and the result could be decisive. After all, if the Raj went up in flames would not the British take badly needed troops from France to secure their Empire?

German action was swift as agents fanned out eastwards spreading propaganda and inciting revolt. They said that the Kaiser had secretly converted to Islam, that Germany would supply them with arms and guarantee their future freedom. Needless to say all these assertions were false, but when Muslims began to desert from hitherto loyal regiments such as the Indian Army's 129th Punjabis, and four entire companies of the 5th (Native) Light Infantry mutinied in Singapore, then London began to worry. The seriousness of the situation can be gauged by the fact that by the middle of 1915 the British Indian Army refused to send any more Indian troops to the Western Front, for fear of spreading disaffection, and thus forced Kitchener to make his infamous call for mass civilian British volunteers – the so-called Kitchener Army with its Pals' Battalions. That Army would die in the mud of the Somme a year later.

Coordinated by the *Reichskolonialamt* (Reich Colonial Office) in Berlin trouble was fomented in the Horn of Africa – Somaliland and still-independent Abyssinia, the Sudan and further north in Egypt, to directly threaten the Suez Canal. At a time when every man and weapon was desperately needed to hold the line in France the War Office diverted considerable forces and material to deal with the very real threat of widespread Muslim rebellion. An invasion of western Egypt in early 1916 by the warlike Sanusi under their leader Sayyid Ahmad was opposed by the entire 1st South African Brigade shipped back to North Africa from England before it could be deployed on the Western Front. A simultaneous attack from Ali Dinar, the Sultan of Dafur in Sudan, was met by Britains' Western Frontier Force while the 'Mad Mullah' of Somaliland, Sayyid Mohammed Abdille Hassan, was countered by the Somaliland Field Force. In a series of campaigns covering thousands of square miles, all three rebellions and incursions were comprehensively defeated by 1917.

However the situation in Abyssinia was of an altogether different magnitude. Here the German government delegate, the wily Leo Frobenius, and his colleague the German Consul in Addis Ababa, von Syburg, encouraged the new Emperor, Lij Iyasu, to ally himself increasingly with Islam and prepare an invasion into British Somaliland. This caused consternation in the War Office particularly as their entire policy in the East had just suffered a huge blow with the loss of 10,000 men under General Townshend at the Battle of Kut in Mesopotamia against the Ottoman Turks. Not for the first or last time it was decided that Britain's interests were best served by removing a foreign sovereign ruler. The result was a British-backed coup in Addis Ababa that deposed Lij Iyasu in favour of his aunt, Zaudita. There ensued a brief but bloody civil war which culminated in the Battle of Sagale on 27 October 1916, in which more than 100,000 men fought. Sagale was a decisive victory for Zaudita, and in the aftermath Lij Iyasu fled into the eastern lowlands where he was eventually captured in 1921. The threat from Abyssinia was over.

The events of 1916 in Muslim Africa shook the War Office, and coupled with the Easter Rising in Dublin, made the British government feel far less secure in its overseas possessions. The threat of a future jihad would not be underestimated.

For Germany the lack of resources and ability to project their power outside of Europe meant their ability to light a bonfire under the British Empire in particular was always going to be an extremely long shot, but it did sow the seeds of future endeavour. Germany had now established a track record of supporting both a pan-Islamic awakening, and Muslim nationalist aspirations, in order to achieve its goals. It would draw on both of these policies again when Hitler launched his war of conquest in 1939.

Nazi racial philosophy

Having established the precedence for German-Muslim cooperation in World War One there remains the question of race, after all, the entire foundation of National Socialist rule in Germany was explicit racism. This racism was not a badge of convenience or a device to gain temporary political advantage, but a heartfelt belief system that dominated every aspect of Nazi policy and German national life. If a future alliance between Nazi Germany and any Muslim populations was to be viable then this circle needed to be squared. The answer was to come from an altogether surprising source, Alfred Rosenberg and the Nazi policy of *Drang Nach Osten* – the Drive to the East!

The Nazis' attitude on race was infamously framed by Hitler in his incredibly turgid book *Mein Kampf* – My Struggle. Hitler expressed the Nazi *Weltanschaung*, their World View, as one entirely based on the innate racial superiority of the Germans and their ethnic cousins in north-western Europe who, in the Nazis' eyes, all sprang from the same ancient Aryan *Volk* – People. It was the destiny of the Aryans, Hitler's master race or *Herrenvolk*, ultimately to rule not only Europe but also to dominate the world, but in order to achieve this it was absolutely necessary for the Aryans to exterminate their most dangerous racial enemies, the Jews, and their political allies, the Bolsheviks. Incredible though it may seem today, this was the founding belief of a political party that was eagerly swept into power in Germany in 1933 by an educated voting populace.

The Nazis' anti-semitism and delusional conspiracy theories were nothing new of course, but were drawn from a rich vein of similar bigotry that had existed across Europe for centuries. What was new with the Nazis was that they were able to move from being crackpot hate-peddlers operating on the lunatic fringes of society to the very pinnacle of national power. They were able to do this without having to hide their political poison, indeed it was central to their appeal, and thus once in government they could turn it into official policy.

Prior to the 1933 election it was Adolf Hitler himself who fulfilled the role of chief racial 'thinker' in the Nazi Party. But after his accession to power he was far less interested in developing Nazi racial theory and far more concerned with its implementation both at home in the Third Reich, and abroad in his war of conquest. This did not mean Nazi racial thinking stopped dead in 1933 however, as there were two senior devotees to the cause in the shape of the bespectacled bureaucrat and head of the SS, Heinrich Himmler, and the Party's own rather grandiosely titled 'racial philosopher', Alfred Rosenberg. As for the rest of the Party, as one would expect the Nazis had always attracted a whole host of anti-Semites who fancied themselves as intellectuals. The reality was that the vast majority were nothing more than crude Jew-baiters, with the bullet-headed Julius Streicher, as the editor of the the violent and semi-pornographic magazine *Der Stürmer*, being a perfect example of the type. The Party were not all violent thugs though, and it did attract a number of educated professionals to its ranks. Alfred Rosenberg was in this latter category.

The 'Reichsheini' and Rosenberg

Himmler, unflatteringly nicknamed the 'Reichsheini' by his detractors on account of his slavish loyalty to Hitler, was a racial fantasist on a grand scale. He held the same core beliefs as his master but was also devoted to evolving and expanding them. Himmler was fascinated by Teutonic paganism and Germanic tribal history and was a firm believer in the outright rejection of Christianity as a source of 'un-German softness'. With the full resources of the Nazi State at his disposal he established commissions, founded museums, funded scientific expeditions and set up entire departments to research, investigate and irrefutably prove the existence and history of the Aryan race and its genetic superiority. He then used some of the spurious conclusions from this work to determine the recruitment policies of his beloved Waffen-SS, the armed wing of his empire. This policy even included Himmler personally vetting photos of every single prospective Waffen-SS officer to ensure no-one was accepted who did not exhibit the required kind of 'Nordic features'. This was on top of the requirement, instituted in 1935, for every SS applicant to prove a 'pure' Aryan genealogy, dating back to 1800 for enlisted men and 1750 for officers. Even in Hitler's 'Aryan Germany' this meant the rejection of 85 out of every 100 volunteers. Himmler even rebuilt, at vast expense, the medieval Schloss Wewelsburg in the German countryside to become in effect an 'SS theme park' with its guest rooms dedicated to historical Germanic heroes such as King Henry the Fowler and the Emperor Frederick Barbarossa. It was Himmler who tried to map the global distribution of the mythical Aryans and who would later use this information to target the foreign volunteer recruitment for the Waffen-SS. Crucially though, it was also he who would distort and disregard his own 'racial science' later in the War in order to try and fill the blood-soaked gaps in the Waffen-SS order of battle, including the large-scale recruitment of Muslims. For Himmler the vision of the Waffen-SS was of a blue-eyed, blond haired order of giants answering the mythical call of their blood and soil, and definitely not a mass of people who answered the call to prayer. This, though, would change.

Alfred Rosenberg, on the other hand, was very different from the pedantic Bavarian Reichsführer-SS. Born on 12 January 1893 (incidentally the very same day as Hermann Goering) in Reval, Estonia's modern day capital of Tallinn, to Baltic German parents, Alfred was a serious young man who studied architecture in Riga, Latvia and then engineering in Moscow as the First World War raged to the west. After completing his studies he returned to his home city where he worked as an architect, indeed many of the buildings he designed are still standing in Tallinn city centre. Following the Russian October Revolution in 1917 and the defeat of the counter-revolutionary Whites in the ensuing Civil War he and his family, as committed anti-bolsheviks, fled west to Germany and settled in Bavaria. There Rosenberg was swiftly drawn into far Right politics and became an extremely early member of the tiny German Workers' Party in January 1919. This was before its name change to the National Socialist German Workers Party, and even before Hitler became a party member that October.

As one of the few highly educated professionals in the fledgling organisation Rosenberg was asked to edit the party newspaper, the virulently anti-semitic *Völkischer Beobachter* ('People's Observer') from 1921 onwards. Under his stewardship the paper steadily built its circulation and allowed Rosenberg to expound his pseudo-scientific racial theories. He went on to briefly lead the Party during Hitler's imprisonment in Landsberg following the failure of the Munich Beer Hall Putsch in 1923, before becoming an elected Reichstag deputy in 1930 and publishing his landmark book, *Der Mythus des 20 Jahrhunderts* ('The Myth of the Twentieth Century'), which dealt with key issues in the national socialist ideology, such as the Jewish question. No doubt avid reading for some fanatics, this hefty tome even bored Hitler, who called it 'stuff nobody can understand'.

Rosenberg turns East

Despite his lofty pretensions Rosenberg lacked both personal charisma or any real political skill or drive, and became increasingly marginalised over time as the Nazis got closer to supreme power from 1930 onwards. This loss of influence was compounded by the fact that he was not on good terms with most of the other Party leaders including Himmler and Goebbels, while Goering positively detested him. But he did manage to wield enough influence over Hitler to reinforce his master's belief that the major threat to the long term future of Nazi Germany lay not in the liberal democracies of the West but in the East. It was the East that Rosenberg saw as the crucible that would decide the fate of the Nazis and where he modelled his 'racial ladder' theory. This theory placed all races in a hierarchy, naturally with the Ayrans at the summit and the Jews at the bottom, alongside black Africans. Significantly for later policy in the Soviet Union he was fairly ambivalent towards the Slavs, believing that they were not the *Untermensch*, the sub-humans, that Hitler thought they were. Indeed he saw them as a potential racial ally. As can be imagined, this was not a popular view in the Nazi Party.

On the Nazis' assumption of power in 1933, unlike Himmler, Goebbels and Goering, who obtained significant portfolios in government, Rosenberg received very little. He was appointed to lead the Party foreign political office and tried to build bridges with Britain, but was little more than an unwanted appendage to von Ribbentrop as the Foreign Minister. With little to do he was fobbed off the following year with overseeing the educational and philosophical beliefs of the Party. The post was universally held in low regard by the Party leadership but Rosenberg fooled himself into thinking that it was a potential beacon for the evolution of Nazi policy. It was this post he held at the outbreak of War in 1939. His self-delusion was then reinforced when he was made head of the the Centre of National Socialist Ideological and Educational Research the following year. It was in this position that Rosenberg would develop his thoughts on what he called the 'religion of the blood' that sought to reject what he viewed as the corrupting influence of Christianity on Germany, and instead draw on aspects of paganism, Zoroastrianism and even Vedic Hinduism. Part of this illusory belief system was Rosenberg's thesis, first proclaimed by an earlier American writer called Chamberlain, that Jesus Christ himself was a member of a Nordic enclave resident in ancient Galilee who struggled against Judaism.

Despite these wild ramblings Rosenberg's position as head of the Centre, and a Baltic German to boot, did bestow on him an unearned reputation as an expert on the peoples of the East and allowed him to play a major part in shaping the future policies of Nazi occupation. In this role Rosenberg was an influential player, and his views set the tone for much of the move to recruit Muslims into the Waffen-SS.

The *Ostministerium* – Ministry for the East

With the invasion of the Soviet Union on 22 June 1941 and the advent of Operation Barbarossa, Rosenberg finally got his wish and was granted a government Ministry all of his own – the clumsily entitled *Reichsministerium für die besetzten Ostgebiete* – Ministry for the Occupied Eastern Territories. This *Ost Ministerium*, as it was more commonly known, was intended by Hitler as the central policy instrument for the Nazis in their new *lebensraum* (Hitler's so-called 'living space' for the Germans) in the conquered East. Rosenberg was to lead this policy formulation but, as became crucial over time, was purposefully given little executive control to turn these policies into practice. Responsibility for that lay with the military commanders in the field and the all-powerful regional governors such as Hinrich Lohse (governor of the *Reichskommisariat Ostland* comprising Estonia, Latvia, Lithuania and Belorussia) and the incredibly brutal Erich Koch (governor of *Reichskommisariat Ukraine*). These men theoretically reported to Rosenberg but in reality were loyal to Hitler, appointed by him to rule their designated areas entirely as they saw fit to serve Nazi Germany's interests. This split between policy and practice was to lead both to the creation of a Muslim Waffen-SS from the Soviet Union's Muslim minorities and to its eventual failure, with far-reaching consequences for the German war effort.

From the start Rosenberg saw the polyglot Soviet Union as an unnatural construct that had to be split up into its constituent ethnic parts. For the majority Slav populations of Belorussia (White, or Little Russia), the Ukraine and Russia proper, this would mean enslavement and subjugation under German rule. But for hitherto minority peoples in the Soviet Union he foresaw the potential for some form of limited self-government under Nazi domination. Overwhelmingly this second and far more lenient approach was envisaged for the populations of the southern Soviet Union, both Christians such as the Georgians and Armenians, but also for the Muslim peoples of the Crimea, the Caucasus and the vast Turkic steppes of central Asia. Rosenberg's plan called for the establishment of a ring of buffer states around Russia by granting independence to the likes of the Baltic states, the Ukraine and Belorussia. There would also be independence for the Soviet Union's Muslim minorities such as the

Crimean Tartars and the various Turkic steppe peoples, albeit under German hegemony. In this respect Rosenberg was a clear proponent of encouraging nationalism among the Soviet Union's ethnic minorities as a counter-balance to Russian central power, even though this line of thinking fell foul of Hitler's personal obsession with the destruction of the Slavs. For both Hitler and his ever-loyal lackey Himmler, the peoples of the East, with a few exceptions such as the Estonians and Latvians, were nothing more than sub-humans fit only for slavery – they were Slavs, after all – or extermination.

II

The War begins

Nazi war strategy

If Hitler had a grand strategy prior to the outbreak of general war, and this is still debatable, then the West's reaction in declaring war on account of his invasion of Poland threw it into complete chaos. The counter-reaction from the Reich Chancellory was nothing if not quick and decisive. The Wehrmacht's *Fall Gelb* operation (Case Yellow) set in motion a *blitzkrieg* assault on the Low Countries and France that effectively knocked all of Nazi Germany's opponents, except Great Britain, out of the War. Hitler could now focus on what he considered to be his true enemy, the behemoth of Soviet Russia. With the British unable to respond following the disaster of the battle for France and Dunkirk, Hitler was confident his rear was secure. Scandinavia was in his pocket and Finland was still smarting from its defeat by Stalin in the previous year's Winter War and willing to side with Germany to secure its northern flank. The only piece of the jigsaw left was to ensure south-eastern Europe and the Balkans were on side and then Hitler could focus all of Germany's might on kicking in the Soviet door.

Using a combination of carrot and stick Hitler and his Foreign Minister Joachim von Ribbentrop managed to win over the majority of states in that traditionally chaotic part of Europe. Despite being the bitterest of enemies, both Rumania and Hungary signed the Nazis' Tripartite Pact (previously an agreement between Germany, Italy and Japan), and even King Boris's Bulgaria agreed to cooperate, though interestingly not to turn its troops against its Soviet neighbour. Albania had been invaded by Mussolini's Italy and effectively annexed several years previously. As for Greece, its diminutive dictator, General Ioannis Metaxas, was pro-Axis but he was also a fierce patriot and the failed Italian invasion of the previous winter necessitated German intervention. But as long as Yugoslavia could be brought into the fold then Greece would remain isolated until overwhelmed. This seemed entirely probable with Yugoslavia having been led from 1935 by the pro-Axis Serb Milan Stojadinovic and his Radical Union Party. Stojadinovic even referred to himself as the *Vodja* (Serbo-Croat for Führer) and set up his own uniformed paramilitary stormtroopers, similar to the Nazi's brownshirted SA, to bully opponents. However he had been replaced earlier in the year by Dragisa Cvetkovic who was not seen in such a favourable light by the Germans. Consequently, what passed for diplomacy in Nazi Germany swung into action and the usual mix of bluff and promises overwhelmed the Belgrade government, which duly signed up to the Pact on 25 March 1941.

All was now set to allow Hitler to begin his momentous invasion of Russia at the very start of the 1941 campaigning season and give his troops the best possible chance of defeating the Soviet Union before the onset of the horrendous Russian winter. With everything in place the entire apple cart was knocked over by the trademark unpredictability of the Balkans. Popular revulsion in Yugoslavia at the signing of the Tripartite Pact led to an uprising against the Regent led by the military High Command, and covertly supported by Great Britain, that saw the government overthrown and an anti-Germany administration swept into power just two days after the Pact was signed in Vienna. At the Chancellory Hitler flew into a towering rage and demanded retribution. Yugoslavia's fate was sealed.

Unternehmen Strafe (Operation Punishment)

The planned German invasion of Greece, codenamed Operation Marita, was hurriedly amended by Hitler's Führer Directive No. 25 that called for an immediate invasion of Yugoslavia which aimed 'to destroy Yugoslavia militarily and as a national unit'. In an incredibly short period of time the existing plans were adapted and on 6 April the invasion of Yugoslavia was heralded by a savage bombing raid on Belgrade carried out by *Generaloberst* (General) Alexander Löhr's *Luftflotte* (Airfleet) IV. In two days of bombardment, reminiscent of the terror bombing of Warsaw and Rotterdam, over 17,000 Yugoslav civilians died. Simultaneously, elements of both the Second and Twelfth Armies and *Panzergruppe* Kleist (Panzer Group Kleist, named after its commanding general) comprising ten corps with 32 divisons, attacked Yugoslavia from Bulgaria, Hungary, Rumania and Austria (the *Ostmark*, as it had been called since the Nazi *Anschluss* of 1938). Even though the Royal Yugoslav Army was over 900,000 men strong it was no match for Nazi Germany's modern forces and *blitzkrieg* tactics and it took the Wehrmacht just twelve days to force the country's surrender, on 17 April. The end of the campaign saw 6,028 Yugoslav officers and 337,684 NCOs and men become POWs, but more than 500,000 soldiers of all ranks refused to lay down their arms and disappeared either back home or into the mountains. Many of them would later become the enemy against which Muslim Waffen-SS men would fight. For the Germans it was a victory bought incredibly cheaply with a casualty count of just 151 men killed, 15 missing and 392 wounded.

In accordance with Hitler's wishes the great dismemberment of Yugoslavia was then carried out. In effect a sovereign nation was carved up between the victors, nothing had been seen like this since the great Partitions of Poland in the seventeenth and eighteenth centuries.

Yugoslavia disappears from the map

The victory belonged to Germany and it was she who divided up the former Triune Kingdom and handed it out to her allies. Montenegro was given to Italy along with most of the Dalmation coast and islands as well as half of Slovenia that lay just across the Italian border. The largely ethnic Albanian Kosovo region was joined with Albania and so in effect also became Italian territory. Bulgaria, who had not sent any troops into Yugoslavia but had allowed the German Twelfth Army to launch its attacks from there, was rewarded with the whole of Yugoslavian Macedonia, while Hungary received the Barania and Backa regions of Yugoslav Vojvodina. As for Rumania, it only acquired some very minor border districts and the ethnic German Banat region which by virtue of its Germanic population in effect became a province of the Reich. Germany herself annexed the remaining half of Slovenia bordering the Ostmark to further extend her borders. As for the rest of the country, Serbia was effectively reduced to its pre-1912–13 Balkan War borders and placed under German control but with its own administration and limited self-defence forces under the collaborationist General Milan Nedic. A new country was also created in Croatia with the amalgamation of the Catholic Croats with the ethnically mixed population of Bosnia-Herzegovina and parts of coastal Dalmatia. Although nominally independent the new nation had permanent German and Italian garrisons and was a puppet state. Outside of Muslim Albania it was in this country that lay Europe's largest indigenous Muslim community.

Bosnia's Muslims

Since it had burst out from the Arabian Peninsula centuries before, Islam's contact with Europe had been little but a litany of blood and violence. Charles Martel's last stand at Tours, Roland at Roncevalles, the *Reconquista* in Spain and of course the centuries of conflict of the Crusades had seen a tradition of conflict between the two religions wherever they met. Nowhere was this tradition of warfare more ferocious than in the Balkans where the Turkish thrust into south-western Europe over the Hellespont had receded over time as the Ottoman Empire gradually atrophied and decayed. There was little large-scale Muslim migration to their conquered lands in Europe, and widespread opposition to Muslim rule led to very few conversions, with one notable exception. Among the independent-minded peoples in the rugged mountain province of Bosnia were a sect of Christians called the Bogomils. An introverted group, they were universally despised by their Catholic and Orthodox Christian neighbours and seen as nothing better than heretics. Prejudice was rife and persecution open but all this changed with the conquest of Bosnia by the rampaging Ottomans. Turkish policy was one of religious tolerance and the Bogomils were afforded a level of state protection hitherto unknown. In an unprecedented act of gratitude towards their Turkish overlords the Bogomils willingly converted en masse to Islam, and in doing so became the only racially European Muslim community on the continent. This act, viewed with delight by the Ottomans but with fury by their Serbian and Croat neighbors, has fuelled a bitter internecine ethnic conflict that has lain near the surface of Bosnian life ever since.

The civil war – Ustasha atrocities

By the time of the German invasion there were over one million Muslims in Bosnia-Herzegovina out of a total population of some two-and-a-half million. Their incorporation into the new *Nezavisna Drzava Hrvatska* (the Independent State of Croatia) under the leadership of Dr Anté Pavelic, an ex-Vice President of the Croatian Bar Association and member of parliament, and his extremist Croatian nationalist *Ustasha* ('Uprising') movement was greeted with a sense of cautious optimism after Pavelic spoke of equality between the state's Catholics and Muslims. However, it soon became clear that any reassurance felt by the Muslim community was totally illusory. From almost day one of its creation the new country was in a state of near civil war.

Many Croats had felt little if any loyalty to the old Serb-dominated Triune Kingdom of Yugoslavia and most wanted at least a measure of autonomy and self-determination. Support for Croat culture and political parties was strong and so when the Wehrmacht invaded they had been actively assisted by a large Croatian 'fifth column' as well as some elements in the *volksdeutsche*, ethnic German, populace. Pavelic and his Ustasha were at the very extreme end of this Croat nationalist spectrum and were overwhelmingly based overseas in Italy and Hungary where they were funded primarily as a terrorist organisation. The German conquest allowed them to return home and wreak their vengeance for years of enforced exile and resulted in the summer of 1941 being turned into a horrific bloodbath that has scarred Bosnia in particular ever since. Trained abroad, the Ustasha cadres were hurriedly armed by the Germans and Italians and then proceeded to turn those weapons on their neighbours, especially the Orthodox Christian Serbs. Pavelic's goal was an 'ethnically pure' Croat state, loyal to him and the Catholic Church, and for the Serbs unlucky enough to find themselves within Croatia's borders the Ustasha solution was simple and brutal – genocide. The oft-quoted line in the new capital of Zagreb was 'one third of Serbs to be driven out as refugees, one third to be converted to Catholicism, and one third to be killed'.

In practice this meant trucks of Ustasha turning up and surrounding Serb villages first thing in the morning. As the black-capped Ustasha men jumped down from the backs of their lorries the locals looked on bemused at the shouting and bawling and the sight of armed men in their midst. But that bemusement turned to fear as the hard-faced Croat fanatics began forcibly herding people out of their houses and farms and into the main square. No-one was exempt, with the local schoolhouses emptied and elderly relatives having to be carried. If the village was lucky the Ustasha commander would then offer them all the opportunity to save their lives by converting to the Catholic faith, and if not the violence would begin. It is not the subject matter of this book to document the mass atrocities perpetrated by the Ustasha but suffice to say it at least equalled the very worst excesses of the Nazis during the War. Whole communities were butchered in orgies of destruction that saw tens of thousands shot, burned alive in churches and homes, thrown off cliffs, or buried alive. Not content with wanton slaughter the Ustasha also indulged in torture and mutilation on a medieval scale, with Pavelic even being sent bags of victims' ears by his crazed militias. One example of Ustasha terror will serve as the epitome of what their rule was all about. As meticulously documented as the Nazis' own *Einsatzgruppen* extermination squads in the East, the Ustasha files captured after the War contain a litany of horror. One such archive from October 1941 is entitled '*Ustachen Werk bei Bjelovar*' ('The Ustasha's activity in Bjelovar'). In this hitherto quiet rural district the Ustasha cadres rounded up the local Orthodox priest, the school teacher and 250 local Serb men. Marched out of their villages they were taken to a wood and told to dig a long trench. When it was considered deep enough they were ordered to get down into it and stand in a line. The Croats then filled the trench in and buried them alive. Any who tried to get out were shot.

Unsurprisingly there was immediate resistance by the Serbs to their attempted genocide and before long moderate Croats were actively opposing what was being done in their name. There were already two major resistance movements in Yugoslavia; the first being the pro-royalist and Serb-dominated chetnicks led by the former Yugoslav Army officer Colonel (later General) Draza Mihailovic, and the second being the communist Partisans led by Josip Broz, Tito. The latter began fighting their occupiers as soon as the Soviet Union was invaded and were not bound to one ethnic group, Tito himself being a Croat. The chetnicks, named after the Serb '*cetna*' guerrillas who resisted the Ottoman Turks, initially fought the Italians, the Ustasha and the Germans but soon began to view Tito's Communists as the real enemy. In general, resistance groups sprang up everywhere as villages banded together to protect themselves, and tens of thousands of former soldiers who had not surrendered and escaped to the hills began to fight back against the Ustasha murder gangs and their German and Italian allies.

Caught up in the middle were Bosnia's one million Muslims who found themselves in the uniquely unenviable position of being persecuted by all sides in this triumvirate war. As royalist Serb chetniks fought Ustasha fanatics and communist Partisans, the Partisans fought the Ustasha and their Axis allies, and the Ustasha butchered atheist Partisans and Orthodox Serbs, it was the Muslims who were viewed by all sides as an enemy. The result was a population in crisis and struggling to survive. It is impossible to get accurate figures but a conservative estimate is that by 1943 250,000 Muslims had been forced to leave their homes and become refugees, and perhaps as many as another 100,000 (that is 1 in 10 of the pre-war population) had been murdered or died from disease or starvation. This was the backdrop to future Muslim Waffen-SS recruitment in Bosnia. But it was not in Bosnia that the Germans first developed a taste for Muslim soldiery; that was to occur in the vast battlegrounds of the Soviet Union.

III

The German Army's Muslim Legions

Muslims in the German Army – the Heer

The Muslims of the Balkans served from the start under the banner of the Waffen-SS, but this was not the case for those Muslim minorities from the Soviet Union and North Africa. A great number of them did eventually come to be part of Heinrich Himmler's empire but initially at least they were recruited, trained, equipped by and fought under the aegis of the German Army, the Heer. To understand the role they played in Nazi Germany's war effort and why they came to fight it is essential to understand their past.

The Soviet Union and the world of Islam

The southern edges of Russia had been the scene of violent confrontation with the expanding Mongol Empire for centuries, and when this was combined with the migration and expansion of the Islamicised Turkic peoples of the Middle East the scene was set for a hostile meeting of Islam and Christianity. Throughout the fourteenth, fifteenth and sixteenth centuries Islamic steppe warriors swept northwards across the Caucasus and east of the Caspian Sea establishing powerful, independent khanates and settling wherever they went. As this centuries-old conflict settled down in the eighteenth century there were three main areas of Islamic habitation to the south of Russia proper.

Tsarist Russia and the Khans

From west to east there was firstly the land of the Crimean Tartars established as a Khanate in 1430 (it would last for more than 300 years). Lapped by the beautiful waters of the Black Sea and with a climate warm enough to grow grapes for wine, the Crimea was almost an island joined to the mainland by thin strips of land. It became an Islamic stronghold which enabled the Tartars to sally out and ravage their Russian and Ukrainian neighbours for centuries. One single raid in 1667 saw the Tartars destroy 300 villages and plunder 50,000 cattle, while their great 1672 raid netted 44,000 Russian slaves. Further to the east was the wild and rugged Caucasus with Europe's highest mountain, Mount Elbrus, crowning its remote fastnesses. Here was the home of some equally rugged Muslim peoples, the Chechens, Ingush and Dagestanis. Finally even further to the east lay the vastness of the central Asian steppes that had once been home to the fabled Golden Horde and which had coalesced into the Khanates of Khiva and Khokand (and its capital of Tashkent), the raiding centre of Geok-Tepe, the Emirate of Bokhara and its fabled city of Samarkand and the remote and isolated Khanate of Merv. The peoples who lived in these lands were from a myriad of tribes speaking a multitude of languages and adhering to a host of differing customs, but due to their common Turkic origins were collectively referred to as 'Turkmen' or 'Turcomen'.

Today they form the independent countries of Kazakhstan, Uzbekistan (containing part of Bokhara and the cities of Samarkand and Taskent), Tajikistan (formerly part of the Emirate of Bokhara), Turkmenistan (containing elements of both Khiva and Bokhara) and Kyrgyzstan (primarily Khokand).

In a series of daredevil campaigns all of the independent Khanates that had existed for centuries along the fabled Silk Route from China to Europe were conquered by Imperial Russia during one of its periodic historical 'land grabs'. Khokand fell to assault in 1865, Bokhara a year later and Khiva in 1873. The oasis of Geok-Tepe was captured in 1881 and the last independent khanate of Merv surrendered the following year without a shot being fired. In less than twenty years more than three centuries of Muslim rule on the central Asian steppes was wiped away. Being thousands of miles away from Moscow the new lands of the Russian Empire were ruled with a fairly light touch and this remained the case until the outbreak of World War One and the disasters it wrought on the incompetent and tottering house of Romanov. As Imperial Russia struggled to deal with the war in the west it failed to realise the trouble that was brewing in its southern possessions, where migration from the Russian heartlands in particular was causing huge local problems over land and water rights. The Kazakhs especially resented what they saw as discrimination against them in favour of the newcomers. Tensions reached boiling point in 1916 and spilled over into a general revolt. Kazakh mobs attacked Russian and Cossack settlements killing all they found and burning homes and crops. Engaged as the Russian Army was with its successful Brusilov offensive against the Austro-Hungarians in far-off Belorussia it still managed to respond to the uprising by dispatching a powerful force to quash the revolt. Retribution was swift and merciless. Within two months the rebels were defeated and some 300,000 Kazakhs were driven fleeing into the mountains or over the border into neighbouring China. When 80,000 of the exiles tried to return the following year they were met by Russian troops who butchered them in their thousands. Brutal treatment of Russia's minorities was not a Stalinist invention, it was part of a long and inglorious tradition stretching back many years.

Communism and Islam

Following the seizure of power by the Bolsheviks in November 1917 and the ending of the war with Germany the former Islamic khanates became semi-independent, like so many of Imperial Russia's ethnic lands, as Lenin and Trotsky struggled to create the Soviet Union. When the new government did establish itself it brought the Muslim lands firmly back into its grasp but did grant them the status of autonomous republics. This status did not prevent Moscow from imposing its hated land collectivization policies on the local people, which had the same results as elsewhere in the new Soviet Union – mass starvation. In the famine of 1921–22 nearly one million Kazakhs alone died of hunger. Alongside this state-sponsored tragedy, traditional Muslim society was further weakened by the dispossession of the old elites of tribal and clan leaders, and worst of all the Bolsheviks imported their atheistic beliefs into these fiercely Islamic lands and oppressed religion. Mosques were closed, imams arrested and the Koran suppressed. Unsurprisingly, there was widespread resistance to Moscow's rule and a vicious guerrilla war between the Red Army and local rebel groups, *basmachi* as they were called, was endemic.

For Turkistan, declared an autonomous Soviet Republic in 1917, even that limited freedom was curtailed in 1924 when the country was officially dissolved by order of the Kremlin. The land had been collectivized into state-owned *kolkhoz* collective farms, religion was crushed and

Russian was imposed as the official language, with all the various Turkic languages and dialects banned.

The Tajiks and Uzbeks fared slightly better as they at least retained their status as republics, although the usual Soviet policies as regards land and religion were still applied.

Worst hit though were probably the Kazakhs who continued to suffer from Russian suspicion and the resulting brutal suppression even after the famine of 1921–22. The net effect was a reduction in the Kazakh population by 22% between the Revolution and the outbreak of the Second World War.

The mathematics of war

Between 1 September 1939 and 31 May 1941 the German Wehrmacht lost 97,000 men killed out of a total 218,109 casualties whilst waging its Polish, Scandinavian, Western European and North African campaigns. An incredibly small number given the enormity of their conquests. The Wehrmacht had then begun the invasion of the Soviet Union on 22 June 1941, Operation Barbarossa, with an unimaginably vast force of 3,400,000 men. By 13 August 1941, only the 53rd day of the campaign, German losses had reached an unprecedented 389,924 with 98,600 of those posted as dead or missing. This was a wholly new type of war for Nazi Germany. By the end of November the casualty list had passed the three-quarters of a million mark and the number of dead and missing had doubled. Over 8,000 officers had been killed, which roughly equates to the entire officer output of the British Army's famous Royal Military Academy Sandhurst for a decade. By 20 March 1942 the German Army's High Command, the *Oberkommando des Heeres* (OKH), listed German losses since the launch of Barbarossa less than a year before, at a staggering 1,073,006 officers, NCOs and men. That equates to almost a third of the entire invading force. True, by the end of 1941 the Russians had lost over 4,500,000 men, but they had vast reservoirs of manpower that were only just beginning to be tapped and as a consequence the Red Army still stood at a strength of 4,255,000 men and growing. For the Nazis it was a different story, Germany was already struggling to keep its field army reinforced and the Ostheer, the German Army in the East, had dropped down at the same time to a total of 3,138,000 effectives. Although still impressive, it was a quarter of a million men short of what the General Staff calculated was needed to win.

This was the manpower backdrop to the war in the East and led directly to the German's first use of Muslim troops.

The *Osttruppen* – Eastern Troops

Almost from day one of Barbarossa the pragmatism of the frontline contradicted the neat racial theories of the desk warriors back in far-off Germany. Wehrmacht commanders desperate for manpower replacements for their hard pressed units that were not forthcoming from the Reich turned to what was on hand and available, and that was the teeming masses of the territories they were overrunning. Barely a fortnight into the invasion in early July 1941 *General* (Lieutenant-General) Philipp's 134th Infantry Division openly signed up ex-Red Army personnel onto its strength, many of whom would stay with the Division until its annihilation in the summer of 1944 in the Operation Bagration battles. But the 134th was not alone, every German unit at the front down to platoon level had its official, or even unofficial, complement of *Hilfswillige* or *Hiwis* for short, literally 'Willing Helpers', who did everything from digging latrines and trenches to carrying rations and ammunition. Very quickly this approach altered dramatically to one of active participation in combat, with the behind-the-lines threat from the partisans usually providing the trigger. By November 1941 over 400,000 square miles of Soviet territory and 65 million people were under German occupation and literally tens of thousands of partisans were being fought by the Wehrmacht's woefully few rear area security divisions. Local militias and self-defence forces were raised to relieve the pressure on the hard-pressed Army and police units, and naturally enough, the distinction between arming the indigenous population to fight partisans and arming them to fight at the front became increasingly blurred.

The birth of the 162nd Turkmen Division

Generalfeldmarschall (Field-Marshal) Fedor von Bock's Army Group B took the lead at the front when it formed a full six battalions of armed Hiwis in November 1941, and a secret order was issued by the Wehrmacht High Command – the *Oberkommando der Wehrmacht* (OKW), that officially authorised the setting up of the newly-christened *Osttruppen* (Eastern Troops) units, initially in groups of no more than 200 men and commanded by their own officers. OKH even authorised German divisions to utilise *Hiwis* for up to 20% of their establishment, and in an average frontline combat infantry division of 12,000 men that meant over 2,000 non-Germans. Kazakhs, Kirgiz, Uzbeks, Tajiks, Tartars, Chechens and Ingush made up a large number of these men. Under Rosenberg's instigation from the *Ostministerium* this was followed swiftly on 30 December 1941 by an order from the OKH establishing the concept of ethnic legions as home units for the non-Russian volunteers such as the Caucasian Christian Armenians and Georgians. Foremost amongst these new units would be Caucasian Muslim legions for the Azeris, Chechens and Ingush as well as Turkic units composed of steppe peoples.

To provide an administrative home to these disparate units it was decreed that they were to be nominally attached to the 162nd Infantry Division, not a frontline unit but a holding formation, who provided a training, political education and logistics base for them at their home depot in occupied Slovenia. It was this relationship with a German 'home' that led to the new formations being collectively referred to as the 162nd Turkmen Division (162 *Infanterie Division* (*turk.*)), and as such becoming the living expression of Alfred Rosenberg's hopes for the occupied territories. The division had its own newspaper *Svoboda – Ezenedel'naja gazeta legionerov* ('Freedom – the weekly newspaper of the legionnaires'). It was commanded by *Generalleutnant* (Major-General) Oskar Ritter (literally 'Knight' and equivalent to British 'Sir') von Niedermayer. Niedermayer had been the Military Attaché in Iran and the Director of the Institute of Strategic Studies in Berlin prior to the War and had developed a keen interest in Islam culminating in his conversion to the faith. Although later replaced as divisional commander due to lack of experience, Niedermayer would go on to take over from *Generalleutnant* von Wartenberg as Commander of Volunteer Units East under the Commander-in-Chief West in 1944.

The Rosenberg plan

Alongside Ostland and Ukraine, Rosenberg envisaged the creation of two further *Reichskommisariats*; that of the *Kaukasus* (the Caucasus) and *Moskau* (Moscow metropolitan area and the rest of European Russia). Rosenberg's vision foresaw these regions as cradles to encourage ethnic nationalism as a counter-balance to Russian power. He launched a 'Free Caucasus' campaign appealing with posters, leaflets and radio broadcasts to the Caucasian soldiers fighting in the Red Army. This was quite successful in attracting recruits to the legions from among the ranks of deserters and POWs, of which there were officially 2,053,000 by November 1941, although the actual figure was probably more than twice that number. Further to this he established a series of 'national committees' for the various ethnic minorities to provide some sort of political legitimacy for the recruitment drive. Each of these committees also maintained a liaison staff at Rosenberg's ministry called *Leitstellen* (leadership offices). All of this effort bore some fruit and could have sown the seeds for large-scale success, had Rosenberg's efforts not been firmly opposed by Himmler and his sprawling SS apparatus. While Rosenberg wanted to stoke the fires of latent nationalism and anti-communism among the peoples of the Soviet Union to help Nazi Germany win the War, Himmler and his minions simply saw the war in the East as one of almost medieval conquest and extermination. For them the local populace was simply a source of entirely expendable human economic material. Himmler gave a speech in 1942 speaking about the enslavement of civilian workers that summed up his attitude:

> Whether 10,000 Russian females fall down from exhaustion while digging an anti-tank ditch for Germany interests me only so far as whether the anti-tank ditch is finished. We shall never be rough and heartless when it is not necessary, that is clear. We Germans, who are the only people in the world who have a decent attitude towards animals, will also assume a decent attitude towards these human animals. But it is a crime against our own blood to worry about them and give them ideas, thus causing our sons and grandsons to have a more difficult time with them.

Crucially, Hitler backed Himmler in this battle of two wildly differing visions for the occupation of the Soviet Union and this effectively sidelined Rosenberg and his Ost Ministerium. It also consigned Muslims to a largely hidden role in the Wehrmacht's conflict with the Red Army. Strangely enough, it would be Himmler and his Waffen-SS who would completely change this picture later on in the War.

Back with the Ostheer

As Himmler and Rosenberg clashed over occupation policy, the Ostheer had to get on with the practicalities of fighting such an enormous campaign and of what to do with the rising number of Muslims volunteering for service with the Wehrmacht. As the Muslim units began to coalesce and recruitment grew, the national legion concept was increasingly turned into reality. For instance, on 13 January 1942 the *Abwehr's* (German Military Intelligence organisation under Admiral Wilhelm Canaris) *Unternehmen Tiger B* group, a special forces unit operating under the joint auspices of the Abwehr and the Foreign Office and composed of a German cadre from the famous

Brandenburg Regiment z.b.V 800 and Muslim Caucasian volunteers from the prisoner-of-war camps, was transformed by OKH command into the *Turkestanisch-Kaukasisch-Mohammedanische Legion* (Turkistan-Caucasian-Mohammedan Legion) as the lead unit for Muslim volunteers from the Soviet Union. At that time the majority of the Legions volunteers were ethnic Azeris and as their numbers swelled they were split out into their own unit, the *Aserbeidschanische Legion* (Azeri Legion) on 22 July 1942. To comply with their status as an affiliated sub-unit of Niedermayer's infantry division the Azeris were then again rebadged on 1 June 1943 as the 314th Infantry Regiment of the 162nd Infantry Division, commanded by an ex-Colonel in the Imperial Tsarist Russian Army, Magomed Nabi Oglu Israfilov. Holding the German Army rank of *Oberst* (Colonel), Israfilov transferred to the SS as a Waffen-Standartenführer later in the War, while also being the Chairman of the Azeri National Committee set up by Rosenberg's Ost Ministerium.

The remaining men from the original legion were likewise renamed, as the new *Turkestanische Legion* (Turkistan Legion) which, as the name suggests was mostly comprised of Turkmen. Separate from this reorganisation but also established in the occupied Polish *General Gouvernement* in January 1942 was the newly-raised *Wolgatatarische Legion* (Volga Tartar Legion), composed mainly of Muslim Volga-Tartars but also a minority of the tiny Volga-Finnish community.

This last unit was also called the *Idel-Ural Legion*, Idel being the Tartar name for the Volga. Propaganda accompanied these attempts at forming Muslim fighting units, and the Germans produced a host of newspapers and journals aimed at the new recuits. Alongside *Svoboda* came *Mili Turkistan* ('The National Turkistan'), *Yeni Turkistan* ('The New Turkistan'), *Tatar Adabijat* ('Tartar Literature'), *Idel-Ural* and *Azerbaican*.

However, the Muslim Legions were only half of the story, as no German general was going to voluntarily turn away willing manpower. For every Muslim who went to serve in the new formations many more stayed with the German frontline divisions that recruited them. Most of these men served as Hiwis and were put on the official ration strength of their German unit, and thereafter were near enough invisible officially, except to the fellow soldiers they served with. But sometimes they were formed into distinct outfits, as in the far south after the conquest of the Crimea by the Eleventh Army when a recruitment drive among the region's five million Tartars saw the establishment of six whole battalions of local troops who were used to fight local partisans, particularly in the bitter guerrilla war in the Yaila mountains.

Fall Blau – Case Blue, the invasion of the Caucasus

Expecting a renewal of the previous winter's offensive against Moscow the STAVKA, the Soviet High Command, was caught by surprise when the Wehrmacht launched its major offensive of 1942 in the south. As the German Army's largest single formation, the Sixth Army, continued its doomed march to Stalingrad the overall offensive was weakened by the dispatching of von Kleist's entire Army Group A to seize the oil-rich Caucasus. With the motorised units of the élite multinational 5th SS Wiking Division in the vanguard, the Germans swept east and south and took the only major oil field north of the Caucasus mountains at Maikop. For the first time since the Crimea the invaders began to come across large populations of Soviet Muslims and found them as well disposed to them as liberators as their fellow co-religionists further west. On November 2 1942, Ewald von Kleist captured Nalchik, the capital of the mainly Muslim Kabardo-Balkiar region and his troops were pressuring Vladikavkaz. Even Grozny, the capital city of Chechnya deep in the mountains, and the fabled city of Astrakhan on the shores of the Caspian Sea were within reach. But as so often before in the Soviet Union's seemingly limitless spaces, the Germans lacked that vital last battalion and their offensive ran out of steam.

Nevertheless in the newly-captured areas the Germans practised a model occupation designed to win over local support. In the Karachai region one of Rosenberg's National Committees was set up under the leadership of the local notable Kaki Baieramukov. The celebration of the Muslim holy day of Bairam on October 11 in Kislovodsk was an occasion that saw the exchanging of gifts between the German commanders and their Muslim hosts. This turn of events was continued in Nalchik on December 18 1942 when Rosenberg's representative in the area, Otto Brautigam, led a German delegation at the Kurman festival and both sides made speeches pledging friendship and cooperation. A Balkiar nobleman even presented one of the famous Balkiar mountain horses to the Germans as a personal gift for Hitler.

The icy Ninth Circle of Hell

For Stalin, his dreaded NKVD secret police and those fighting the Wehrmacht, the warmth of this relationship between some Muslims and the invaders was anathema. Brutal as the fighting on the Eastern Front always was, it tended to reach its zenith when former countrymen came to blows. One incident is indicative of the merciless nature of the fighting between these former countrymen. In that winter of 1942, south of the Kuban River in the Caucasus, as the great German offensive ground to a halt there were bitter battles on the 'Stalin Highway' from Saratovskaya and Krasnodar, as the Soviets strove to cut the Germans only withdrawal route north. Fighting alongside the German 97th Jäger Division (literally 'hunter' but used to describe élite light infantry, usually mountain-trained) was a company of Turkmen volunteers who were based in the long-abandoned village of Severskaya. One morning the Turkmen could not be raised by radio and a German patrol was sent to investigate. As the patrol neared the village, they became uneasy as they noticed the unusual quiet and so, like the veterans they were, they prepared for possible action. There was no need. The patrol commander went into the first house and reeled at the sight. The Turkmen still lay in their beds but minus their heads. The hut was awash with blood. Every building was the same. The entire company had been decapitated, and scrawled in chalk on the walls of the peasant *isbas* (huts) was the legend: 'Traitors will not escape revenge!'

Muslims in combat

Hundreds of miles north on the mighty Volga, the cataclysmic battle of Stalingrad was in full flow. Both sides had their contingents of Muslims, although they seemed to be having different experiences. The Red Army was throwing any and every man it could lay its hands on into the desperate fighting to try and retain a hold in the city. For the Muslims of central Asia there was an enforced levée en masse, as the NKVD, the Soviet secret police, rounded them up by the thousand and pressed them into battalions at the front. The Kazakhs alone contributed five entire rifle divisions. By November 1942, almost half of Chuikov's 62nd Army fighting von Paulus's Sixth Army was made up of barely-trained Uzbeks, Kazakhs and Crimean Tartars. Air attack, artillery and armour unnerved them and they were liable to panic. This lack of understanding of modern technology, coupled with problems with the Russian language, were grave handicaps. One Russian lieutenant commanding Muslim conscripts commented: 'It is hard for them to understand things, and it very difficult to work with them.'

Huge numbers died without even knowing the names of their officers. The Red Army's Muslim 196th Rifle Division for example was almost entirely wiped out, and thousands of other Islamic conscripts simply deserted in an attempt to escape the horror. One Crimean Tartar from the 284th Rifle Division decided he had had enough and as night fell he crawled out of his trench and across no-man's land towards the German positions. Disorientated in the darkness he actually doubled back on himself and crossed back into the lines of the neighbouring Soviet 685th Rifle Regiment. He walked into a command bunker to surrender to find it full of Soviet officers. As the Red Army report stated, 'The traitor was executed.'

On the other side, the Germans had a far smaller Muslim contingent but it made its mark. Sixth Army had over 50,000 Hiwis in its ranks including three entire battalions of Turkmen. Following their encirclement by the Red Army in the winter of 1942–43 all three Turkmen battalions fought to the last man in the snow and rubble of the city rather than surrender. Alongside them in the first week of January 1943, as the Sixth Army was in its death throes, other Muslim volunteers fought equally well. One German officer in the hotly contested factory district reported: 'Especially brave were the Tartars. As anti-tank gunners using a captured Russian weapon, they were proud of every Soviet tank they hit. These fellows were fantastic.'

Better trained, better led and perhaps better motivated, the German Army's Muslims died in the snow with their comrades of the Heer. For those that survived the final conflagration in the city there were only the tender mercies of the NKVD's well-trained 10th Division in their distinctive blue-piped uniforms waiting for them. Whole companies of the secret police combed the still-smoking ruins and the columns of skeletal prisoners, and any Muslims who were found were either shot out of hand or marched off to their imminent deaths. There was to be no mercy on the Volga that winter.

As for the Muslim populations overrun in von Kleist's Caucasus offensive (disparagingly called by the troops involved, *Kaukasus hin und zurück* – Caucasus there and back offensive), the hasty German withdrawal back north over the winter of 1942–43 was a disaster. Rightly fearing Stalin's revenge, thousands of them abandoned their homes and took to the roads. After only knowing the Wehrmacht as an occupying force for a matter of months, the refugees packed their belongings either into carts or piled on their backs and hurried westwards through the gathering snows. Needless to say many died on the way from the cold, hunger and vengefull partisan attacks.

Hitler tries to hold back the waves

Despite their increasing importance in the German Order of Battle the Osttruppen continued to be a source of immense disagreement in the Nazi hierarchy. Hitler especially did not want to acknowledge that

Germany needed Eastern *untermensch* to fight the Red Army. After all, not so long ago, on 16 July 1941, he had addressed his generals on the subject of arming volunteers from the East:

> It must always remain a cast-iron principle that none but Germans shall be allowed to bear arms. Even when, at first sight, it might seem expedient to summon foreign peoples to arms, it would be folly to do so. One day it would be sure to prove our absolute and irretrievable undoing.

Doing his best King Canute impersonation, Hitler issued an order on 10 February 1942 forbidding the enlistment of any more Osttruppen, but no sooner had it been transmitted than it was already being almost universally ignored, a situation that the Wehrmacht would have done well to remember when it laboured under Hitler's infamous 'hold ground at all costs' orders later on in the War. If nothing else, the Osttruppen issue proved that a slavish obedience to every utterance from Hitler was not always necessary. No German officer was disciplined for disobeying the February decree and Muslims continued to pour into the ranks of the Ostheer. Perhaps a reason behind Hitler's leniency on the issue was his knowledge that neutral Turkey was looking on to see how their ethnic cousins, the Turkmen, were treated. Hitler had already entertained General Erkilet of the Turkish General Staff in the autumn of 1941, who prevailed upon him to be lenient with Red Army POWs of Turkic ethnicity. Hitler's fantasy of bringing Turkey into the War on the Axis side, as in the First World War, was always to play in the back of his mind when it came to the subject of Muslim volunteers.

The Osttruppen mainstreamed – pay and rations

By mid-summer of 1942 the use of Osttruppen was so prevalent that it was decided by OKH that they needed to be regularised in terms of pay, rations, ranks, decorations and dress. Decrees of 14 July and 18 August laid down standards of uniform and rank and even instituted a special war decoration, the 'Decoration for Bravery and Merit of the Eastern People', available in five grades and awarded with swords for action at the front and without swords for rear area non-combatant merit. It must be remembered that this privilege was not afforded to the much-vaunted western European legions serving at the front, indeed, the Dutch contingent were even banned from wearing their own 'Mussert Cross' medal all together. In addition, the Osttruppen were made eligible for all German awards. As for the often vexed question of uniforms, in essence the Osttruppen used whatever uniform was to hand, most often based on the Wehrmacht patterns used by the Turkestani formations affiliated to the 162nd Infantry Division but with distinct differences between nationalities. The one item that Hitler drew the line on was that the *Hoheitabzeichen* emblem, the German eagle clutching a swastika that every member of the Wehrmacht wore above the right breast pocket, was not to be worn by the *Ostvolk*, the eastern people. No doubt this symbolic gesture made his reliance on the so-called Slavic *untermensch* a little more palatable to Hitler. However, even that directive was only followed occasionally, after all, in the mud and fire of the Russian Front, who really had time to care about the niceties of a tunic emblem?

For rank insignia there were two systems in operation, both modelled on the Russian and not German patterns. The first was used for the Ukrainians and Cossacks and the second for the ethnic legions from Armenia, Georgia and the Muslim minorities. Each legion had its own cap cockade and arm shield, usually in their national colours and often depicting a national symbol. The Turkmen for instance often sported an arm shield depicting a famous mosque from the legendary city of Samarkand.

In August 1942, *General* (Lieutenant General) Ernst Köstring, like von Niedermayer another former Military Attaché, this time in Moscow, who had been born and brought up in Russia and spoke fluent Russian, was appointed Inspector General of Turkic and Caucasian Forces. Potentially of huge significance, this bold move was lessened in importance by the fact that his entire assigned staff consisted of one *Hauptmann* (Captain) staff officer, one driver and a single clerk. Köstring's remit was broadened out four months later on 15 December when his function became the 'Inspectorate of Osttruppen'. He had no command responsibilities for the Osttruppen but at least provided some coordination and he remained in post until his retirement from service in January 1943, whereupon his command was given to *General* Heinz Hellmich, a non-Russian speaker with no specialist knowledge of the East at all. The appointment was not a success and Köstring was prevailed upon to come out of retirement in June and return to head up all Turkic and Caucasian units. Although not quite in the same league as Guderian and his hugely powerful Inspectorate of Panzer troops, these were still significant steps in formalizing what was fast becoming a huge part of Nazi Germany's war effort in the East. By the end of 1941 there were some 150,000 Osttruppen serving with the Wehrmacht, and this figure ballooned so that by September 1943, official German Army estimates placed the number of Osttruppen at over half a million grouped in more than 78 battalions and 122 independent companies. Whilst this number is enormous it was dwarfed by the summer of 1944 when close to a million Osttruppen were officially recorded across the Heer, Luftwaffe and even the Kriegsmarine. Even though most German units kept little official record of their Hiwis, it is clear that without them the Ostheer would not have been able to hold out against the growing might of the Red Army as long as it did.

Spades not rifles

It wasn't just at the front that Soviet Muslims made such a valuable contribution to the Nazi war effort. Given the Soviet Union's vast spaces and lack of infrastructure, the Nazis concentrated an enormous amount of effort on improving the often scant road and rail networks and increasingly, as the Wehrmacht passed onto the defensive, the building of defensive lines and fortifications. Huge numbers of Muslims were involved in these endeavors, including by the middle of 1943, some 111 companies of Turkmen (over 20,000 men), 21 companies of Azeris and 15 of Volga Tartars.

The German Army's North African and Middle Eastern 'stormtroopers'

Although it was in Soviet Russia that Muslim soldiers came to the fore for the Wehrmacht, it was not the only theatre of operations where the Axis looked to put Islam in uniform. With Rommel driving east to Suez and the Ostheer looking to move south into the Caucasus, the Middle East and North Africa assumed important geographical positions for the Reich. A small number of Arabs from a range of Middle Eastern countries; Egypt, Iraq, Palestine, Transjordan and Syria were floating around the system until the appointment of the Luftwaffe General, Hellmuth Felmy, on 21 June 1941, as the Wehrmacht's head of Arab affairs. The so-called Special Staff F. Felmy, was initially involved in trying to support the Iraqi revolt, but with that failure he turned his attention to recruiting and training a cadre of Arabs who could be utilised to further Nazi Germany's cause.

The 288th Training Battalion

Initially established at the Döberitz training ground just outside Berlin, the new cadre unit was designated the 288th Training Battalion. Another base was then organised in Sunium, Greece where the inflow of recruits was to undergo initial military training. This was not popular with the exiles who regarded military discipline as unduly harsh and the physical 'toughening-up' process as too much like hard work. The German training staff did not help matters, as they were mainly men who had lived and worked in the Middle East prior to the War and tended to view Arabs as second-class citizens.

The British offensive of November 1941 in the Western Desert forced OKH to amend its plans and send the still-forming 288th to aid Rommel in blocking the whirlwind British advance. This left a rump of some 30 Arab volunteers at Sunium to continue their training. They were joined in April 1942 by a further 103 men, many of whom had 'volunteered' from the teeming POW camps of North Africa. They arrived to find a far different set-up than was originated in late 1941 with a new commander, *Hauptmann* Schober, making a radical difference. New uniforms with a 'Free Arabia' armband had been issued, training had been standardized and made more professional and some of the equipment deficiencies had been rectified. Altogether this made the recruits feel much more like soldiers of the Reich than they had before.

Arabs in Russia

The summer advance of von Kleist's Army Group A into the Caucasus in 1942 was seen as an opportunity by the OKH to deploy the Arabs and hopefully stir their fellow Muslims into open support of the invaders. Consequently, the original Battalion, now upgraded with the addition of more than two battalions of German troops as well as heavy weapons companies to become the 287th Special Regiment, was transferred in August to Stalino in southern Russia in readiness to intervene when the German advance reached the southern Caucasus. This it never did and the Arabs were not used to bolster the collaborationist efforts of their co-religionists. So bad was morale among the Arabs that Schober had to parade them and remind them of their oath of service to try and instil some sort of order in their increasingly fractious ranks. With von Kleist then in retreat, the Arab battalion was withdrawn from theatre and sent to Sicily, while their German comrades were sent to Budenovsk where they helped to counter an attack by the Red Army's 4th Cavalry Corps.

Operation Torch

The Anglo-American landings in French North Africa in November triggered a change of view for the Arabs, who had now spent the better part of a year being shunted around the Nazi empire without ever seeing any action. Taking the short trip across the Mediterranean to Tunisia the Arabs were now reorganized, again, into the *Deutsch-Arabisches Bataillon Nr 845* (the 845th German-Arab Battalion). Somewhat surprisingly the Allied invasion had prompted a few hundred local North Africans to volunteer for service with the Axis, and enough men were forthcoming to raise two battalions of Tunisians, and one each of Algerians and Moroccans. Motivation though was not centred on belief in the Axis cause but the fact that service was seen as a way out of hunger and grinding poverty.

Having said that, most of the recuits had previous military experience in one of the colonial armies and one man had even served as an NCO in the Imperial Ottoman Army in the First World War. Companies in the newly-raised battalions were strong with generally about 150 men in each commanded by German Afrika Korps officers with Teutonic ex-French Foreign legionnaires acting as the NCO cadre. However, due to the tenuous supply situation of the time the troops were poorly equipped with mainly ex-French Army weaponry and training was fairly rudimentary. The whole set-up then suffered a major blow when its commander, the now-promoted Major Schobert, and his superior *Oberstleutnant* (Lieutenant-Colonel) Meyer-Ricks were killed during an airstrike on 24 February 1943. Effectively beheaded, the Muslim soldiers floundered, and with the building pressure being exerted by the Allies from both east and west, the Axis command had little energy left to focus on its newest local additions.

Beggars can't be choosers though, and Montgomery's advance in late February and early March necessitated the use of every available man at the front. Consequently the Tunisian battalion was deployed forward and ordered into the line. Led forward by guides into an exposed position on a hill during a cold and wet night, the Tunisians settled into their new positions by lighting fires to try and warm themselves against the chill. As this was entirely contrary to much more disciplined German practice the neighbouring units in the line thought the Allies had taken the position and opened fire on their Muslim comrades-in-arms. Noting the disarray in the Axis line the British reacted swiftly and launched an immediate attack. The Tunisians were hit by the veterans of the Eighth Army and sent streaming back off the hill. German units had to mount desperate local counter-attacks to stabilise the front and make up for the deficiencies of their latest allies.

From then on the majority of the Muslim battalions were used on rear area duties and the building of defensive positions. Three companies were however deemed good enough to be posted to act as the tactical reserve of the 999th Light Division (Africa). Employed on the northern sector of the line near Mator, the Muslims acquitted themselves rather better than their cousins on the front facing the British Eighth Army. Fighting alongside the veterans of the Luftwaffe's Hermann Goering Division and Witzig's élite para-engineers, the Islamic troopers fought well in repelling attacks from the fresh-faced American First Army units. As the Axis bridgehead in North Africa shrank they retreated backwards towards the coast and eventually assembled at Porto Parina, north of Tunis hoping to be evacuated before the end came.

It was not to be, and so along with around 4,000 other German soldiers gathered at the small port, they were taken captive by the victorious Allies in May as Germany's entire 300,000-plus army in Africa was finally overwhelmed.

The 845th German-Arab Battalion in Yugoslavia

Disastrous though the intervention in North Africa had been for the 845th, enough of a cadre had been withdrawn before the final capitulation to enable the battalion to be reconstituted and sent on again, this time to the Balkans. Stationed in Greece under the control of *Heeresgruppe E* (Army Group E) the Battalion fought Greek partisans in the region south of Lamia during the spring and summer of 1944. In the autumn of that year, with the Red Army looking as if it might cut off the entire German southern wing, the decision was taken by OKW to evacuate the Aegean area. Fleeing towards the north-west as fast as they could the Germans were harried by Tito's men and local partisans of all colours as they scented blood. The 845th was one of the rearguard units selected to try and keep these incessant attacks from slowing the retreat.

Here at last the Arabs did themselves justice in combat. The terrain was not the deserts they had been trained to fight in but the cold, dark hills of the Balkans. Nonetheless they fought hard against an experienced enemy who was buoyed by the knowledge of impending victory. Operating in territory only recently evacuated by their fellow Muslims of the SS-Handschar, the Arabs were involved in bitter fighting around Uzice in Serbia, where in deep snow and biting cold they seized a prominent local feature, Hill 734, from Tito's men to allow the retreat to continue. They relinquished ground inch by inch until by early 1945 the remnants of the Battalion were between the Danube and Sava Rivers north of Bosnia (in fact, again very near the remnants of the SS-Handschar). Exhausted, low on supplies and having taken debilitating casualties, the few survivors surrendered to local partisans in May. Amazingly they were not shot out of hand, as happened to so many Axis troops in the Balkans, and were eventually sent to a POW camp. Kept behind the wire for about a year they were then quietly released and returned home to their various countries with little fanfare. For many of them their experiences with the Nazis would actually stand them in good stead, as the Muslim countries of the Middle East, and to a lesser extent North Africa, prepared to try and destroy the infant state of Israel.

IV

The 1st East Mussulman SS-Regiment – Himmler's first Muslim SS (Ostmuselmannisches SS-Regiment 1)

The 1943 Waffen-SS expansion

Himmler had been working assiduously since the outbreak of the War in 1939 to expand the armed, Waffen-SS wing of his empire. The advent of Barbarossa in all its vast scale had speeded up this process and 1943 was a watershed year in the growth of the Black Guard. Previous recruitment and formational strictures, imposed by the Wehrmacht high command, which had hitherto acted as a brake on growth, were either greatly relaxed or dispensed with. The result was an explosion in the overall number of Waffen-SS personnel and type of units. This was especially true of foreign recruitment, which prior to 1943 had primarily been focused on either providing small-scale battle casualty replacements to the existing SS field divisions, or more importantly in setting up and manning the various Waffen-SS national volunteer legions. These SS legions; the Norwegian *Legion Norwegen*, the Danish *Freikorps Danmark*, the Dutch *Legion Niederlande* and the Flemish *Legion Flandern*, were all recruited for an initial two-year engagement and in 1943 this was ending.

The performance of the legions had been mixed, with issues around training and treatment of volunteers damaging performance. But the Russian Front was a formidable school for a soldier to learn his trade and two years on from their inception there were enough signs of optimism from the legions to convince the SS authorities that the foreign volunteer experiment should be continued. What was also clear, was that a complete restructuring was needed. The legions themselves were too small as units to maintain viability at the front. Casualties in Russia were so high that anything less than brigade or regimental size was quickly worn down to nothing and became combat ineffective. Consequently, the conclusion was not that fewer foreign volunteers were needed, but more. The aim now then was to use the surviving veterans as cadres to expand the old legions into much larger SS regiments or full blown SS-*Sturmbrigades* (assault brigades), such as the French SS-*Frankreich*, Belgian Walloon SS-*Wallonien* and the Belgian Flemish SS-*Langemarck*. These units would then be used to form either new divisions in their own right, or to act as significant reinforcements for the existing premier SS formations, thus the Wallonien fought with the SS-Wiking and the Langemarck with the SS-Das Reich.

Himmler takes a hand

But even this major expansion was not enough for the Reichsführer-SS Heinrich Himmler, and he cast his acquisitive eye still further afield to fill the Waffen-SS order of battle. Himmler, just like his master in the Reich Chancellory, was rabidly anti-Slav and still could not bring himself to agree with the playwrite Schiller's view on Russia; '*Russland nur durch Russland überwunden*' (roughly translated, 'Only Russia can overcome Russia'). This was still a step too far for the bespectacled Bavarian bureaucrat, but the host of Muslims already serving in the German Army at the front were a different ball game as far as he was concerned.

For Himmler, the bravery of the Muslim soldiery in von Kleist's Caucasus invasion had been encouraging, especially their performance during the winter retreat when they had fought doggedly as part of the rearguard of Army Group A. This positive impression was reinforced during Manstein and Hausser's crucial check to the charging Red Army at the battle of Kharkov. When the city was initially abandoned, contrary to Hitler's latest 'hold to the last man' order and prior to the counter-attack led by the SS panzer corps, a Turkmen battalion had lost its beloved German commander killed in action and had actually voluntarily re-entered the doomed city to retrieve his body for an honourable burial. This was the kind of act that Himmler could appreciate and firmly planted in his mind the potential for an SS Turkic Muslim division. As so often when Himmler had an idea that needed action to become reality, he turned to his arch-fixer and close confidant, the seemingly tireless Swabian SS-Gruppenführer Gottlob Berger and the recruiting machinery of his *SS-Hauptamt* (SS Main office responsible for all foreign volunteer recruitment).

Berger had been Himmler's main ally in building the Waffen-SS since before the War and for him this was another opportunity to dutifully answer his master's call. After putting out some feelers and speaking to various members of his own staff and that of OKH, Berger began to look closely at an existing German Army unit; the *verstärkt Turkestanisches Infanterie-Bataillon* 450 (reinforced Turkistani Infantry Battalion 450).

Colonel Reinhard Gehlen
and Major Andreas Meyer-Mader

On the whole, the Wehrmacht juggernaut that thundered across the border into the Soviet Union on 22 June 1941 was anti-Slav in outlook and thinking. This was especially pronounced of course in the Waffen-SS formations. This antipathy, prevalent though it was, was not universal. From the beginning there were members of the Army officer corps who agreed fundamentally with Schiller's comment above on how to defeat Russia. Many of them had initimate knowledge of Russia, having either served there in the past, being Russian-born or of Baltic German parentage like *Reichsminister* Rosenberg himself. This admittedly small group of enlightened junior officers (none was above the rank of Colonel) found a spiritual home in *Oberst* (Colonel) Reinhard Gehlen's *Fremde Heere Ost Abteilung* (Enemy Armies East Section) in the *Abwehr* intelligence service. Here they expounded their belief that the best, and indeed only, way of winning the war in Russia was to turn the seething discontent of the Soviet masses against their own communist government. For Gehlen and his compatriots the Slavs were not enemies but potential allies in crushing Stalin.

One officer with such an outlook, although not a member of Gehlen's staff, was the Austrian *Major* (Major) Andreas Meyer-Mader. Meyer-Mader had had an interesting career to date, having already commanded foreign troops when he was posted as a liaison officer before the War to the Chinese Nationalist Generalissimo Chiang Kai-Shek. Initially intended to carry out a purely technical advisory role in Chiang Kai-Shek's long running war with Mao Tse-Tung's Communists, Meyer-Mader had ended up commanding Nationalist troops in the field during Mao's now-famous Long March.

Meyer-Mader's experiences in China would probably have been nothing more than a fascinating interlude in his military career, except that he went on to serve with the Seventeenth Army in southern Russia during the early winter of 1941. He was there when the decision was taken by *General* Russwurm (at the same time as von Bock was making the same decision to the north with Army Broup B) to raise two battalions of local Hiwis to supplement the strength of his 444th *Sicherungs* Divison

(Security Division) made up of older men and tasked with combating partisans in the rear areas. One battalion was Christian and the other was Muslim, the latter being designated the 444th Turkmen Battalion. Casting around for a suitable commander, Russwurm alighted on Meyer-Mader as an officer with just the right experience to lead foreign troops and he was duly appointed. The Battalion was immediately thrown into the ruthless barbarity of the Russian *Bandenkrieg* (guerrilla war) and under Meyer-Mader's command soon earned an unenviable reputation for horrendous behaviour over the winter of 1941–1942. Despite this, the experiment was judged enough of a success to separate out the Turkmen and expand the size of the unit. The result was the creation of the *verstärkt Turkestanisches Infanterie-Bataillon* 450 (reinforced Turkistani Infantry Battalion 450).

The *verstärkt Turkestanisches Infanterie-Bataillon 450*

Withdrawn from the front in southern Russia at the beginning of January 1942 the Turkmen were sent by train over a thousand miles north to the old Polish fortress town of Modlin in the *General Gouvernement fur die besetzten Polnischen Gebiete* (General Government for the Occupied Polish Region), more commonly known simply as the General Government. For the Turkmen it was the first time that any of them had been outside the Soviet Union; equally, the local Poles were extremely curious about the new arrivals, but there was no time for pleasantries, as no sooner had they arrived in Modlin than they were sent on to the small town of Legionowo some thirteen miles to the east. It was here that the Turkmen were officially designated the *verstärkt Turkestanisches Infanterie-Bataillon* 450 on 13 January 1942. Still under Meyer-Mader's command the new unit was built up with fresh drafts of volunteers, many of them ex-POWs desperate to escape the horrors of German captivity, and put through its paces on the training grounds with stocks of captured Soviet weaponry. Within a few weeks the unit boasted a strength of 822, comprising a German cadre of 10 officers, 52 NCOs and 31 other ranks (filling specialist and support roles), with a mainstay of 620 Turkmen other ranks, 102 NCOs and also seven officers. To have so many command appointments filled by Turkmen was truly remarkable. By comparison the Flemish SS-Legion Flandern, comprising some thousand men of all ranks, went into combat the previous November with only a solitary Flemish NCO, the rest being German. To have almost as many Turkmen officers as Germans was also worthy of note, this was clearly not to be a unit of cannon-fodder Turkmen commanded solely by Germans. The new unit was established with three battalions; Companies 1–4 in I Battalion, Companies 5–8 in II Battalion and Companies 9–12 in III Battalion.

Following its training period in Poland the new unit was again dispatched to southern Russia, this time to reinforce the German Army's largest field formation, Friedrich von Paulus's massively powerful Sixth Army. As the Sixth Army thrust eastwards in the Wehrmacht's renewed summer offensive of 1942 the Turkmen followed in its wake acting as rear area security, although in the huge expanses of the southern steppes and in the chaos of cut-off Soviet formations this often meant in effect frontline combat against Red Army men as well as partisans. When the Sixth Army finally arrived at the gates of Stalingrad in late autumn Meyer-Mader's men were one of several units tasked with keeping open the vital rail link back west to the logistics and communications centre of Kharkov in the Ukraine. This was a thankless job but not as hard as the death struggle von Paulus's men were engaged in on the banks of the Volga, but even so Meyer-Mader seemed incapable of maintaining basic discipline in the unit and their behaviour deteriorated until atrocities against local civilians were commonplace.

The Soviet counter-offensive that saw Sixth Army encircled, pushed the Turkmen and their German allies back westwards and ended *Heeresgruppe Süd's* (Army Group South's) patience with the Austrian major and his men. Meyer-Mader himself was relieved of command for incompetence and the battalion was withdrawn from service until further notice. Unlike many other units of Muslim volunteers fighting in the same theatre with both von Paulus's men and von Kleist in the Caucasus, this particular unit was a disaster. In truth, German commanders did not know what to do with it and were unwilling to waste either precious trained German cadre personnel or modern weaponry on it. For the moment they would let it kick its heels in the rear.

SS-Obersturmbannführer Meyer-Mader and the 94th SS Regiment

It was at this time that Gottlob Berger began to express an interest in the Turkmen and one can only guess at the feelings of relief that this investigation evinced in the harried staff officers of Army Group South. As a result, it was made known to Berger that there would be no Army opposition to recruiting the Turkmen into the Waffen-SS. Berger was also interested in the Turkmen's former commander and set up a meeting in November 1943 between his boss the Reichsführer, Meyer-Mader and the Mufti of Jerusalem (more information on the Mufti is included in the next chapter).

The agenda was the ability to raise, train and lead a combat division of Turkic Muslim SS. The Mufti's role was to give the proposed formation his blessing and spiritual guidance, and for him to lend practical recruitment support to Meyer-Mader who was to be induced to transfer to the Waffen-SS and lead the new unit. The first meeting went well and was followed up on 14 December 1943 by a second where Meyer-Mader was promised a promotion, a free hand in recruiting and an increase in pay, rations and equipment scales for his new troops. The Austrian officer agreed and overnight became SS-Obersturmbannführer Andreas Meyer-Mader, regimental commander of the 94th SS Regiment formally established on 18 December 1943.

Based in the Poniatowa/Kaposvar area the new regiment was made up of recruits lured over by Meyer-Mader from the now-defunct and disgraced *verstärkt Turkestanisches Infanterie-Bataillon* 450 (a transfer the Army were only too pleased to see). Meyer-Mader also recruited men from existing Turkic Osttruppen units such as the 480th, 782nd, 786th and 791st Turkestanische Battalions, as well as the Azeri 818th and Volga Tartar 831st. POW camps were trawled as well as the teeming ranks of Hiwis and soon there were some 3,000 men in training in the unit. Redesignated the 450th Eastern Regiment, with a complement of three infantry battalions of three strong companies each, the formation continued its work-up training in spring 1944 but was hampered by lack of equipment. Although some first-class German arms were forthcoming as promised, the supply situation in the Third Reich was such that it was difficult to see how the unit was ever going to receive anything other than the scraps from a pretty meagre table. Even uniforms were scarce and many men had no boots. In an attempt to remedy the situation the Regiment was transferred to the Trawniki base area near Lublin, which had been used for some time as the training centre for non-German concentration camp personnel. The move did mean that some of the worst deficiencies of kit were made up, but it did not bode well for how the Turkmen were viewed by the SS authorities, or how they were to be trained. This was an establishment that oversaw the arming and preparation of some of Nazi Germany's most brutal and barbarous thugs.

Combat in Belarus – *the Ostmuselmannisches SS-Regiment 1* (the 1st East Mussulman SS-Regiment)

Alongside this less than helpful geographic move, and as ever on the merry-go-round of Waffen-SS nomenclature, the Turkmen then underwent another name change at the beginning of March 1944 when they were officially re-titled the *Ostmuselmannisches SS-Regiment* 1 (the 1st East Mussulman SS-Regiment). This was intended as a precursor to their envisaged expansion into a full Turkic SS division. It was also decided that some of them at least were ready to take part in an upcoming anti-partisan offensive in Belorussia. Shipped to the town of Yuratishki near Minsk the Turkic SS men were supplied some weaponry and uniforms from the SS logistics depot at Bobruisk and prepared for combat, although it seems only the relatively small number of 550 men were considered fit for action at the time and the majority of the Regiment did not move out to take part in the fighting.

Belorussia itself had the dubious distinction of suffering the highest per capita casualty rate of any country in Hitler's war, higher even than Poland, the Ukraine and Yugoslavia. Fought over by local nationalists, separatist Poles and Ukrainians, as well as the invading Nazis and liberating Soviets, the fertile land and thriving cities of Belorussia were reduced to bloody ruin in more than three years of total war. By the spring of 1944, unrest in the country was endemic due to the savagery of German oppression and STAVKA's (the Soviet Supreme Command) policy of stirring up resistance in the Wehrmacht's backyard to disrupt German effectiveness at the front. The terrain, with its almost limitless forests and swamps, made it relatively easy for large numbers of partisans to operate and unbelievably some 150,000 were estimated to be doing so according to the German OKH by early 1944. They were organized into approximately 150 brigades and 49 separate detachments. The result for the Germans was chaos and real concern about the vital rail and road links to the frontline in the east. For example, the main Lida to Minsk rail line was attacked an average of 40 times a month. Something had to be done, and that something was planned to be a co-ordinated offensive between elements of Third Panzer Army and the rear area security formations of Belorussia' s Higher SS and Police Leader SS-Gruppenführer Curt von Gottberg's *Kampfgruppe von Gottberg.*

Dirlewanger, Kaminski and the death of SS-Obersturmbannführer Meyer-Mader

The proposed offensive was targeted at the Lepel-Usaci area north-east of Minsk and west of Vitebsk. There were believed to be about 14,000 partisans in the region including the 3,000 man-strong Alexejew Brigade and the 2,500 men of the Melnikov Brigade, among others. The plan was to surround the partisans to deny them an escape route, then to destroy them before they could link up. The first part of the operation was named

Unternehmen Regenschauer – Operation Rainshower, and was an attack by units of Third Panzer Army west (including three armoured trains and a security regiment), launched on April 11, to push the partisans back and establish a secure stop-line on the Lake Gomel to Lake Beloje axis. The second part of the offensive was codenamed *Unternehmen Frühlingsfest* – Operation Spring Festival, and was aimed at attacking the compressed guerrilla formations and annihilating them. Involved in the latter operation were a real menagerie of units, including some of the most notorious ever to wear SS uniform, such as the the convicted felons of SS-*Sonderkommando Dirlewanger* (SS-Special Commando Dirlewanger), the turncoats of the *Kaminski* Brigade, the killers of SS-Police Regiments 2, 24 and 26 (and SD Battalion 23), as well as the locally-recruited auxiliaries of two *Schutzmannschaft* Battalions. Kampfgruppe von Gottberg was divided into four attacking columns for the assault; Krehan, Kaminski, Anhalt and Rehdans, with Meyer-Mader's available Muslim SS men placed in Gruppe Anhalt under the tactical control of the mass murderer SS-Standartenführer Oskar Dirlewanger. Dirlewanger's unit, originally intended as a penal unit for convicted poachers was only 434 men strong when the attack started (including only eight officers) and so the addition of the 550 Muslims was welcomed. However, from the start the deployment of the Turkmen did not go as planned.

The advance of Gruppe Anhalt was characterised by 'clearance' operations that saw civilians seized for transport to the Reich as slave labour, their villages burned and livestock confiscated. Anyone who objected was summarily shot. Given such a barbaric example the Turkmen responded in kind and soon vied with the criminals of the *Sonderkommando* for the level of atrocity they could commit. As before, Meyer-Mader could not control his charges and to all intents and purposes it was Dirlewanger who led the Turkmen in their first taste of action as SS men.

Bitter fighting soon broke out as the SS advanced north and the villages of Hornowo-Sswatki, Hornowo II and Hornung-Asory III were hotly contested during the last two weeks of April and into early May. There was further fighting at the village of Horowo-Wiercinski on 2 May and it was here that SS-Oberstumbannführer Andreas Meyer-Mader, late German Army major commanding the 450th Reinforced Turkistani Infantry Battalion and first commander of the 1st East Mussulman SS-Regiment, was reported as 'Killed in Action'. Meyer-Mader's death is shrouded in mystery. He was the only German reported killed in the action, no-one else was even wounded, and none of his Turkmen seem to have been involved in any combat that day either. The entire SS-Sonderkommando only lost 19 men killed and 43 wounded during the whole month-long operation. What is clear was that by this time Meyer-

Mader had become an embarrassment to the Waffen-SS. He had not learnt from his failures of command in the Army and his men had ran amok seemingly even in excess of Dirlewanger's killers. Perhaps he was killed in a partisan attack, but equally possible was that Dirlewanger had ordered for him to be shot to spare the further blushes of his SS bosses. Whatever the truth the result was that morale within the 1st East Mussulman SS-Regiment, which was fragile at best, plummeted with the death of their beloved leader. Meyer-Mader was militarily incompetent but he was also adored by his Turkmen soldiers. He made a concerted effort to understand them, their cultures and traditions, and to learn at least bits of their languages, but he was unable to translate this affinity into the creation of an efficient fighting unit, even when other Turkmen formations had been a success. In particular his record was besmirched by a horrendous litany of atrocities committed by his men stretching from the Don Region and southern Russia in 1942 and 1943 and into Belorussia in the spring of 1944.

Fritz Sauckel, the Reich Plenipotentiary for Labour and Manpower and ex-Gauleiter of Thuringia, even went so far as sending Dirlewanger a warning order on 8 May suggesting the entire regiment of SS Turkmen were going to be permanently attached to his Sonderkommando in late June, and that a further 1,000 Turkmen were in Oslo in Occupied-Norway awaiting transport to join their fellow-countrymen in Belorussia. This turned out not to be true, although Muslim units would continue to serve alongside, or in association, with Dirlewanger's murderous gang for the rest of the War. This was forever to their detriment as they were continually embroiled in the horror that was Dirlewanger's war.

As it turned out after Meyer-Mader's death, and with the suspension of Regenschauer and Frühlingsfest on 10 May 1944, the Regiment was wholly withdrawn from action and confined to barracks for a desperately needed reorganisation.

Reorganisation and retribution

With Meyer-Mader dead a new commander for the Regiment was found in the form of the much lower ranking SS-Hauptsturmführer Billig. Billig's lack of seniority did little to reassure the unhappy Turkmen, but much worse was to come when the abrasive SS-Hauptsturmführer decided that the only way to stiffen the unit's resolve was to weed out elements he considered 'undesirable'. He consequently convened an SS military court and tried large numbers of the Regiment for insubordination. A staggering 78 were found guilty during these pretty dubious legal proceedings and were summarily shot. Even the SS authorities, not renowned for their squeamishness, found this bloody episode difficult to swallow and Billig was hurriedly replaced by SS-Hauptsturmführer Herman after less than a month in charge, in an attempt to sweep the whole embarrassing and brutal episode under the carpet.

The 1st East Mussulman SS-Regiment and Operation Bagration

Following the Turkmen's inept performance during the fighting in April and May there was little enthusiasm at OKH to re-deploy the Regiment into combat, but everything changed on the morning of 22 June 1944. On that fateful date, exactly three years to the day since Nazi Germany launched Operation Barbarossa, the Red Army launched Operation Bagration, its biggest offensive of the War so far. Named after the famous Tsarist prince who helped defeat Napoleon's Grande Armée in 1812, the sheer size and scale of Bagration was truly awesome. The STAVKA had amassed over 2,500,000 men supported by 5,200 tanks, 5,300 aircraft and a staggering 31,300 artillery pieces. In opposition *Generalfeldmarschall* Busch's Army Group Centre could only deploy 580,000 men equipped with 900 tanks, 775 aircraft and 9,500 artillery guns. Bagration's aim was to destroy *Heeresgruppe Mitte* (Army Group Centre) completely and liberate all of Belorussia, and from day one of the attack the Red Army set about doing just that.

The Ostheer struggled to respond effectively to the offensive as the sheer weight of the assault swept the German defences away. As he was wont to do, Hitler decided to 'aid' the Soviets by removing his commanders' freedom of action and imposing one of his 'hold to the last man' orders. The result was that whole regiments and divisions were wiped off the face of the map by the Red Army behemoth.

In these circumstances, fighting the partisans became of secondary importance and every man who could hold a rifle was called to the front. This included the rear area troops of Kampfgruppe von Gottberg who were thrown into the path of the advancing Soviets east of Minsk near Smilovici as part of Heinrici's Fourth Army. The Kampfgruppe included SS-Police Regiments 2, 4, 17, 22, 26, 34 and 36 among others. Prominent among the Kampfgruppe was SS-Sonderkommando Dirlewanger, and again attached to it were the Turkmen of the 1st East Mussulman SS-Regiment. Still 4,000 men strong, the Regiment should have been a stalwart of the defence but was becoming more of a liability as time went on. Under pressure from the advancing 26th and 83rd Guards Rifle

Divisions Kampfgruppe von Gottberg was pushed westward towards Lida and away from Minsk as it struggled to help stem the Soviet tide. But its intervention was only ever going to be a sticking plaster for an increasingly desperate Army Group Centre. By 29 June, only a week after the offensive had started, the Germans had already lost 130,000 men killed, 60,000 captured and almost all of its 900 tanks destroyed.

With the loss of Minsk, the Belorussian capital city on 3 July, the entire German front was effectively split and a race was on to strengthen the northern and southern shoulders of the huge hole through which the Red Army was pouring, even as the Ostheer's entire Fourth Army was finding itself surrounded east of the city. If they could hold their flanks then at least they could look to contain the breach and try to seal the front with counter-attacks. That was the plan, and as part of it Kampfgruppe von Gottberg was ordered north-west to join VI Corps, part of neighbouring *General* Reinhardt's Third Panzer Army from Operation Regenshauer days, falling back on Vilnius in Lithuania. This the SS men did, but then pointedly refused to join the Corps and instead fell back on the main railway line to Warsaw at the village of Ivye on 5 July. Why von Gottberg did this is not clear, although it has been speculated that he and his units were keen not to be cut off by the rampaging Soviets and wanted to stay close to the railway as an escape route. Seemingly by accident the Kampfgruppe was now the only cohesive force between Fourth Army and *General* Jordan's Ninth Army. Whatever the reason, unsurprisingly OKH was furious, but events overtook matters as the Soviet 31st Army (part of Chernyakovsky's 3rd Belorussian Front) attacked the dug-in Germans and their allies on 6 July. In desperate fighting SS-Sonderkommando Dirlewanger and the Turkmen threw themselves into a counter-attack on the flank of the assaulting Soviet 26th Tank Corps, and to everyone's surprise checked the Russian advance.

Would this be the time when the men of the 1st East Mussulman SS-Regiment would cover themselves in glory? Unfortunately not, as the counter-attack proved to be more of a last gasp than the start of a fighting reputation. The Soviets soon got over their initial shock and renewed their assault on 8 July with the 3rd Guards Cavalry Corps leading the charge. Lida fell to the onslaught on the same day and the Turkmen withdrew west with orders to dig in on the city of Grodno, north-west of Bialystok, along with the 3rd SS Panzer Division Totenkopf. By now though it would seem the Turkmen believed that orders were more of a guide rather than compulsory instructions and so instead of Grodno, the Regiment continued to retreat west to Lyck in East Prussia, 50km southeast of Rastenburg. There they found themselves out of the maelstrom that was savaging Army Group Centre and they watched as the whole centre of the German front in the east went through its death throes. For Army Group Centre, Operation Bagration brought nothing less than extinction. The Ostheer lost a staggering 27 divisions including 20 infantry, 3 panzer-grenadier, 2 Luftwaffe field, 1 security and 1 panzer division wiped off the order of battle, in total 350,000 men were killed. It was the worst ever defeat suffered by German arms and eclipsed even the calamity at Stalingrad.

For the Turkmen it had offered a rare glimpse of what they could do on occasions, but this momentary shaft of military competence from their counter-attack at Ivye was all too soon to be forgotten due to the infamy of their next campaign.

Shame and horror in Warsaw

At 5pm on 1 August 1944 the Warsaw Uprising began. Under its leader, General Bor-Komorowski the 34,000 strong Polish *Armia Krajowa* (Home Army) in the capital rose up to secure their city before the arrival of the communist Red Army. The Poles hoped to quickly expel the exhausted Germans and then establish a free government with which to receive the liberating Soviets and save them from swapping one occupation for another. They miscalculated from the start. Stalin was not prepared to see a non-communist regime in Poland, the Western Allies were in no position to help the insurgents and the Nazi beast was far from dead. Warsaw would be left by the Russians to its own devices and the tender mercies of the man appointed by Himmler to crush the rising, SS-Obergruppenführer Erich von dem Bach-Zelewski. As the former supremo of Nazi Germany's anti-partisan conflict in occupied Russia von dem Bach-Zelewski was no stranger to the barbarism of war, but in beautiful Warsaw the battle he was to lead was to plumb new depths in depravity, and its memory will forever stain the reputation of the Wehrmacht and the Waffen-SS in particular.

From the start, Muslim soldiers in the Wehrmacht were involved in the bloodbath. On the Uprising's first day, as groups of German soldiers all over the city were attacked, a unit of Azeris were surrounded in their barracks on Koszykowo Street. The Azeris put up fierce resistance but were running out of ammunition when called upon to surrender by the assaulting Poles. With their hands raised high the Azeris came out of their barracks and into the street, only to be butchered where they stood by having their throats slit. There was to be no mercy on the Vistula that August.

Azeris were to be further involved in the battle as *Hauptmann* (Captain) Werner Scharrenberg led the five officers and 677 men of the 1st Battalion of the Azeri 111th Regiment throughout the struggle and *Oberleutnant* (Lieutenant) Mertelsmann led the Azeri 2nd Battalion 'Bergmann' (minus its 7th Company). These men were not the only Muslims in Warsaw as the first two battalions of the 1st East Mussulman SS-Regiment were also sent from Lyck to take part in the suppression of the revolt under their new commander, SS-Obersturmbannführer der Reserve Franz Liebermann. The rest of the Regiment was meant to move to Kaposvar in Hungary for refitting, but instead ended up in Slovakia.

Very few records of the fighting were kept by the Germans so it is tremendously difficult to know exactly what units took part in what fighting during the two months of the Uprising, but suffice to say that the litany of atrocities carried out by the Nazis beggars belief, and it is clear that the Muslim SS played a part in it. The Nazis practised wholesale slaughter of the people of Warsaw, coupled with horror on a medieval scale. Civilians, including women and children, were burnt alive, thrown from roofs, skewered on bayonets, hung upside down from windows and generally exterminated. By the time of the capitulation on 2 October some 15,700 members of the Home Army had been killed along with an incredible 150,000 civilians. How much was directly attributable to the Muslim SS cannot be accurately identified, but as in Belorussia they were fighting alongside Oskar Dirlewanger's murderers and his unit was responsible for some of the very worst acts. It is impossible to believe that their hands were not stained with blood.

The last act – uprising in Slovakia

The Poles were not the only people in revolt in August 1944. To the south, Germany's ally Slovakia, saw the writing on the wall as the Red Army advanced to its borders. The result was a general uprising on 27 August led by disaffected elements of the Slovak Armed Forces. As the Germans struggled to contain and then extinguish the rebellion, under the command of Gottlob Berger of all people, many of the units that had participated in the butchery in Warsaw were then deployed to take part in the campaign. Those elements of the 1st East Mussulman Regiment not involved in suppressing the Warsaw Uprising were there already and they were soon reunited with their comrades who came south on Dirlewanger's coat-tails. By this stage in the War, reporting was often quite chaotic and distinctions between Dirlewanger's 'regulars' and the Muslim SS men were blurred so it is unclear as to exactly what sub-units did what and when during that inglorious and bitter sideshow conflict in the autumn of 1944. What is certain is that although the fighting was nowhere near as brutal as the mass murder that went on in Warsaw it was still a vicious conflict where the distinctions between combatants and civilians were not always observed and butchery, rape and looting were commonplace.

As the fighting ebbed, the Regiment remained in Slovakia in the run up to Christmas that year, ostensibly carrying out further training. At that time Liebermann went the way of Billig and Hermann before him, and was replaced by a new regimental commander. This time the SS-Hauptamt thought they had hit on a winner in the form of SS-Standartenführer Harun al-Raschid Bey (formerly Wilhelm Hintersatz). As with Meyer-Mader the Regiment's new commanding officer was an Austrian who had extensive knowledge of Islam, indeed as his name suggested he had become so enamoured of Islam that he had converted to the faith. He had been an observer attached to the Turkish General Staff and then a liaison officer with the Mufti of Jerusalem. This would seem to be the perfect background for the role, but in reality Hinterstaz's appointment was an unmitigated disaster. The Turkmen took against him immediately following his assumption of command on 20 October, and from then on the situation only worsened. The Regiment was mooted for transfer to the German-controlled Russian National Liberation Army of General Andrei Vlasov, but for the Turkmen this was seen as a betrayal of their nationalist, anti-Russian aspirations. Even when this ill-conceived idea was consigned to the dustbin Hintersatz was unable to win the sullen soldiery over and on Christmas Eve 1944 the whole issue came to a head with an armed mutiny. Led by home-grown officers, Waffen-Obersturmführer Gulum Azimov (a former Red Army Turkic NCO) and Waffen-Untersturmführer Asatpalvan, some 450 members of the Regiment's 1st Battalion killed several NCOs of their German cadre and fled their barracks to join the resistance in the hills. Azimov himself was a veteran of the Russian Front and had earlier been awarded the Iron Cross for bravery, but he had become disillusioned with the Germans, and Hintersatz's incompetence was the straw that broke the camel's back. The Turkmen marched into the mountains but soon some lost heart and almost 300 turned back and returned to face the punishment of their German masters. Azimov was not among them. He led the remainder to make contact with the partisans who promptly shot him on the spot before accepting his men into their ranks. Perhaps the Slovak guerrillas thought this was one betrayal too many.

The mutiny forced Himmler into action and he immediately dismissed Hintersatz and ordered the 1st East Mussulman SS-Regiment to be disbanded. The Turkmen were not to be abandoned altogether though, but reformed and reorganised into a new formation, the *Osttürkischen Waffen-Verbände der SS* (the East Turkic SS Armed Detachments – see Chapter VIII).

Reprise of the 1st East Mussulman SS-Regiment

It is difficult to understand how of all the Turkmen units in the German Army Berger alighted on the one with by far the worst combat record and with a commander, in Meyer-Mader, who was patently not up to the job. There were a host of other Turkic formations that would have been far better suited to act as the base unit for an SS formation, indeed bringing them together under one banner may well have increased their combat effectiveness, as long as racial differences were understood and strong leadership given. All the lessons that the Waffen-SS had learned in dealing successfully with foreign troops over more than two hard years seems to have been disregarded in the case of the Turkmen and unsurprisingly led to muddle, confusion, military ineffectiveness and worse of all, unspeakable brutality. Tens of thousands of Turkmen fought with the Germans during the War, figures of 50,000 dead and 12,000 wounded are sometimes quoted but this would seem extraordinarily high, and many of them fought with courage and great fortitude in the completely false hope that Nazi Germany would help them establish independent homelands. This was not so for the 1st East Mussulman SS-Regiment which was a total disaster from start to finish and some of whose members forever damned themselves by involvement in some of the worst atrocities of the War.

V

Bosnian Muslims – The History of the 13th SS Mountain Division 'Handschar' (13. Waffen-Gebirgs Division der SS Handschar (kroatische Nr.1))

Back in the Balkans 1941–1942

The winter snows of 1941 finally brought an end to the summer and autumn of slaughter that had gripped the new Ustasha kingdom of Croatia. Few though they were – at its height in 1942 the movement only numbered some 60,000 adherents – their reign of terror was complete. The country was hopelessly divided and riven by bitter hatreds brought on by the mind-numbing barbarities of the black-clad Croat fanatics. Whole communities were now nothing but ruins and the survivors had banded together and armed themselves with whatever they could find to protect themselves and their families. The Serbs sought refuge in the ranks of the royalist chetniks or Tito's Partisans, while the embattled Muslims formed scratch militia units such as Major Muhamed Hadziefendic's brigade in Tuzla. Pavelic's Minister for Culture and Education, Mile Budak, might have stated that: 'The Croatian state is Christian. It is also a Muslim state where our people are of the Mohammedan religion.' But this simply wasn't believed by the Muslim community who saw an administration completely domainted by Catholic Croats, with only 2 out of the 20 state Ministers and 13 of the 206 Peoples' Representatives being Muslims. Pavelic did order the building of a new mosque, to be called the 'Poglavniks mosque', to reassure the Muslims, but it was seen as little more than an empty gesture. In fact, Islamic opinion on the conduct of Pavelic's government was hardening fast and in response to the horrors visited on Bosnia by the Ustasha. Gatherings of Muslim leaders in Sarajevo, Mostar and Banja Luka issued three separate *'fatwas'* (Islamic decrees) from October to November 1941 denouncing Nazi/Ustasha atrocities against the Jews and Serbs.

As the unrest continued in the spring of 1942 and beyond, increasingly German and Italian troops had to intervene to maintain some sort of order and this was an unacceptable drain on men and material that were desperately needed on the Russian Front. Locally-based German officers were vociferous in their condemnation of the Ustasha. The German Plenipotentiary General in Croatia, *General* Edmund Glaise von Horstenau, wrote to OKW in Berlin complaining of the '…unspeakable swineishness of this gang of murderers and criminals'. As early as July 1941 he commented that 'According to reliable reports from countless German military and civilian observers…the Ustasha has gone raving mad.'

On the ground, while locally raised self-defence units were a necessary stopgap they were considered by the Germans as no substitute for well-trained, well-equipped regulars who would be able to defeat the various resistance forces and carry out the two tasks deemed as vital by Berlin. The first of these was to safeguard the production and transportation of bauxite from local mines to feed Germany's war industries; the second was to protect the ethnic German volksdeutsche communities in the northern areas of the country around Srem, that numbered around 700,000 people all told.

Russia in 1942 – Stalingrad

The summer and autumn of 1942 had been a rerun of the events of 1941 with Bosnia gripped by tit-for-tat sectarian killings with no end in sight. To the Germans, it was clear that Pavelic and his thugs could not keep order in the country, let alone run the state efficiently, and therefore it was going to be down to them to pacify the land and achieve victory. But how to do that when every single man was needed in Russia? After all, the rapid German advances of the summer had now been replaced by the unutterably savage street fighting in Stalingrad. Worse still, the most powerful German military formation on the planet, Friedrich von Paulus's Sixth Army with its five entire panzer divisions and multiplicity of infantry divisions was now cut-off and encircled in the ruined city and the rest of the retreating Ostheer faced possible encirclement and disaster between the Don and Dnieper Rivers. In these circumstances there was no way German troops were going to be released for the sideshow in the Balkans.

These issues were of especial interest to Heinrich Himmler who believed he saw an opportunity for further expansion of his beloved Waffen-SS while at the same time defending far flung ethnic German homelands – the perfect coincidence. So with thousands of Germans and their allies dying of cold and hunger in their foxholes in Stalingrad in December 1942 the Reichsführer-SS met with Hitler and presented to him the idea of recruiting a Bosnian division to fight the Partisans on their own turf. Himmler cunningly cloaked the ethnicity of the proposed recruits by alluding to the Italian anthropological investigations of the early 1930s that indicated that the Bosnians were actually descendants of Aryan Gothic invaders and not native Slavs – utter nonsense with no basis in fact. However it did make their recruitment more palatable to the racially obsessed Nazis. Hitler approved of the concept and saw it as a potential answer to his Balkan headache. Himmler was encouraged and sent SS-Obersturmbannführer Letsch from his staff to meet the local German envoy in Croatia, Siegfried Kasche, to discuss the idea.

The genesis of the SS-Handschar

Thus was born the idea that over time would become the largest and longest serving Muslim Waffen-SS formation of the War. This division of Bosnian Muslims, whether it liked it or not, was to be the totem representing all Muslims in the Black Guard. Its story would be one of troubled recruitment, the one and only ever mutiny in a Waffen-SS unit and one of the most controversial combat records of any of Himmler's battle formations. It was to be this unit that was to dominate the relationship between Islam and Nazism for the rest of the War.

Himmler and Islam

The draw for Himmler however was not only about solving a pressing manpower issue, or even the chance to add another division to the Waffen-SS order of battle. There was another element to his motivation in looking at Bosnians Muslims and that was their religion itself.

While men in the Heer and Kriegsmarine were served by their own chaplains, both the Luftwaffe and the Waffen-SS had no such pastoral care. While Himmler did not actually ban Christianity in the Black Guards the approved status was 'Gottgläubiger' – 'believer in God', rather than any specified denomination. Religion and the Waffen-SS has always been a subject with a certain amount of duality. On the one hand, Himmler was patently anti-religious, but this antipathy seemed only to extend as far as Christianity. He had a romantic belief in paganism and its associations with the old barbarian Teuton tribes and he saw

Christianity as a weakening and corrupting influence with its adherence to non-violence and tolerance. This was not his view of Islam, indeed he enthused about it and its applicability to the profession of arms. In a conversation with the Reichminister for Propaganda, Joseph Goebbels, he said:

> I have nothing against Islam, because it educates the men in this Division for me and promises them heaven if they fight and are killed in action. That's a highly practical and attractive religion for soldiers!

For Himmler then, Islam was not a barrier to membership of the Waffen-SS, in fact it was a spur to entry. Having learnt lessons earlier in the War about the sensitivity required in handling foreign volunteers the Reichsführer was determined that this time round due note was paid to religious and cultural differences. This firmly applied to the spiritual wellbeing of the envisaged formation and it was resolved that the division was to have its own staff of imams down to battalion level. To cater for this, two schools would actually be established to train SS imams, one at Dresden and the second co-located with the SS Cavalry School at Göttingen. As a further support to build bridges with the Muslim community in Bosnia, Himmler decided to enlist the help of one of the most controversial Islamic figures of the last century.

Mohammed 'Haj' Amin al-Husseini (also spelt Husayni) – the Mufti of Jerusalem

Born into a rich and powerful aristocratic Arab family in Jerusalem in 1895, young Amin was the son of the senior Koranic scholar in the city, called the Mufti. His family had held the post almost unbroken since the seventeenth-century. Sent to study at the prestigious Al-Azhar University in Cairo (long considered the premier Arab learning institution in the world) he began his lifelong dedication to the cause of anti-semitism by establishing a small anti-Jewish society. In 1913 aged just eighteen he then went on pilgrimage to Mecca and received the honorary title of 'Haj' in recognition of his devotion, before going on to further study at the Istanbul School of Administration, the acknowledged heart of Ottoman Turkish imperial rule. With the outbreak of the First World War he joined up, and was commissioned as an artillery officer in the 47th Turkish Brigade based at the beautiful and bustling multi-ethnic Anatolian port city of Smryna. Claiming disability in November 1916 – on account of what, it is difficult to surmise – he left

Smyrna and returned to Jerusalem where he stayed for the remainder of the War. With the Allied conquest of Jerusalem and most of the Middle East towards the end of the War he switched sides and even helped to recruit volunteers for the Allied-backed army of Faisal bin-Husayn (he of Lawrence of Arabia fame).

With the War over he agitated for the creation of an Arabic mega-state in the Middle East comprising modern-day Israel, Syria, Lebanon, Jordan, Iraq and even Cyprus and parts of Turkey. This clearly came to nothing. He then founded his own anti-Jewish society, *'El-Nadi al-Arabi'* – the Arab Club, and began to openly attack the Jews and Jewish immigration to Palestine. This culminated in riots in March 1920 during Passover, when local Muslim mobs set upon and murdered Jewish civilians in Jerusalem. The British administration, headed by the legendary High Commissioner, Sir Herbert Samuels, was outraged and al-Husseini was forced to flee to Damascus. Nevertheless he was tried in absentia, convicted of incitement and sentenced to ten years in prison.

Election to Grand Mufti

The following year Amin's brother Kamil, who had taken over his father's role as Mufti in Jerusalem, died. The subsequent election for the post, gerrymandered as it was, installed Amin as the new Mufti. Seeing an opportunity to calm tensions and build some bridges Samuels accepted the election and pardoned Amin. This was a huge mistake. From the moment of his inauguration al-Husseini transformed the post from that of a pre-eminent and learned Islamic scholar into a strident political platform from where he attacked the British and the Jews. Centuries of Islamic tolerance and learning were wiped away in a matter of months by a hate-filled fanatic. He said of his views: 'The Zionists will be massacred to the last man. We want no progress, no prosperity. Nothing but the sword will decide the fate of this country.' Israel and Palestine still live in the shadow of hatred spawned by men like this. At the time sporadic violence flared up as al-Husseini stoked up the Arabs sense of grievance, with 40 Jews alone being killed in inter-communal fighting in May 1921, although British troops shot dead several dozen Muslim rioters to try and stem the trouble. At this time al-Husseini adopted the self-created title of 'Grand Mufti', and established the World Islamic Congress to try and further his own influence and power. While this attempt at self-aggrandizement failed, due to the opposition of fellow Muslims, he continued to act as the self-styled leader of anti-semitism in the Arab world, inspiring murder and mayhem on a growing scale through the 1920s and early 1930s. Recognising a kindred anti-semitic spirit, al-Husseini even sent a telegram to Adolf Hitler on his election to the Chancellorship in January 1933 saying: 'I look forward to spreading your ideology in the Middle East.' Eventually the British had had enough and moved to arrest him again in 1937, whereupon he fled Jerusalem for Mecca. He then went to Lebanon before finally settling in Iraq in late 1939.

Revolt in Iraq

Seized by Britain from the Ottoman Empire at the end of the First World War, Iraq was a backwater, albeit one of growing importance in the 1930s after the discovery of oil. The Anglo-Iraqi Treaty of 1930 cemented Britain's stake in Iraq by giving it bases in Baghdad and Basra and major interests in the newly-found oilfields of Mosul and Kirkuk. It also established an independent Iraqi state, with its own army of five divisions, controlled by the pro-British Nuri es-Sa'id Government which ruled the country on behalf of the King.

However, nationalist Iraqis were unhappy with this stance and in March 1940 a new pro-Axis Government under the premiership of Rashid Ali al-Kilani was installed. Backed by the so-called 'Golden Square' society of rightwing Iraqi army officers, al-Kilani took an antagonistic approach to Britain that resulted in him losing power later that year as Britain's Desert Army under Wavell, thrashed Italian forces in the Western Desert. However the stunning Axis victories in Yugoslavia, Greece and Crete in early 1941 were seen as portents of Britain's future defeat and with al-Husseini's backing, a military coup was launched that put al-Kilani back in power on 3 April 1941. Even though hard pressed in the desert and with thousands of men lost in Greece and Crete the British were swift to respond and prepared to intervene. Churchill's instructions to the commander on the ground, Air Marshal Smart, were clear: 'If you have to strike, strike hard.' This he did.

At dawn on 2 May the British attacked. A British battlegroup built around the magnificent Arab Legion attacked east from Transjordan, while the soon-to-be-famous Bill Slim led the 10th Indian division as it landed in the south at Basra. The action was brief but sharp with Iraqi opposition collapsing under the onslaught, as first Fallujah fell to assault and then Baghdad itself was taken. The Axis was caught unprepared and even though efforts were made to get weapons and supplies through to the Iraqis it was all too little too late. By the end of the month Iraq was conquered and al-Husseini was again forced to flee.

Iran, Syria and Lebanon – a postscript

In neighbouring Iran, another backwater at the time, the king (or Shah) Reza had declared the country neutral but was overtly friendly to the Axis. Britain and the Soviet Union decided to take no chances and in the only example of its kind in the War launched a joint operation on 26 August 1941 to occupy the country. The Russians threatened the north and the British crossed the border from Iraq defeating a tribal revolt in the south as they went. Resistance was short-lived and Reza forced to abdicate. His son, Mohammed Reza Shah Pahlavi was installed as ruler in his stead under the firm guidance of the British. His own rule would end 36 years later in Iran's Islamic Revolution of 1979.

As for the French imperial possession of Syria and Lebanon they were invaded on 8 June in collaboration with Foreign Legionnaires fighting for de Gaulle under the Free French banner. In a vicious re-run of the Spanish Carlist War of the nineteenth century the fighting centred on foreign legionnaire versus foreign legionnaire. As with the Iberian struggle it culminated in a fratricidal battle between legionnaires this time in Damascus and not Barbastro. The result was an Allied victory that saw Syria and Lebanon conquered by 14 July, Bastille Day for the French.

Al-Husseini in Nazi Germany – the Eichmann connection

Al-Husseini himself stayed temporarily in Iran (wherever he went disaster seemed to follow), before travelling through Turkey, Bulgaria and Italy to finally reach Nazi Germany in November that same year. He was warmly received in the Reich. Previously, al-Husseini had met the infamous Adolf Eichmann himself back in Jerusalem and the two men shared a common bond of virulent anti-semitism. Now several years later it was Eichmann who helped, along with von Ribbentrop whom he met on 20 November, facilitate a meeting between al-Husseini and Hitler. This meeting duly took place on 28 November 1941 at which time al-Husseini pressed the Führer to publicly declare his support for Arab-Muslim independence. Al-Husseini made a positive impression on Hitler with his reddish blond beard, dapper appearance and confident command of English, Arabic and Turkish, although not German which hampered him a little. Hitler was unwilling to openly align himself with al-Husseini's cause, but he dropped enough hints to let him know that once Nazi Germany had reached the Middle East, through either the Western Desert or the Caucasus, he would not only look upon Arab independence favourably but would want the physical destruction of the Jews living there. This was music to the Mufti's ears and he pledged his support for the Nazis.

While the Germans wandered how best to use the Mufti they gave him an elegant villa in the fashionable south-western Berlin suburb of Zehlendorf and organised a stipend paid for by both the SS and the Foreign Office. Al-Husseini, and his mainly Iraqi entourage, settled down to a very comfortable existence while they extended their networks and tried to get the Nazis on side with their own agenda for the Middle East. During this time it was noted by several German observers that al-Husseini was guarded by a strange character indeed. This man was a Bedouin dressed in European clothing who was perpetually armed and never left the Mufti's side. He would stand outside the door and bar entry to the room whenever the Mufti was praying, and at night he would sleep outside blocking the doorway like a faithful guard dog. The Germans found it quite bemusing.

The Mufti talks up the Handschar

For al-Husseini, 1942 was a quiet year. It was only when 1943 dawned and the concept of a Muslim SS division began to be floated that he came into his own. With Hitler's formal approval for the division given on 13 February 1943 at his *Wolfschanze* (Wolf's Lair) headquarters deep in the East Prussian forests of Rastenburg, it was all systems go for the SS-Handschar and for al-Husseini's official involvement.

A conference to launch the new formation was organised in Berlin for the 24 March and just days prior al-Husseini gave a speech lamenting the fate of Muslims in Bosnia.

> The hearts of all Muslims must today go out to our Islamic brothers in Bosnia, who are forced to endure a tragic fate. They are being persecuted by the Serbian and communist bandits ... They are being murdered, their possessions are robbed, and their villages are burned. England and its Allies bear a great accountability before history for mishandling and murdering Europe's Muslims, just as they have done in the Arabic lands and in India.

Exile had clearly not mellowed his view on Britain in particular.

Croatian obstacles

Between Hitler's sanction in mid-February and the Berlin confer-ence there were high level discussions between the Germans and the Poglavnik's government in Zagreb to smooth the creation of the new division. That was the German intent anyway, but it was not that of the Croats. From the very beginning, the Ustasha viewed the raising and arming of a division for the Waffen-SS from Muslim subjects of their new country as an affront and a potential danger to their own flimsy sovereignty. They were happy to see the Germans train, equip and arm a force of Croat nationals as a source of support to the flag-ging existing Croat armed forces, and if some of these men happened to be Muslim then so be it. But they were decidedly unhappy about the creation of an independent force entirely out of their own control that drew exclusively on their Muslim minority, this was a threat to Catholic-Croat hegemony.

Enter Phleps

To lead the initial recruitment and establishment phase Himmler and Berger settled on a man they viewed as the ideal candidate – SS-Obergruppenführer Artur Martin Phleps. Phleps was by then the commander of the 7th SS Freiwilligen Gebirgs Division Prinz Eugen, recruited from Yugoslav volksdeutsche (mainly from the Serbian Banat), having previously commanded the Dutch/Flemish SS-Westland Regiment in the Wiking Division during the fighting in southern Russia in 1942. He was a Romanian volksdeutsche having been born in Birthälm (modern-day Biertan, northwest of Ploesti – Rumania) as a member of the ancient Transylvanian Saxon community. Having commanded the SS-Westland, and then having successfully raised a new division in the Balkans, he was considered by his superiors to be just the man for the job. It was not a view he shared. Phleps himself was involved in *Unternehmen Weiss* (Operation White) in Bosnia at the time, where his division, along with several others was trying to destroy the Partisans in Bosnia. Time away from the offensive was not conducive to military success, and he saw the creation of the SS-Handschar as an unnecessary distraction to that task. Despite his personal feelings Phleps came to an agreement with the Croats which, though far from perfect, allowed the recruiting effort to start in earnest on 20 March 1943.

Recruitment

As the Waffen-SS recruiters toured Bosnia their message was clear. The glorious tradition of the old Austro-Hungarian Bosnian regiments was being reborn, and with it would come security for the Muslim communities beset on all sides by the chetniks, Partisans and Ustasha. Desperate for relief from the depradations of the ongoing civil war, a host of volunteers came forward, so that less than a month later some 8,000 men had volunteered. This perhaps, was not the monumental flood that the SS authorities had expected but it was pretty respectable given the fact that the world was still coming to grips with the Wehrmacht's catastrophe at Stalingrad, and there was widespread mistrust of the Germans in Bosnia after two years of official indifference to the plight of the Muslim community. Indeed, by far the biggest recruiting sergeant for the new division was the ongoing spectre of ethnic violence. Every time an Ustasha, Partisan or chetnik attack targeted the Muslim community more young Muslim men signed up to what they believed was the best defence they could get – German uniforms, German training and above all, German weapons.

The effort was helped by al-Husseini who, true to his word in Berlin, toured Bosnia from 30 March to 14 April drumming up support by meeting with local Muslim leaders and speaking in mosques, exhorting his audiences to take advantage of the German offer and join the fledgling division.

A new commander, a new name and a new uniform

Phleps's month or so in charge of the new formation was now at an end. It was abundantly clear that he was needed back with the SS-Prinz Eugen, and a new full-time leader was necessary for the thousands of recruits being collected across northeastern Bosnia and sent onwards to initial recruit training at Wildflecken, northeast of Frankfurt-am-Main, Germany. On 1 April 1943 the post was given to a former regimental commander in the specialist mountain formation the 6th SS-Gebirgs Division Nord, SS-Standartenführer (later Oberführer) Herbert von Obwurzer. Von Obwurzer was a tall, imposing, former Austrian jäger who, although not envisaged as the long-term answer to the command issue, was considered to have the right background to deal with the cultural sensitivities of the new intake. He would be replaced on 9 August after just four months, and would go on to command the hard fighting Latvians of the 15th SS Division before being captured by the Soviets in northern Russia towards the end of the War. Von Obwurzer formed a strong relationship initially with his Chief of Staff, fellow Austrian SS-Sturmbannführer Erich Braun, with whom he intended to forge a solid anti-partisan division.

This point is crucial to understanding the combat record of the Handschar. The new Muslim division was never intended as a frontline unit destined to fight the Red Army. Instead, it was absolutely focused on defeating the far more lightly armed and far less trained Partisans of Tito's growing force. This meant equipment scales, training and cadre were all geared towards that goal, and not combating the highly mechanized and aggressive Soviets.

That cadre was drawn overwhelmingly from Phleps' SS-Prinz Eugen and was primarily Swabian volksdeutsche from the Banat. This weakened the Prinz Eugen just as it was starting to come to grips with the Partisans, but was unavoidable given the desperate shortages of both officers and NCOs for the new division. The intention was to fill as many of these posts as possible with indigenous Muslims with prior Royal Yugoslav Army experience, but Serb domination of the pre-war Army was so strong that there were very few Muslims who had served as anything other than privates or very junior NCOs. There were a number of Muslims who had held rank in the old Habsburg Austro-Hungarian Imperial Army, but they were a pretty elderly bunch by 1943. The barely juvenile Croat armed forces were dredged for suitable candidates (much to the annoyance of the Ustasha authorities), as was the likes of Major Muhamed Hadziefendic's self-defence legion from Tuzla, although this approach hit a bit of a dead end when the Major himself was killed in action, along with 55 of his men, in a particularly bloody battle with the Partisans. The end result was a relatively high proportion of Germans, both *reichsdeutsche* (Germans from the Reich – i.e. pre-war Germany and Austria, as opposed to those ethnic Germans from outside its borders) and volkdeustche in the division, including an all-German Signals Battalion. Numbers of native Bosnians were sent on command courses, coincidentally, several ended up training with French Waffen-SS NCO candidates at the training school in Posen-Treskau (see *Hitler's Gauls* for more detail), but the fact was that throughout its short life the division would be reliant on Germans, both Reichs and Volksdeutsche, for much of its command and control element.

The 'sword of Islam'

As for its name this was the subject of a myriad of debate and changes, with the Ustasha keen to avoid overt references to a separate Bosnian-Muslim identity, and Himmler keen to do the exact opposite. The working title of the division started out as the *Kroatische SS-Freiwilligen-Division* (Croatian SS-Volunteer Division), and this title lasted until July when it was amended to the *Kroatische SS-Freiwilligen-Gebirgs-Division* (Croatian SS-Volunteer Mountain Division) – to be honest both variations on a theme. Further names came and went, including the *SS-Freiwilligen-Bosnien-Herzegowina-Gebirgs-Division (Kroatien)* and the 13.*SS-Freiwilligen-Bosnien-Herzegowina-Gebirgs-Division (Kroatien)* when it was finally given a divisional number in the official Waffen-SS order of battle. Finally, months later, in May 1944 the detail-obsessed SS hierarchy settled on the 13 *Waffen-Gebirgs Division der SS Handschar (kroatische Nr.1)*, the 13th SS-Mountain Division 'Handschar'. The nomenclature was important in so far as explaining the division's ethnic composition, as by being entitled a '*Division der SS*' meant that, whilst being volunteers, the men were not Aryan, in the Nazi world these things mattered a great deal. The Bosnian Muslims were allowed to be members of the SS, carry the weapons and shed the blood, but they would never be the same as the men from the Reich.

For ease of reference, from now on the division will be referred to simply as the SS-Handschar. The term 'Handschar' itself is a derivation of the Arabic word for a long dagger, the 'khanjar' (and was the official name of the weapon carried by pre-war Imperial Ottoman policemen), and this warlike nomenclature was echoed in the unit collar tab that included a scimitar gripped by a firm hand. It was the ubiquitous Gottlob Berger who suggested the name.

Uniforms and insignia

As the first, and largest, of the eventual three Waffen-SS Muslim divisions, and as one would expect from the SS, much thought was put into the minutiae of uniform and insignia. The approach taken with the men of the Handschar would come to be the benchmark for all other Muslim Waffen-SS formations, and in its adherence to detail and willingness to defy previous convention, would yet again demonstrate that the Handschar and sister Muslim units were no mere flash in the pan for the Black Guard.

Basic uniform was initially field grey with subsequent issuing of the standard, and much-famed, Waffen-SS camouflage. A special collar patch was designed and introduced showing a hand holding a curved scimitar (the proverbial handschar itself) with a small swastika underneath. German cadre staff were entitled to wear the full SS runes emblem on their left breast below the chest pocket. The national arm shield on the upper left arm below the disputed Hoheitabzeichen Nazi eagle was the red/white chequered board of Croatia (two versions were produced), although some of the Kosovan Albanians wore the Albanian eagle, that they subsequently took with them to the Skanderbeg. As a mountain division the Handschar men were allowed to wear the prestigious *edelweiss* insignia on their upper right arm. Also for the first, but not the last time, permission was given to wear a most un-Aryan piece of headgear, a fez.

To those of a certain age, including myself, the fez will always be associated with the likes of comedian Tommy Cooper and a genre of madcap comedy, but in the Forties it was a common sight all over the Balkans and the Near East. As with so much in the formation of the Handschar Himmler was keen not to antagonise local sensitivities and 'fitting in' was important. So the order went out. No field caps – it was to be the fez. Two types were issued; the first was the field grey version, and the second was dark red for dress wear. Both were made of compressed felt and were unlined. They had sweatbands on the inside rim and a dark tassel on the top.

Transfer to France – a bad move

In accordance with the wishes of the Ustasha Government, the division was set to have Zemun (some 30 miles southeast of Novi Sad on the Duna River) as its establishment area, in effect, where all the unit's recruits and equipment would be concentrated when specialist training was complete and it could begin its work up to combat readiness. However it was clear to von Obwurzer, following an inspection of the facilities available that Zemun was unable to fulfil this role, especially given the fact that the Germans were also using it as the establishment zone for the Heer's new 117th Jäger Division. Von Obwurzer made a representation to Berlin, due to the inadequate facilities at Zemun, and finally headquarters in Berlin made the fateful announcement on 6 June; the SS-Handschar was to form up in occupied France. The Muslim SS were to be formed in the same country that was now being subjected to the largest seaborne invasion the world had ever seen.

Despite the invasion, the German reasoning was simple, it would enable the division to be raised unmolested by the growing Yugoslav communist Partisan threat and give access for the unit to far better training facilities than were available at home. But these advantages were overshadowed by the fact that the majority of the recruits saw joining the Handschar as the best hope of protecting their homes and families, and by moving to France they were in effect abandoning their loved ones when in desperate need. From then on, every attack on a Muslim village back in Bosnia, reported in the papers or in a letter from home, would visibly drain morale. France may have been seen as heaven by German troops stuck in the slaughter of the Russian Front, the constant phrase used by the average German *landser* (the German equivalent of the British Tommy, French *poilu* and Soviet *Ivan*) was '*Leben wie Gott in Frankreich*' ('living like God in France'), but for the Muslim SS men the War meant Bosnia and little else.

Arrival and training in France

The division was to be quartered in the *départments* of south central France, with its headquarters initially in the city of Le Puy-en-Velay (*départment* of Haute-Loire), before being moved in short order to neighbouring Mende (*départment* of Lozere). From 1 July transports of volunteers began to arrive from their initial staging points in Germany and Poland, such as Wildflecken and Goslar, and were allocated out to their various garrison and training bases. These were widely dispersed; from the combat engineers in Villefranche-de-Rouergue (*départment* of Aveyron) in the west through the *gebirgsjäger* (mountain infantry) bases in Rodez and Millau; north to the *panzerjäger* anti-tank men and anti-aircraft artillerymen back in Le Puy-en-Velay and down to the divisional Signalmen and headquarters staff in Mende. It is a huge area, predominantly rural, with few major towns and cities and the population overwhelmingly living in villages and hamlets dotted across the lush countryside. It is a beautiful and undisturbed part of France. Now it was to be home to the Waffen-SS's first official Muslim soldiers for the next three months.

For both sides in the area it was a curious and sometimes unsettling experience. The Bosnians were mainly poor farm boys from the rugged mountain villages of their homeland. To them the prosperous towns and villages of southern France, relatively untouched by war, were another world. The French on the other hand had gotten used to seeing German uniforms over the last three years since the invasion, but they were in no way prepared to see these strange SS men in their midst with their fezs and prayer mats.

But there was little time for introspection, for as soon as the men arrived they began training. And this wasn't Sunday drills but Waffen-SS training; that meant as good as it got with death a real possibility if you made a mistake. Whilst the reichsdeustche had grown up in Germany's national militaristic system of tiny young *Pimpfen* to Hitler Youth to Labour Service to full military service, and the volksdeustche had already been through training in the SS-Prinz Eugen, the Bosnian volunteers had in the main, no military experience at all. The German methodology kicked in immediately and the young Muslims found themselves going through the most advanced and comprehensive training system in the world. As ever with the Waffen-SS the emphasis was on their three pillars of military excellence; physical fitness, weapon handling and marksmanship and character development, this last being encouraged through self-reliance, initiative and aggression.

Right from the start training was carried out with live ammunition. A Waffen-SS innovation, conceived by one of the fathers of the Black Guards Felix Steiner, it did lead to casualties in training but saved a lot more on the battlefield. At the time it was revolutionary but is now considered normal – modern armies owe some legacies to the likes of the armed SS that not many like to acknowledge.

A new commander arrives – the *Schnellchen* ('Speedy')

By now the previously good relationship between the two Austrians leading the division, von Obwurzer and Braun, had broken down irrevocably with Braun making formal complaints about his superior. In Berlin, Himmler received these reports pretty dispassionately as he had always envisaged replacing von Obwurzer at some point. The decorated Waffen-SS cavalry commander, Hermann Fegelein, was the Reichsheini's first preference to replace von Obwurzer but he was persuaded by Maximilian von Herff, the head of the *SS-Personalhauptamt* (SS-Main Personnel Office responsible for officer and other personnel records), that *Oberst* (Colonel) Karl-Gustav Sauberzweig of the Heer was the man for the job.

Sauberzweig was not your typical Waffen-SS commander. A meticulous Prussian, short in stature, hook nosed and bespectacled, although he only had one eye having lost one in World War One. He was not a member of the Nazi Party, did not speak Serbo-Croat, had not served in a mountain formation, had not served in the Balkans or with foreign volunteers of any kind, and had never commanded a division. Not exactly the ideal candidate on paper. But what he had in his favour was a wealth of combat experience, having won both the Iron Cross 2nd and 1st Class in the First World War (both by the age of just 18), and gone on to higher command during Hitler's invasion of the West and the East in the previous four years. During this time he confirmed his reputation as a brave and diligent leader of men who would work tirelessly on their behalf and would never throw their lives away needlessly. From the moment he arrived in Mende as a newly transferred and promoted SS-Gruppenführer and took over command from von Obwurzer on 9 August 1943, he began to form a bond with the officers and men of the division that would still be cherished by veterans more than 50 years later. Nicknamed the *Schnellchen* (the Speedy) due to his irrepressible energy, Sauberzweig immediately set himself to getting round his dispersed command and getting to know his officers and men. Roaring around the French countryside in his staff car he injected pace and belief into the division. The men, constantly worried about events back home in Bosnia, were reassured that they would be back there as soon as they were ready and that everything they were doing was to prepare them to defend their homes and families.

The Handschar order of battle

One of the first tasks Sauberzweig undertook was to construct the order of battle of the Handschar, which was to be as a standard mountain division, there was to be no armour, no tanks or assault guns, this was not a formation designed to fight the grand battles of movement on the Eastern Front. The Handschar was to be formed around the muscle of two *gebirgsjäger* (mountain infantry) regiments, each hopefully of three battalions. Normally Waffen-SS divisions were composed of three regiments, but this was dropped to two in mountain divisions, due as much to shortage of men as the demands of military doctrine. Each regiment was designed to be able to fight as an entity in its own right, and in support of these lead sub-units there were to be five other teeth units to multiply its effective combat power.

The most important of these was the division's artillery regiment of four battalions. It was this gun park that would provide the SS-Handschar with reach and weight of steel. Its heavy howitzers could throw a 150mm high explosive shell over eight miles into the hills and wreak havoc. To help find the targets for these guns the division had its own reconnaissance battalion. The eyes and ears of the division, the German methodology was that the Recce Battalion was an élite within its structure and was usually mechanized or at least motorised. In Handschar's case with its heaviest integral combat vehicles, a series of 8-wheeled SdKfz 221 armoured cars. The modern British Army favours this doctrine too, with the Recce Platoon in every infantry battalion usually hand-picked from the best of the rest and vehicle borne for mobility.

Next came more guns. Firstly a battalion of anti-aircraft cannon. An anomaly really, as Tito never managed to expand his wartime JANL into the air although the Allies were starting to send aircraft to support the Partisans, but mostly these men and their weapons were firmly trained on the ground where their high velocity automatic firepower could be devastating. The last of the divison's guns were those of the *panzerjäger* (anti-tank) battalion. Tito wasn't exactly awash with fleets of tanks, only ever having a few outdated vehicles (usually whatever he could capture from the hapless Italians), but the towed 50mm anti-tank guns were equally adept at bunker busting and firesupport as well as taking on the odd captured Italian tank (disparagingly called 'herring cans' by their previous Italian crews due to their vulnerability). Last but not least were the combat engineers of the *Pionier Bataillon*. German doctrine at the time emphasised the role of these troops as hugely effective multi-purpose fighters of immense combat value. The hitherto impregnable Belgian Eben-Emael fortress was captured by the paratroop version of this sub-unit back in 1940. Waffen-SS combat engineers were trained much the same way as modern-day British Royal Engineers are today, including the laying and clearing of obstacles such as mines, bridge building, explosives, fortification and defensive construction, but crucially the Wehrmacht also used these men as specialist close-quarter assault troops. In the United Kingdom this dirty job is left to the infantry alone.

The division also had the usual service support and logistics troops, including veterinary staff to look after the pack animals, so necessary for operations in the trackless mountains of north-eastern Bosnia.

The full order of battle was as follows:

Divisional Commander	SS-Gruppenführer Karl-Gustav Sauberzweig (ex-Heer regimental commander)
Divisionsstab (Divisional Headquarters)	Feldpost Number 57400
Ia (Divisional Operations Officer)	SS-Sturmbannführer Erich Braun
IIa (Divisional Adjutant)	SS-Hauptsturmführer Götz Berens von Rautenfeld (promoted to SS-Sturmbannführer as of 9 November 1943)
IIb (Quartermaster)	SS-Hauptsturmführer Karl Liecke (future Knight's Cross winner)
IVb (Divisional Medical Officer)	SS-Sturmbannführer Dr Albrecht Wiehler (also commander of SS-Sanitäts-Abteilung 13 medical battalion of doctors, medics and vets for the divisions animals)
Divisional Imam	Abdullah Muhasilovic (after standard bearing for the division he eventually

led the Divisional Staff Security Company of 101 men in open mutiny to head home and protect their families in late 1944.)

Waffen-Gebirgsjäger-Regiment der SS 27 (kroatische Nr.1) – SS Mountain Rifle Regiment 27 (Croatian no.1) – Feldpost Number 59054

Commander	SS-Obersturmbannführer Mathias Huber (Huber was succeeded on 9 November 1943 by the future divisional commander SS-Obersturmbannführer Desiderius Hampel. Hampel was an ethnic German from Croatia and was eventually one of the four men from the Handschar decorated with the Knight's Cross on 3 May 1945)
Regimental Imam	Hasan Bajraktarevic

I/27 – 1st Battalion – Feldpost Number 1–6 Companies 57130 A–F

Commander	SS-Hauptsturmführer der Reserve Karl Liebermann (promoted SS-Sturmbannführer as of 9 November 1943 – this was the same officer who was to serve with the Turkmen Waffen-SS men)

Battalion Imam – Fadil Sirco

II/27 – 2nd Battalion – Feldpost Number 7–12 Companies 56013 A–F

Commander	SS-Hauptsturmführer Karl Fischer (promoted SS-Sturmbannführer as of 20 April 1944 – Hitler's birthday and so often used for promotions)

III/27 – 3rd Battalion – Feldpost Number 59583

Commander	SS-Hauptsturmführer Karl-Hermann Frenz

Due to manpower shortages this battalion was not activated during the division's formation, and only really came into being in June 1944. It only lasted until October when it was dissolved due to desertion and casualties.

IV/27 – 4th Battalion – Feldpost Number 57295
Commander   SS-Hauptsturmführer Heinz Jägers
Like its sister battalion the 3rd the lack of troops meant this sub-unit
only really existed in name until it was finally wiped off the order
of battle in June 1944 during the divisional reorganisation.

Waffen-Gebirgsjäger-Regiment der SS 28 (kroatische Nr.2) – SS
Mountain Rifle Regiment 28 (Croatian no.2) – Feldpost Number 57347
Commander   SS-Standartenführer der Reserve Franz
                                  Matheis (an elderly officer, Matheis,
                                  who had served in the First World War
                                  in the Austro-Hungarian Army, was
                                  replaced in the autumn by the highly
                                  experienced Hellmuth Raithel)
Regimental Imam   Husejin Dzozo

I/28 – 1st Battalion – Feldpost Number 1-6 Companies 56329 A-F
Commander   SS-Hauptsturmführer der Reserve
                                  Walter Bormann
Battalion Imam   Ahmed Skaka

II/28 – 2nd Battalion – Feldpost Number 7–12 Companies 59128 A–F
Commander   SS-Sturmbannführer Egon Zill

III/28 – 3rd Battalion – Feldpost Number 57872
Commander   SS-Hauptsturmführer Hans-Heinrich
                                  Kaltofen. (Kaltofen was also nomi-
                                  nally in command of IV/28 but as
                                  with its mirror battalions in Regiment
                                  27 both the 3rd and 4th Battalions of
                                  Regiment 28 suffered from the divi-
                                  sion's continual manning problems.
                                  The 3rd never properly formed until
                                  the reorganisation in June 1944 and
                                  was then dissolved in October that
                                  same year, while the 'phantom' 4th
                                  only lasted on paper until June 1944.)

With both mountain rifle regiments struggling to fill more than
two battalions at any one time it was clear that the combat power
of the division was going to be restricted. Mountain fighting, just
like fighting in urban areas and thick woodland, soaks up men on

a huge scale. To try and increase the unit's overall fighting strength each mountain battalion had a heavy support company armed with a platoon of three guns of the obselete but effective 3.7cm Panzerabwehrkanone (PAK 36 – anti-tank gun). Against the T-34s of the Red Army these guns were as useful as chocolate fireguards, but against the JANL they were still powerful. The difficulty of the terrain, and the problems with bringing firepower to bear, always means that a few determined men can hold up a much larger attacking force, and the only maxim that counts then is 'God is always on the side of the big battalions'.

Waffen-Gebirgs-Artillerie-Regiment der SS 13- SS Mountain Artillery Regiment 13
Feldpost Number 59297

Commander	SS-Sturmbannführer der Reserve Alexander von Gyurcsy. (von Gyurcsy was also the 4th Battalion commander in charge of the division's heaviest guns whose very size kept them relatively roundbound and necessitated their usual co-location with regimental headquarters anyway. An arrogant man of advance years he was not liked by his subordinates and was later replaced).
Regimental Imam	Haris Korkut

Three of the four artillery battalions used lightweight mountain artillery that could be broken down and packed by mule and manpower, but to add firepower the IV Battalion was equipped with one battery of long range guns and two batteries of heavy howitzers equipped with the massive 15cm (5.9in) schwere Felfhaubitze (sFH18 – heavy field howitzer), with a range of about 8 miles/13 km. If used well these big guns would give the SS-Handschar a real advantage.

I/AR 13 – 1st Battalion – Feldpost Number 1-4 Companies/Batteries 57452 A-D

Commander	SS-Sturmbannführer Bozidar Dobrinic
Battalion Imam	Hasim Torlic

II/AR 13 – 2nd Battalion – Feldpost Number 5-8 Companies/ Batteries 56388 A-D

Commander

SS-Hauptsturmführer der Reserve Friedrich Kreibich (promoted to SS-Sturmbannführer as of 21 June 1944, was subsequently killed in action on 6 September 1944)

III/AR 13 – 3rd Battalion – Feldpost Number 9-12 Companies/ Batteries 59136 A-D

Commander

SS-Sturmbannführer der Reserve Hermann Behrends. (Hermann Behrends had a 'colourful' career, starting out as the first ever commander of the feared Sicherheitsdienst (SD – the SS's own security service) in Berlin, he then moved to become Werner Lorenz's deputy at the Volksdeutsche Mittelstelle (VOMI) – the Ethnic German Main Assistance Office. He served in the Handschar in two separate stints; the first from 13 October to 9 November 1943 as the commander of the 3rd Battalion in the Divisions artillery regiment as it trained up, and then again from 12 January to 15 April 1944 in Bosnia in the same role as it became operational. Following this he went on to become the Higher SS and Police Leader in Serbia, Montenegro and the Sandzak until October that same year. This was possible due to the fact that while he was only a Sturmbannführer der Reserve in the Waffen-SS, in the police he was a Gruppenführer und Generalleutnant. After the War he was arrested in Flensburg by the British and interned at Special Camp 11 on the old Neuengamme Concentration Camp site alongside several other ex-SS-Handschar officers including his own divisional commander Sauberzweig. Extradited back to Yugoslavia, he was tried for war crimes, convicted and

executed by firing squad in Belgrade
on 4 December 1948).

IV / AR 13 – 4th Battalion – Fledpost Number 57822
Commander   SS-Sturmbannführer der Reserve
                                  Alexander von Gyurcsy

SS-Gebirgs-Aufklärungs-Abteilung 13 – SS Mountain Reconnaisance
Battalion 13 Feldpost Number 58907
Commander   SS-Hauptsturmführer Emil Kuhler
Battalion Imam   Salih Sabanovic
A cadre from this battalion went on to form the basis of the SS Kama
division's reconnaissance battalion under Sepp Syr. The reconnaissance battalion had a heavy anti-tank platoon that was equipped
with three of the excellent towed 75mm Panzerabwehrkanone
40 guns – anti-tank PAK 40. With a range against tanks of 2000m
and against infantry of 7500m, this high velocity gun gave the
unit at least a modicum of punching power. Detached from division - along with several other sub-units - in September 1944 to act
as corps troops for II SS Cavalry Corps, the battalion was partly
equipped with the Leichte Panzerspähwagen (MG) (SdKfz 221
– light armoured car), a four-wheeled armoured car armed with a
machine-gun and manned by a crew of two. A good, lightweight
vehicle ideal for mountain warfare.

SS-Panzerjäger-Abteilung 13 – SS Anti-tank Battalion 13 – Feldpost
Number 58861
Commander   SS-Hauptsturmführer Gerhard Dierich
                                  (promoted SS-Sturmbannführer as
                                  of 30 January 1945 – the anniversary
                                  of the Nazis accession to power in
                                  Germany and again used for promo-
                                  tions. The battalion was equipped for
                                  its first year with the towed PAK 36
                                  5cm (2in) gun, a good all-round gun
                                  served by a crew of three, well able to
                                  deal with anything the Partisans were
                                  armed with. In summer 1944 these
                                  were replaced by the heavier PAK
                                  40 7.5cm (3in) guns that were prov-
                                  ing so effective on the Narva at the
                                  same time, hundreds of miles north,

when handled by men such as Remy
Schrijnen (see *Hitler's Flemish Lions*).

Battalion Imam   Kasim Masic

SS-Flak-Abteilung 13 – SS Anti-aircraft Battalion 13 – Feldpost
Number 58056

Commander   SS-Obersturmbannführer Husejin
                                Biscevic (one of the few Bosnian
                                Muslim officers in the division,
                                Biscevic was another retread from the
                                old Austro-Hungarian Army)
Battalion Imam   Dzemal Ibrahimovic (born in Sarajevo
                                in 1919 Ibrahimovic went to the pres-
                                tigious madrassa (Islamic school), Gazi
                                Husrevbegova before service in the
                                Royal Yugoslav Army. He would serve
                                with the Handschar to the end).

The battalion was equipped with a whole company/battery of the
famed 88mm gun. Originally designed as an anti-aircraft piece by
chance the Germans had realised it was even more effective in the
anti-tank role. Able to destroy almost every tank on the battlefield at
a range of two kilometres it became feared by the Western Allies and
Soviets alike as a 'wonder weapon'. The mainstay of the battalion
though was the ever-versatile towed 3.7cm Fliegerabwehrkanonen
(Flak 36/37), the guns were very effective used as fire-support
weapons against infantry.

SS-Gebirgs-Pionier-Bataillon 13 – SS Mountain Assault Engineer
Battalion 13
Feldpost Number 56975

Commander   SS-Obersturmbannführer Oskar
                                Kirchbaum
Battalion Imam   Halim Malkoc

(Kirchbaum was to be murdered by his own men on 17 September
1943 during the infamous mutiny, while Malkoc was so instrumental in defeating it that he was awarded the Iron Cross 2nd Class by
a grateful Heinrich Himmler. After the War the Yugoslavs were not
so grateful and he was executed in Bihac on 7 March 1947).

SS-Gebirgs-Nachrichten-Abteilung 13 – SS Mountain Signals
Battalion 13
Feldpost Number – 58229

Commander   SS-Hauptsturmführer Hans
Hanke

(The Handschar had a reasonably high number of German-speakers, both volksdeustche and reichsdeutsche, and with the language of command being German it was decided that the entire Signals Battalion was to be German to avoid communication problems).

SS-Nachschubsführer 13 – SS Divisional Supply Train 13
Commander   SS-Obersturmbannführer Ajanovic
(Ajanovic was, along with Biscevic, the highest ranking Bosnian Muslim officer in the division as well as an ex-Austro-Hungarian officer, but he was unable to make an impression on his command and was replaced. Unlike in most SS divisions the support services were not parcelled out into separate battalions on the order of battle but concentrated into one bloc. This included the Medical Battalion commanded by SS-Sturmbannführer Dr Albrecht Wiehler. The Battalion had two ambulance platoons and a stretcher-bearer company to service two medical companies and were equipped with trucks).

SS-Feldersatz-Bataillon 13 – SS Field Replacement Battalion 13
Commander   SS-Obersturmführer Hermann
Schifferdecker

This was the replacement battalion of the division designed to act as a depot unit to prepare men to go to the Handschar as and when necessary. The battalion had a Headquarters and four jäger companies and eventually became a shared resource across the Handschar and Kama. Further details about this interesting sub-units history are included in the chapter on the SS-Kama.

The SS-Handschar as a fighting force

A Wehrmacht mountain division was traditionally a powerful military force. This combat power did not come from masses of heavy equipment and high degrees of mechanization and mobility, such things would have been redundant in the terrain mountain troops were trained to fight in. No, the combat effectiveness of a mountain division lay in the human material it contained, which was almost always excellent, combined with their superior motivation and training. This superiority lay in its command structure too, with officers and NCOs being from the very top drawer. The proof for this can be seen in the wartime record of the German *Gebirgsjäger* (mountain troops) which was universally of the very highest class. Wherever they fought they excelled, and right up until the end of the War they were some of the toughest opponents the Western Allies and Soviets had to face.

This was not the case with the SS-Handschar. It was already struggling to fill its command cadres of officers and NCOs and this was before a shot had been fired in anger. To an extent, sheer numbers could have helped make up for this shortfall in leadership but the division was having to turn to compulsion and the call-up of reservists to try to fill the ranks. Even then four whole infantry battalions were either just skeletons or completely struck off the establishment. On equipment, the story was much the same. Like its elder sibling the SS-Prinz Eugen, it was getting the 'bottom shelf' kit, much of it captured from armies the Wehrmacht had rolled over earlier in the War. French, Czech and Russian weaponry was delivered as well as some modern German arms, anything to fill the inventory. While this did see the division equipped, it did not make for combat efficiency. If the division was going to become a proud addition to the Waffen-SS order of battle it would need a fair wind from now on to achieve it. Not only did this not happen, but an event was to occur that was to send shock waves through the whole Waffen-SS and would colour the reputation of the Handschar for ever.

The only ever Waffen-SS mutiny

From its inception, both the SS and Croat authorities had worried about the potential for Tito's men in particular, to infiltrate the fledgling division, receive excellent training and equipment, cause disruption and spread discontent among other recruits and ultimately return to the JANL (Tito's Yugoslav National Liberation Army) as first rate partisans having benefited from the best training regime in the world. The move to southern France had, in part, been to mitigate this threat. The rigid observance of Islamic customs as regarding food, alcohol and religious ceremony, along with the adoption of some Bosnian dress, were also intended to counter this possibility. However there was always the chance that some *agent provocateurs* would slip through the net and all ranks were told to stay vigilant just in case. As it turned out all of these measures were not as effective as was hoped and the ultimate SS night-mare came to pass – mutiny.

Four men, two of them Muslim and two Catholics, had joined the division separately but soon found they were kindred spirits and became determined to subvert the unit when the time was right. The two Catholics, Bozo Jelenek and Nikola Vukelic, were both intelligent and motivated with Jelenek already promoted to officer cadet rank in the division and Vukelic thought of as a potential company commander. Jelenek was a member of the Yugoslav Communist Party and had joined the division under an alias after serving a prison term for his politics. Vukelic it seemed, had no overt political views but had just become severely anti-German. The two Muslims were Lutfija Dizdarevic, a 22-year-old Sarajevan and Ferid Dzanic, the ultimate ringleader of the whole enterprise. The 25-year-old Dzanic came from a well-to-do family in Bihac and briefly served in the Royal Yugoslav Army facing the Wehrmacht invasion in 1941. Escaping imprisonment, like so many of his compatriots he joined the Partisans in 1942 and was subsequently captured by the Germans while patrolling in Bosnia. As proof that not all prisoners were immediately shot out of hand, Dzanic was sent to a prison camp outside Sarajevo from where, unbelievably, he was allowed to volunteer for the Handschar and was released and sent to join them. But this was no 'road to Damascus' conversion and Dzanic was set on continuing the fight against the Germans from within the ranks of their very own armed élite.

All four conspirators were in the same sub-unit; Oskar Kirchbaum's SS-*Gebirgs-Pionier-Bataillon 13*, based in the picturesque town of Villefranche de Rouergue. Having made contact with the local Resistance through sympathetic staff at the Hotel Moderne (also the quarters for the Battalion's officers) the four leaders concocted a plan whereby they would first seize and execute their German commanders, before lead-ing the Battalion on to Rodez, some 30 miles to the west along the River Aveyron. Here they would raise *Waffen-Gebirgsjäger-Regiment der SS 27* in revolt and proceed to go from garrison town to garrison town until the entire region was aflame. After that they were unsure whether to head for the south coast and try to escape to Allied North Africa or fight across the Alps back into Croatia – the mind boggles at their naivety.

Their long-term plan may have been nothing more than fantasy but the mutiny itself was well thought out and fairly meticulous. Dzanic was rostered as the Battalion Duty Officer for 16–17 September 1943, and he ensured that all the men on guard were Dizdarevic's. All was set for when night fell. Just past midnight it erupted, with the guards first arresting the German NCOs in the two pioneer training companies before moving on to secure key points across the town, including the Battalion Headquarters. Lastly Vukelic and Dzanic led their troops on to the Hotel Moderne where they awoke the sleeping officers and bundled them all into Room 4 where they were kept under guard. The middle-aged Kirchbaum was then called out of the room and asked if he would side with the mutineers, when he replied no he was promptly shot dead. The same happened to SS-Hauptsturmführer Heinrich Kuntz and SS-Obersturmführers Gerhard Kretschmer, Anton Wolf and Julius Galantha. Only two officers survived the slaughter; SS-Obersturmführer Alexander Michawetz punched his guards and made a break for it, swimming the Aveyron to safety, and Dr Willfried Schweiger was told he would be spared so as to minister to the mutineers.

Imam Halim Malkoc turns the tide

The Battalion Imam, Halim Malkoc, then appeared on the scene, first reassuring Dr Schweiger that he had known nothing of the mutineers' plan, before speaking to the men of First Company, telling them they had been deceived by their leaders and that their only hope lay in following his orders. He went on to release and re-arm the imprisoned German NCOs and together they took back the town. The two Muslim leaders, Dizdarevic and Dzanic, were killed in the resultant fighting, and Vukelic was captured. The last one, the Catholic Jelenek, fled as soon as it became clear that the mutiny had failed. He managed to escape retribution and served with distinction in the French Resistance until returning to Yugoslavia in late 1944. He survived the War and became a Captain in Tito's army before passing away peacefully in May 1987 at the age of 67.

With two of the ringleaders dead, one in custody and the last on the run, the heat went out of the mutiny and the Bosnians allowed themselves to be disarmed and placed under guard. Having started just after midnight, the whole thing was over and done with by mid-morning on 17 September. The German authorities moved swiftly as soon as they heard about the revolt and sealed off Villefranche, while immediately disarming neighbouring Bosnian units to stop the potential spread of the mutiny. With Villefranche back in loyal hands, Sauberzweig initiated an immediate investigation and the divisional judge advocate, Dr Franz von Kocevar, arrived to start proceedings on the morning of 18 September. SS justice was swift and by that afternoon fourteen Bosnians including Vukelic had been found guilty of mutiny and sentenced to death. The entire pioneer battalion was paraded to watch the sentences carried out in a field opposite the town cemetery. One by one, the condemned men were led to a stake in the field, tied and then shot by firing squad. The vengeful Germans were convinced the town's residents had aided and abetted the mutiny and it was only a stout rebuttal by the one-armed Mayor, Louis Fontages, that saved Villefranche from summary retaliation. Following the executions, four other Bosnians deserted over the next few days but were hunted down, brought back to Villefranche and shot.

Aftermath – move to Germany

On being told of the mutiny Phleps went into near apoplexy, claiming the division was riven with Titoists and that it needed a huge injection of German Waffen-SS men to ensure its future loyalty. Himmler was far more sanguine, acknowledging his disappointment but insisting it was an isolated incident and the division was still basically fine. Just to be sure though there was to be a purge of 'unsuitable' elements and the divison was to be transferred out of France to Neuhammer in German Silesia. Some 825 Bosnians were culled from the ranks and sent to Dachau Concentration Camp. From there, most were press-ganged into joining the German paramilitary labour organisation, *Organisation Todt*, as forced labourers, while the hold-outs were sent on to Neuengamme Concentration Camp. Most never returned to their homeland alive.

Shock waves from Villefranche

Considering the fact that by the War's end over half of the Waffen-SS was non-German, and that a high proportion (up to 25% of its total strength) were not volunteers, it is perhaps more surprising that there was only one mutiny. But only one there was and it was among the Muslim Waffen-SS. Most mutinies occur after long periods of acute unhappiness and resentment among the soldiery, and are then triggered by one act that tips the balance. They tend to be spontaneous and after an initial orgy of violence against those in command, the mutineers usually descend into torpor as they have no plan as to what to do next and no leaders to take charge. The Handschar mutiny did not fit this pattern. The move to France had been unpopular, and there was fear in the ranks for their loved ones back in Bosnia, but the arrival of the hugely energetic Sauberzweig and the reality of hard, military training had dealt

The Muslim Waffen-SS at prayer. (Cody Images)

One of the more exotic officers of the Wehrmacht who served with the Muslim Waffen-SS, *SS-Standartenführer* Harun al-Raschid Bey (formerly Wilhelm Hintersatz) had been a *Heer* observer with the Turkish General Staff and then a liaison officer with the Mufti of Jerusalem. This unusual Austrian officer converted to Islam before taking over command of Meyer-Mader's Muslim SS men following his rather suspicious death.

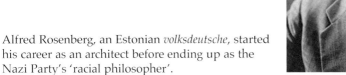

Alfred Rosenberg, an Estonian *volksdeutsche*, started his career as an architect before ending up as the Nazi Party's 'racial philosopher'.

Alfred Rosenberg receives traditional welcoming gifts of bread and salt from people 'liberated' from Stalinism. Unlike the rest of the Nazi leadership he believed it was necessary to harness the hatred for communism harboured by most peoples in the Soviet Union in order to win the War. His views were ignored and Germany paid the price.

Five central Asian Muslim auxiliaries pose for a photo. Every German division serving on the Eastern Front had their contingent of these Hiwis, with up to 20% of every German division in the East being comprised of these hardy but always expendable soldiers. (Courtesy of *OstBattaillon 43*)

A proud recruit to the Turkistan Legion clearly sporting the 1942 version of the armshield depicting the famous mosque at Samarkand and the legend *Biz Alla Bilen*. (Courtesy of Sandtrooper)

Turkic volunteers like this one, with his distinctive Turkistan armshield, formed the majority of the *Osttürkischen Waffen-Verbände der SS* and the 1st East Mussulman SS-Regiment.

A Caucasian officer (with characteristic Muslim kindjal on his cap) inspects a Turkic *Osttruppen* unit in 1941 on the Eastern Front.

General Heinz Hellmich, the 'Inspector of *Osttruppen*' from January to June 1943, reviews some of his Muslim troopers at the Front. Hellmich had no specialist knowledge of the East and was not a Russian speaker; his appointment was not a success.

An SS-*Haupsturmführer* of the Handschar Division.

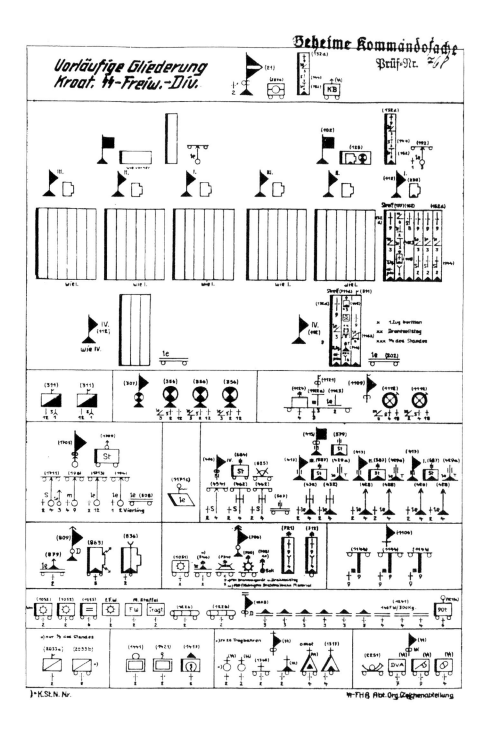

Original organization chart for the Bosnian Muslim SS-Handschar Division.

The Bosnian Muslims were Europeans who had willingly converted to Islam in gratitude for the tolerance shown of their earlier Bogomil faith by the Ottoman Turkish Empire. Across their homeland were distinctive Bogomil tombs like these, reminding them of their lineage and history.

SS-Handschar recruits at morning roll-call.

The Mufti, on one of his visits to the SS-Handschar during its training in
Germany in the winter of 1943–44, talks to a young volunteer and the giant
Bosnian Muslim officer Husejin Dzozo (in fez), the Imam of Regiment 28.
The bespectacled officer to the Mufti's right is the Divisional Adjutant,
SS-Sturmbannfuhrer Götz Berens von Rautenfeld.

The Mufti meets with some of the first recruits to the Muslim 162nd Turkmen Division, the NCO in the foreground is an Azeri, as identified by his armshield.

The self-styled 'Grand' Mufti of Jerusalem, Mohammed 'Haj' Amin al-Husseini with a very young Bosnian Muslim Handschar volunteer. Al-Husseini served as an artillery officer in the Imperial Ottoman Army but never saw any action himself.

A young Asiatic Muslim Hiwi on the Eastern Front. Without them the Wehrmacht's war effort against the Red Army would have collapsed far sooner.

A Turkic Waffen-*Sturmmann* in the most-famed of all the early the Islamic units, the 162nd Turkmen Division (*162 Infanterie Division (turk.)*).

A recruiting poster for the SS-Handschar. Advertisements like these were plastered all over northeastern Bosnia to encourage volunteers, along with tours by the Mufti and German officials.

Albert Stenwedel before the War as an SS-*Obersturmführer*, commanding 6. Kp II. Btl SS-Regiment 'Der Führer', Graz 1938. He would go on to become one of only five Knight's Cross winners in the SS-Handschar, winning the award for bravery on 3 May 1945 as the War came to a close. (Courtesy of James Mcleod)

SS-Sturmbannführer Albert Stenwedel (seated at head of the table) when he
commanded the II/27. Regiment of the SS-Handschar in Yugoslavia, May 1944.
(Courtesy of James Mcleod)

Albert Stenwedel, third from the left, with fellow officers from his II/27.
Regiment of the SS-Handschar, Yugoslavia, summer 1944. (Courtesy of
James Mcleod)

SS-Untersturmführer Rudi Sommerer of the SS-Handschar, one of the division's German cadre. (Courtesy of James Mcleod)

SS-Untersturmführer Rudi Sommerer of the SS-Handschar, sporting both the divisional fez as well as the hand and scimitar collar tab. (Courtesy of James Mcleod)

Sommerer of the 6.28 Regiment with one of his NCOs, the Bosnian Muslim Waffen-*Sturmmann* Nazir Hodic. (Courtesy of James Mcleod)

The men of the Bosnian Muslim SS-Handschar on parade. (Cody Images)

Following the Italian change of sides in 1943, thousands of reluctant conscripts simply abandoned their weapons and equipment and headed home. For the Partisans, scenes like this in Dubrovnik were a god-send as they literally scooped up piles of discarded arms.

Dr Anté Pavelic: Member of the Bar, elected Deputy in the Yugoslav parliament, Croatia's Poglavnik and mass murderer. He survived the war and lived out his life in Franco's Spain.

The German Army's Muslim *Osttruppen*, vital though they were, were kitted out with any uniforms and weapons to hand and were hardly the image of 'Aryan' military precision.

SS-Obergruppenführer Artur Martin Phleps (born 29 November 1881 in Rumanian Transylvania – killed in action 21 September 1944). The highest ranking *volksdeutsche* in the entire Waffen-SS, and the man who created the feared *SS-Prinz Eugen* division and led the ultimately unsuccessful German war against Tito and his Partisans.

Artur Phleps, recently promoted to command V SS Mountain Corps, on a visit to the SS-Handschar, north-eastern Bosnia 1944.

Jubilant Ustasha men stand over the bodies of massacred Serbs. Their litany of atrocities even appalled the Germans, who were not known for their squeamishness. (Cody Images)

A band of Pavelic's Ustasha pose threatening a prisoner with decapitation by handsaw. Unbelievable though it might seem, hundreds of Serbs, Roma and Jews met their deaths in this way at the infamous Jasenovac concentration camp. (Cody Images)

SS-*Brigadeführer* Karl-Gustav Sauberzweig, the *Schnellchen* himself, confers with two of his officers.

General Slavko Stanzer, head of the Croat Domobran home guard and then all of Croatia's armed forces, inspects one of his Muslim units. Captured by the Partisans in 1945, Stanzer was tried and sentenced to death but cheated the gallows by dying in his cell of natural causes the night before his execution.

These *Osttruppen* are Azeris, many of whom participated in the brutal suppression of the Warsaw Rising in 1944 in units such as the 111th Regiment.

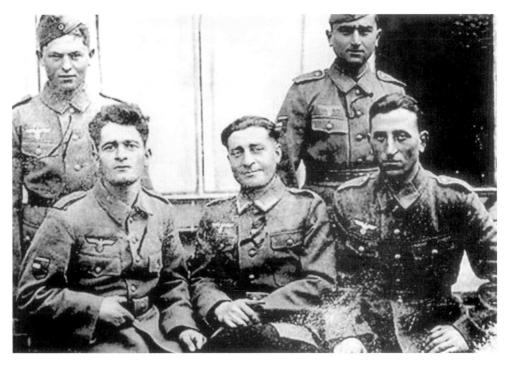

Azebaijanis in the Wehrmacht, 1944. Azebaijani volunteers were dispersed across different battalions as a precaution against rebellion. (Cody Images)

Waffen-SS Mountain Division "Skanderbeg" (Albanian No. 1)

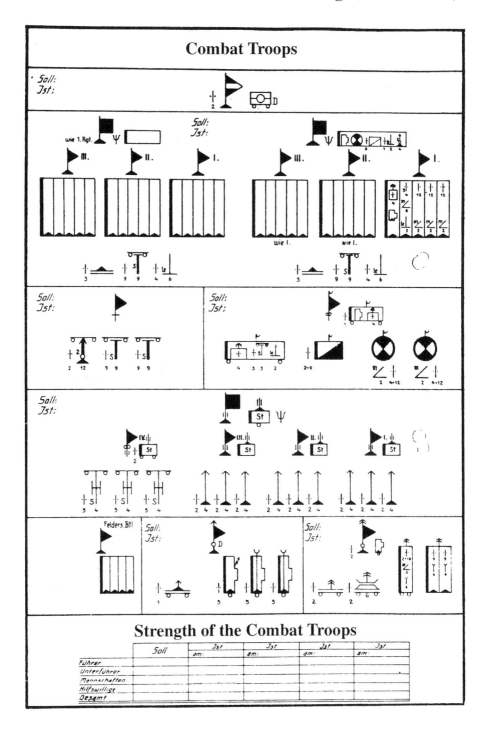

Combat Troops

Strength of the Combat Troops

	Soll	Jst am:	Jst am:	Jst am:	Jst am:
Führer					
Unterführer					
Mannschaften					
Hilfswillige					
Gesamt					

Waffen-SS Mountain Division "Skanderbeg" (Albanian No. 1)

Geheime Kommandosache
Prüf-Nr. tr..

Supply Troops

Soll:
Jst:

Soll:
Jst:

| Soll: Jst: | Soll: Jst: | Soll: Jst: | | Soll: Jst: | Soll: Jst: |

Strength of the Supply Troops

	Soll	Jst am:	Jst am:	Jst am:	Jst am:
Führer					
Unterführer					
Mannschaften					
Hilfswillige					
Gesamt					

Total Strength of the Waffen-SS Mountain Division "Skanderbeg"

	Soll	Jst am:	Jst am:	Jst am:	Jst am:
Führer					
Unterführer					
Mannschaften					
Hilfswillige					
Gesamt					

Waffen	Soll	Jst am:
Pistolen		
m. P.		
Gewehre		
le. M.G.		
s. M.G.		
m. Gr.W.		
s. Gr.W.		
Fm.W.		
Werfer		
s. Panz. Buchs.		
3.7 cm Pak		
5 cm Pak		
7.5 cm Pak		
7.5 cm Pak (Sf.)		
le. J.G.		
s. J.G.		
2 cm Flak		
2 cm Flak (Vierl.)		
3.7 cm Flak		
8.8 cm Flak		
Beob. Gesch. 36		
le. F.H.		
le. F.H. (mot Z.)		
s. F.H. (mot. Z.)		
10.5 cm K (mot Z.)		

Pz.-Fahrzeuge	Soll	Jst am:	Jst am:	Jst am:	Jst am:

Pferde	Soll	Jst am:	Jst am:	Jst am:	Jst am:
Reitpferde					
Bergreitpferde					
Tragtiere					
Packpferde					
le. Zugpferde					
schw. Zugpferde					
schwste Zugpferde					

gez. Zeichenabt. ₩-FHA Org. Abt. Iª/II.

Original organization chart and strength return for the Albanian Muslim
SS-Skanderbeg division.

Atrocities like this one were a standard feature of the fighting in Albania and Kosovo, the homelands of the SS-Skanderbeg. (Cody Images)

They say, blood will have blood. Two-thirds of the ethnic Albanians recruited into the Skanderbeg Division were from Kosovo-Metohija. The division's systematic murder of the Serb Orthodox Christian and Jewish populations there would lead to another massacre in the 1990s.

These three officers served in the short-lived SS-Kama division which lasted a
mere six months from establishment to dissolution. By that stage of the War there
were few willing volunteers in Bosnia who wanted to back the side that was
clearly losing.

23rd Waffen-SS Mountain Division "Kama" (Croatian No. 2)

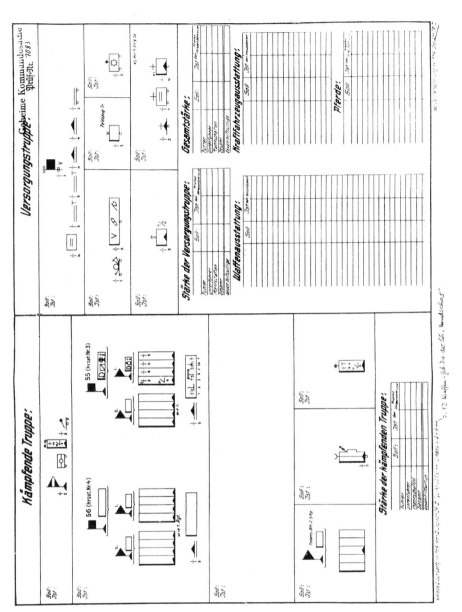

Original organization chart and strength return for the second of the Bosnian Muslim SS-divisions, the Kama.

Very rare photo of a Crimean Tartar, serving with the Germans, receiving hospitality from a local inhabitant in the Crimea. Stalin and Beria would punish this collaboration with exile for the entire people in late 1944.

Crimean Tartar *Osttruppen* carry out weapons drills on the Eastern Front. Thousands would die fighting in the ranks of both the Red Army and the *Ostheer*, and the pro-German survivors would never see their homeland again following their exile to central Asia for their supposed treachery.

Wearing their distinctive tropical uniform, men of the Indian SS-Legion keep watch over the coast of France down in the Bay of Biscay. As it turned out they never fought any Allied troops.

Rudolf Hartog was an official translator with the Indian Legion when it was part of the *Heer*, and remained with it when it was absorbed by the Waffen-SS, although personally he did not transfer to the Black Guards and remained a private in the *Heer*. This picture shows him with his wife celebrating Christmas in 1944. He is wearing the tropical uniform of the SS-Legion. (Courtesy of James Mcleod)

Heinz Bertling. A former Foreign Ministry official and long-time member of the SS, Bertling took over command of the Indian Waffen-SS in August 1944, but was deeply unimpressed by the posting and showed little interest in his men. This pre-War picture shows Bertling as an *SS-Sturmbannführer*. (Courtesy of James Mcleod)

Indian SS men are trained on the 75mm field gun by their German instructors during February 1944, but despite receiving this training the unit was militarily useless.

Franz Ausmeyer was posted to the *Indische Freiwilligen Legion der Waffen-SS* in December 1944. This photo was taken before the War when Ausmeyer was an SS-*Sturmmann* (lance corporal) in the élite SS-*Germania* Regiment. (Courtesy of James Mcleod)

The Calcutta lawyer Subhas Chandra Bose, the Netaji, with some of the men of his collaborationist Indian National Army. (Courtesy of *OstBattalion 43*)

A volunteer in the Indian SS-Legion, in the tropical issue uniform. (Courtesy of *OstBattalion 43*)

Indian Legion volunteers on parade with their distinctive 'leaping tiger' armshield and its legend, Freies Indien. (Courtesy of *OstBattalion 43*)

Indian Legion volunteers construct barbed wire obstacles during their garrison duties on the French coast in 1944. (Courtesy of *OstBattalion 43*)

The Mufti inspects Bosnian Muslim SS men from the SS-Handschar. After the war the Mufti fled to Egypt and stoked the growing Arab-Jewish conflict in the region.

Albert Stenwedel at an OdR (*Oredensgemeinschaft der Träger der Ritterkreuz* – Knight's Cross Winners Society) reunion dinner in 1959, with the legendary *Leibstandarte* commander, Sepp Dietrich. (Courtesy of James Mcleod)

with these issues to a large extent. The Handschar mutiny was a different affair, one of those rare beasts, a planned and organised event by men whose very reason for joining the formation was insurrection. This also doomed the rebels from the start as they were not riding a popular wave of anger among the troops but rather seeking to use them to cause as much trouble for the Germans as possible. The majority of Muslim soldiers were just as aghast at the attack as were their German comrades and it was not a symptom of a wider malaise within the division.

Nevertheless it had huge consequences for the Handschar and hundreds of thousands of other foreign 'volunteers', especially the Osttruppen. In September, Hitler informed a stunned OKH that the Osttruppen were to be dissolved forthwith. A crisis ensued in the German High Command as the generals told Hitler that without the hundreds of thousands of official, and unofficial Hiwis the Russian Front would collapse and Nazi Germany would lose the War in short order. Unsurprisingly Hitler ranted. Eventually a compromise was reached that saw dozens of eastern units swapped for German formations serving in the West. By the beginning of June 1944 one in six battalions defending the vaunted Atlantic Wall was composed of Osttruppen. Hence why in the 12 weeks following D-Day the Western Allies captured over 20,000 of these reluctant beach defenders in Normandy.

It is impossible to say with any certainty that Hitler's decision was motivated by the Handschar mutiny, but it is likely that it played a part. If Eastern troops among the dedicated ranks of the Black Guard could turn on their German masters, then how could the masses of Osttruppen in the Ostheer be trusted? The end result was disaster. Huge numbers of men, whether willing volunteers or not, were sent from the East to the West. In the East they at least understood who they were fighting and why; in the West all of this was gone. Karl Wilhelm von Schlieben's 709th Infantry Division, based in Cherbourg on the Cotentin peninsula, was typical of this mass redeployment, with one in five of its ranks filled by a Hiwi. Von Schlieben was very sceptical about the transfer: 'We are asking rather a lot if we expect Russians to fight in France for Germany against Americans.' He was to be proved entirely right. When the Allied invasion came, the Osttruppen fared badly. *Oberst* (Colonel) Walter Köhn, a regimental commander in the Cotentin, said of them: 'They fell to pieces completely. They held out for quite a while, but when things became critical, they took to their heels too.' Without this policy would the Wehrmacht have held out longer in Normandy? Who knows, it is almost certain it would have done little more than delay the inevitable, but wars often hinge on half-chances and maybes.

Final training at Neuhammer

By 1 October the division was moving by rail to its new home far away to the north-east. Here at the Neuhammer training ground in the safe confines of the Third Reich, the division underwent a wholesale reorganisation following the nightmare of Villefranche. Even though a recent recruitment drive back in Bosnia had garnered another 1,000 or so volunteers it was clear that the division was struggling to fill its establishment. Sauberzweig accepted the reality and disbanded the third battalions of both jäger regiments as well as a slew of smaller sub-units, and used their personnel to bring other core units up to strength. Fresh drafts of German officers and NCOs arrived, including two entire companies from the 6th SS Gebirgs Division Nord. These new men, overwhelmingly, were younger, fitter and more motivated than their predecessors. Their presence began to stitch the division back together after the debacle of France, and in a few short months the SS-Handschar started to look and feel like a division nearing combat readiness. The festivities of Bairam, to celebrate the ending of the fasting month of Ramadan, were greeted with much jubilation in the division. By now everyone knew how bad things were back in Bosnia and they were extremely eager to finish their training, get home and safeguard their families and friends. The divisional Imam, Abdulah Muhasilovic, addressed the division:

> As we observe this Bairam feast with good food, and even havla, an entire army of our brothers, our refugees, wander about from city to village, wrapped in rags, barefooted, hungry and cold. Their Bairam feast will be spent in misery and distress. It is even sadder that cetniks and Partisans carry on their activities, murdering and plundering wherever they go. But we call out to them, 'You can murder and plunder, but the day will come when the tables are turned!'
>
> And to you, dear and beloved Bosnia, we appeal to you, our beloved parents, wives and children – be patient and ask our God that we finish our training quickly. We will then return and thrash our enemies with the courage of lions, and liberate our cities and villages, our Bosnia.

That day of return was swiftly approaching. Himmler visited the division on 21 November and was impressed, as was Amin al-Husseini who brought gifts of scarce honey and tobacco for the men (the Nazis had tried to ban women from smoking in the Reich to ration limited stocks of cigarettes), and by the beginning of December its strength had climbed to 21,065 men (its establishment was meant to be around 26,000). The old problems persisted though, with only 2,078 NCOs out of a complement of over 3,000 and a shortfall of 294 officers from the establishment of 671. But little could be done about this now. The training was almost over and Germany's military situation was growing ever more precarious. By the new year of 1944 the men had had about as much preparation as they were likely to get and January 1944 saw Sauberzweig report the division officially ready for combat.

Hundreds of miles to the south, Pavelic's Croatia was in a state of perpetual chaos with the Ustasha government failing even to feed the populace properly let alone tackle Tito's rampant Partisan forces. The overthrow of Mussolini and the subsequent switching of sides by the Italian armed forces had resulted in a sea change in the civil war. The Italian divisions in Yugoslavia may well have been pretty ineffective but at least they had managed to keep a lid on the JANL. With the downfall of the fascist state, thousands of dispirited but relieved Italian soldiers had simply dumped their weapons and headed for the coast to try and get home across the Adriatic. The Partisans took full advantage. They stormed into garrison towns and emptied the arsenals, scooping up huge numbers of all types of small arms, along with for the very first time, many heavy weapons as well. Partisan commanders press-ganged Italian gunners and tankers into teaching their men how to use their new bounty, and soon began to turn Italian artillery, mortars, heavy machine-guns and even light tanks and armoured cars onto the remaining Germans. The 19,000 or so Ustasha troops (5,000 of whom were permanently stationed in Zagreb to secure the capital) were now hugely outnumbered and outgunned and the few local Muslim militia detachments were fighting an uneven battle – the SS-Handschar with its thousands of well-trained *gebirgsjäger* and stocks of military hardware was desperately needed back home.

Tartars in Croatia

It is interesting to note that the Handschar was not the only Wehrmacht Islamic unit looking to fight Tito. As early as mid-1943 a unit of Tartar Osttruppen had been transferred from the Eastern Front to combat the JANL. The Tartars fought in Croatia near the town of Senj and in the nearby Papuka mountains. However this was small scale stuff. The future depended on the clunking fist of the Handschar.

A year on – the SS-Handschar returns

Having been established in February 1943, it was almost a year to the day when the largest ever Waffen-SS Muslim formation began to board freight trains at the rate of six a day to take it back to its homeland and to one of the most brutal and vicious theatres in the whole War.

The journey itself lasted some six or more days before the trains pulled into stations in north-eastern Bosnia and the men formed up in their concentration areas prior to the commencement of operations. From the start, the Handschar men began to realise what they would be facing. On entering Croatia the trains slowed dramatically to watch for mines on the track and other sabotage. When they stopped it was straight into an all-round defence battle formation with machine-gun crews setting up a perimeter in case of attack. Back in France they had been spread over a huge area with little need for anything other than local security, but here in Bosnia the division's sub-units were tightly focused around the Zupanje – Vinkovci – Sid triangle. Just north of Tuzla and Brcko and astride the modern E70 highway, the area was home to volksdeutsche communities as well as Bosnians and had been the target of multiple Partisan attacks already. The arriving Handschar men noted that every train station was fortified, wrecked carriages littered the lines and military installations were pockmarked with bullet holes. Having alighted from their trains the men hungrily stared south across the Sava River towards their homeland – it was time to go home.

Artur Phleps – the architect of the big sweep

Having led the SS-Prinz Eugen during the anti-Tito offensives of *Unternehmen Weiss* and *Schwarz* (Operations White and Black) in early 1943, Phleps proceeded to hand over command of his beloved division to SS-Brigadeführer Karl Reichsritter von Oberkamp on 21 June. In recognition of the Prinz Eugen's excellent combat record during his tenure, Phleps was awarded the Knight's Cross on 4 July 1943, one of seven members of the division to receive the coveted award during the War. Phleps was then promoted to SS-Obergruppenführer and given command of the newly-formed *V SS Gebirgs Korps* (5th SS Mountain Corps) covering Bosnia-Herzegovina. This Corps had his old division, the Prinz Eugen under command, as well as the Heer's 181st Reserve Division and the newly-formed 118th Jäger Division, the Croatian 369th Division and the SS-Handschar.

Nominally then Phleps had a pretty respectable five divisions to take on the Partisans in Bosnia, but the reality was far different. The SS-Prinz Eugen was the most experienced and most capable of his formations and as such was constantly being tasked by higher command to operate out of area in Serbia or Montenegro or wherever else it was needed. The 181st Reserve Division was exactly what its name suggested, a division of reservists; old men not suitable for the frontline who were best suited to guarding railway lines and had somehow ended up in one of the bitterest struggles of the War. The 118th Jäger was still shiny new and learning its trade, as of course was the SS-Handschar. It was down then to the Croats of the 369th to provide some punch for the Corps. This it did, being a successor unit to the 369th Croat Regiment that had fought so bravely in Russia before being annihilated at Stalingrad as part of Sixth Army. Using base personnel and recovered wounded, as well as fresh drafts of volunteers, the unit had been rebuilt into a division and kept its old number, also acquiring the name of the old Austro-Hungarian 42nd Croat Division along the way, *Vrazja Divizija* – Devil's Division.

This structure did not fit Phleps's concept of anti-partisan War at all. He was a 'big battalions' man who favoured large scale aggressive sweeps carried out by divisional sized groupings who were tasked to fix Partisan formations in place and then use superior firepower to destroy them. For Phlep's plans he needed many men. A great innovator in counter-insurgency warfare he was not. For Phleps, the civilian population in any area were at best a nuisance, if not a hindrance to operations, and were to be treated harshly if suspected of aiding the guerrillas. His views were more akin to the Napoleonic French in Spain than Gerald Templer's in Malaya. This would have mattered less had he had sufficient manpower to overwhelm the enemy and continue to dominate the ground at all times, but as we have seen he did not. Phleps's grand sweeps would merely push the Partisans from one area to another and as soon as his relatively few men moved on, as they invariably did, the Partisans would simply come out of hiding and re-infiltrate the region. Houses would be rebuilt, bases re-established and local attacks on German supply routes and positions would start up all over again.

What Phleps's orthodox military mind never came to grips with is the fact that to a guerrilla fighter, and Tito was one of the finest ever exponents of the art, success was in survival. Conventional forces under men like Phleps were always trying to kick off the decisive engagement, the one battle that would determine the campaign, because if they could do that they knew their superior training, organisation and firepower would ensure victory. This is precisely why any insurgency fighter worth their salt will avoid such confrontations like the plague, unless they are in a position to win them. The French would learn this harsh lesson at Dien Bien Phu in Indo-China in 1954, and the Americans would spend years learning it all over again in the same country in the 1960s and 70s. The key in tackling insurgents was, and still is, to take away their most important advantage – the support of the local population. This is the basis for 'hearts and minds' whereby the populace realises that its best interests, whether that be future freedoms / security / wellbeing, are best served by backing the authorities and not the insurgents. British Army policy in Northern Ireland was predicated on this for years with the majority of the population, both Protestants and Catholics, being given every reason to back the government and effectively keep a lid on the conflict until the politicians came to a solution acceptable to all.

Inadvertently, the deployment of the SS-Handschar in its home area could have delivered a lasting change in the balance of conflict in the area if it was allowed to, in effect 'rule' north-eastern Bosnia. With thousands of well-armed Muslim men guarding their communities the Partisan threat would wither on the vine. The question was, would the Islamic SS be allowed to take on this role?

Unternehmen Wegweiser – battle at last

The SS-Handschar's mission was clear from the start – destroy the Partisans in north-eastern Bosnia between the Sava, Bosna, Spreca and Drina Rivers, secure agricultural production and safeguard the volksdeutsche enclave around Srem to the north. This last objective in particular would free the SS-Prinz Eugen from worry about the homes many had left behind and allow them to move freely around Croatia, Serbia and Montenegro as the German's main offensive weapon in the country.

The first operation slated for Sauberzweig's men was the clearance of the Borsut Forest. This marshy, heavily wooded area a few miles south of Sid held half a dozen towns like Lipovac, Batkovci, Visnjicevo and Jamena that had been in Partisan hands for a long time. Using it as a base location, the Partisans had frequently sallied out and cut the vital Belgrade – Zagreb railway line a few miles to the north. As soon as German troops arrived they would then slip away south back to the forests and the Germans would be left chasing shadows. Communist strength in Borsut was estimated at some 2,000 to 2,500 men from two or more brigades under Sava Stefanovic. *Unternehmen Wegweiser* (Operation Signpost) was designed as a 'sandwich' assault. In essence Raithel's Regiment 28 was to advance from the west, and Hampel's Regiment 27 from the east. Their mission was to destroy any and all Partisan units they found. Faced with being attacked from two sides, the communists would obviously try to escape either north or south and wait until the Handschar assault had blown itself out. To prevent this, blocking formations were placed to the north (the mixed German Heer Jäger Regiment 40) and the south (the Croatian river boat the *Bosna*) to stop the escape of the Partisans. Their role was vital. If they failed to hold their lines then the Handschar men would advance into nothing.

On 10 March 1944, at 0400hrs the SS-Handschar went into action for the very first time. Supported by its heavy artillery, including 88mm flak guns firing in the ground role and a platoon of *Sturmgeschütz* assault guns from SS-Batterie 105, the Muslim jägers swept forward taking town after town across the area. Against four battalions of the Handschar and their heavy weaponry the Partisans soon realised they were outmatched and looked for a way out. Their escape route north was blocked but the line on the Sava River was porous. Using local boats, the mass of Stefanovic's men crossed to the southern bank and disappeared into the thick woodland. There they licked their wounds and waited for the inevitable Bosnian withdrawal. In three days it was all over and Wegweiser was declared finished on 13 March. The Partisans had taken a hit; Sauberzweig claimed 573 had been killed and a further 82 captured, proving again that immediate execution was not always the 'Balkan way'. But even on the German's own intelligence estimates, up to 2,000 had escaped, mainly to the south. While the operation had been a limited success and the Handschar had perfomed well, Signpost demonstrated the flaws in the Wehrmacht's strategy. Large, powerful formations carrying out grand operations would always defeat the Partisans, but they would not stay and fight but instead would retreat, regroup and then re-enter the lost territory when the operation was deemed over. Small towns like Visnjicevo would see their first Axis troops for a long time, but within days they would be gone and the Partisans would filter back and take up where they left off.

Unternehmen Save – the SS-Handschar 'invades' its homeland

With Borsut Forest temporarily cleared and the division's left (eastern) flank secure, the Handschar could turn its nose south across the River Sava to the homeland most of them had not seen for almost a year. On the southern bank of the river stretching away through Bijeljina – Tuzla – Zvornik and Zenica all the way to Konjic – Sarajevo – Gorazde were the mountains and villages of Bosnia that were the very heart of the division's recruiting area. With the Italians gone and the Ustasha cooped up in fortified barracks and unwilling to venture out, the Partisans had had the run of the region. As many as 10,000 Muslims had joined Tito, but that had not saved their communities which had been devastated in see-saw fighting between the warring sides with tens of thousands forced on the road as refugees. For the SS-Handschar men this was the moment they had volunteered and trained for, all in preparation for crossing over the Sava and liberating their country from the communists who threatened to destroy it.

Situation Enemy Forces

Facing the Handschar was the entire Partisan III Bosnia Corps. This comprised a first line of the 16th and 36th Vojvodina divisions, and a second of the 17th, 27th and 38th East Bosnian divisions. As it was this Corps that comprised the majority of Tito's forces in the Handschar's home area, they were to form the backbone of the resistance to Sauberzweig's men for the remainder of the Division's operational time in north-eastern Bosnia. In particular the 16th Vojvodina Division would come to be the nemesis of the Handschar following on from the Battle of Lopare later in the summer.

Partisan formations might have been called brigades and divisions but their strength bore no relation to what is understood in German terms. On paper it looked as if the Handschar would be outnumbered by a factor of five to one in the region, but this was not the case. The Handschar was an understrength gebirgsjäger division of just over 21,000 men, but in comparison a Partisan division was lucky to muster a tenth of that number, while a brigade (in British Army parlance usually about 3,000 men strong) was usually only a few hundred men. Indeed one of the Handschar's own intelligence reports, of 28 May, put total Partisan strength in the area at just 10,200 to 10,500 men, with the 27th East Bosnian Division for example at just 1,200 men strong. This evened up the odds, but it was still clear that the Handschar would be widely spread and could be outnumbered locally if the Partisans could concentrate their formations effectively. Given that this would have presented Phleps with an unbelievably juicy target there was little willingness to do this on the communist side, however what it did mean was that there was always the danger of the Partisans being able to achieve local superiority and hit the Handschar hard – this was the seed of the defeat at Lopare.

For the Muslims it meant that if well handled they could take on each Partisan formation in turn and defeat them in detail as long as they could exploit their superior tactical command, mechanised mobility and firepower in time for each battle.

Back on the Sava, Sauberzweig understood completely the significance of the moment for his men and before they crossed the river he wrote an open letter to the division with instructions that it be read out to all ranks:

> We have now reached the Bosnian frontier and will begin the march into the homeland.
>
> I was recently able to travel throughout almost all of Bosnia [Sauberzweig had carried out a personal recce prior to Wegweiser]. What I saw shocked me. The fields lay uncultivated, the villages burned out and destroyed. The few remaining inhabitants live in cellars or underground shelters. Misery reigns in the refugee camps as I've never before seen in my life. This must be changed through swift and energetic action...
>
> Before long, each of you shall be standing in the place that you call home, as a soldier and a gentleman; standing firm as a defender of the idea of saving the culture of Europe – the idea of Adolf Hitler.
>
> I wish every one of you 'soldier's luck' and know...that you will be loyal until the end.

Signpost had only been over for two days when *Unternehmen Save* (Operation Sava), was launched on 15 March. The Partisans were dug-in and waiting. This was not a simple river crossing with the troops marching over a bridge. Even though this was theoretically part of the Nazi empire, the SS-Handschar was forced to fire an extensive artillery barrage to cover the division as it crossed the Sava in assault boats and inflatables. Hampel's men crossed at Bosanska Raca in the east where the Drina meets the Sava, while the rest of the division's fighting units went over at Brcko a few miles to the west. Regiment 27 advanced south-west taking the town of Bijeljina on 16 March, resistance was light and casualties on both sides were few. Raithel's Regiment 28 met a very different situation and were fighting from the moment they landed on the southern shore. Pushing south towards Lopare the two jäger battalions were engaged in heavy fighting with strong Partisan formations from the 16th and 36th Vojvodina divisions. Nevertheless, the Handschar was equal to the task and captured Pukis, then Celic, Koraj and Zabrde. A communist counter-attack on the evening of 17 March was repulsed with heavy losses, some 201 Partisans being killed in the failed attack. Further counter-attacks followed and although they slowed down the Handschar advance they failed to stop it. One Partisan commander wrote:

> On 19 March we were ordered to retake Zabrde. The enemy had dug in and we are unable to dislodge them. We fought until noon when our

ammunition was exhausted. The enemy pressed the attack but we had to escape. We had heavy losses. In these four days the Brigade suffered 50 dead, 82 wounded, and 40 missing.

Muslim tenacity, coupled with heavy weaponry and superior training, made the Handschar a powerful force and by 20 March the Partisans had retreated south leaving their dead on the battlefield.

Consolidation was then the order of the day for the Muslim SS men, but it was frustrating as all they wanted to do was to keep on going, find and fight the Partisans, beat them and liberate their homeland. Even though Operation Sava was officially over, some fighting continued with Kuhler's Recce Battalion attacking Partisans at Gornje Rahic and killing 124 of them, with further positions in the Bukvik – Vujcici area being assaulted too.

Two operations in, the performance so far

Overall the SS-Handschar had performed well. Many accounts of the Muslim SS-Handschar state plainly that the formation had no redeeming military qualities, never did anything other than commit atrocities and definitely didn't carry out successful operations in the face of stiff opposition. Signpost and Sava prove this is a modern myth. True, the Bosnians were not up against the might of the Red Army, but they had not been trained or equipped for that theatre. They were an out-and-out anti-partisan division conceived to fight Tito, and the month of March 1944 was their baptism of fire. In that time they had cleared a notorious Partisan stronghold in Borsut, made an opposed river crossing of the Sava south back into Bosnia, and then advanced against dogged resistance to the foot of the Majevica mountains. In so doing they had killed, wounded and captured hundreds of Partisans and completely changed the military situation in north-eastern Bosnia. What was previously a communist stronghold was now the hunting ground of Nazi Germany's first ever Muslim SS division.

The third operation – *Unternehmen Osterei* (Operation Easter Egg)

The SS-Handschar had now established a firm foothold in its designated area of operations and given the Partisans a bloody nose. It was no time to slacken off and Sauberzweig knew it. His next step was Operation Easter Egg. This was not a set-piece attack like the previous crossing of the Sava but rather a continuation of the advance south with the intent of further damaging Partisan formations as well as securing the Tuzla salt mines and the Ugljevik coal mines.

Easter Egg and its aftermath would showcase the two entirely different strategies available to the Axis in Yugoslavia. On the one hand, Sauberzweig – more by accident than by design – would show the value of limited military goals backed up by concerted administrative and political activity to win over the population, whereas back at Corps Headquarters Phleps and the higher SS authorities were concerned only with the next 'big op', *Unternehmen Maibaum* – Operation Maypole.

Launched at 0300hrs on the morning of 12 April, Easter Egg saw Regiment 27 continue its push south by capturing Janja, and then hook west to take the Ugljevik mines. Regiment 28 pushed south-east to meet its sister regiment in a local pincer attack that saw Priboj taken after fierce fighting. As with the previous two operations it was Raithel's men that bore the brunt of the battle, but again, as in Signpost and Sava both regiments acquitted themselves well, and although casualties were taken they were not heavy. Life was not so rosy for the Partisans who pulled the hard-pressed 16th and 36th Vojvodina divisions back south over the Tuzla – Zvornik road. Further west the Recce Battalion pushed out to take Srebrenik and then Gradacac and expand the division's right flank.

New tactics – the *Jagdkommados*

It was a facet of the Yugoslav war that even though by 1944 much of the fighting was done by fairly large formations, the situation on the ground was never truly conventional, with the hardcore of Tito's units, supported by thousands of local militia types and units, often splintering and re-forming with many men left behind by accident or design. This meant frontlines were pretty meaningless and in modern parlance led to an 'asymmetric battlefield', i.e. the enemy was not only in front of you, but behind, to the sides and even amongst you. Iraq, post-Saddam Hussein, is a modern example of such a war. The effect on the ground in Bosnia was that even as the Partisan main units were shoved away by the Handschar, there were still a host of them hiding out in the forests and hills waiting for their chance to reappear. Dispatch riders, lone vehicles and sentries would fall prey to them, as well as small patrols and outstations. The effect manpower-wise was not great, but the effect on morale was immense – no-one ever feels completely safe in such a war.

To combat this situation the Handschar innovated in a manner that would become commonplace in anti-partisan warfare in the future, especially in the West's retreat from empire post-Second World War.

Sauberzweig took to organising so-called *Jagdkommandos* (literally hunter commandos). These were usually company strength patrols (sometimes up to battalion size) in which the men would ditch their heavy equipment and transport and seek to use rapid movement and their superior training to find and destroy the Partisans on their own ground. Without their cumbersome logistical tail the Muslims could use the ground and terrain just as effectively as the communists. They could then dominate the ground, remove the Partisans' freedom of movement and then literally hunt him down and kill him. The results were impressive; on the 21 April Jagdkommandos killed 91 enemy and captured another 92, on the 23 April more than 200 enemy were killed south of Bijeljina. The tactics were working; large scale offensives by conventional forces to push the Partisans out of an area were followed up by light forces finding and killing stay-behind guerrillas. The missing piece in what would become classic counter-insurgency warfare practice was the immensely important reaching out to the local populace. Achieve all three in sequence and victory is there for the taking.

Sauberzweig's plan for the people

Given Sauberzweig's traditional military background, and the truly appalling record of the Wehrmacht in dealing with occupied areas, his next move was nothing less than revolutionary. On his own initiative he issued a comprehensive plan as to what was going to happen administratively and economically in the newly-conquered zone. There was no room in this plan for the discredited Ustasha government which was rightly seen as a barrier to success in the campaign, but Zagreb kicked up enough of a fuss to the likes of Berger back in Berlin that the concept of an 'SS Government' in north-eastern Bosnia was put on the back burner. But alongside this plan Sauberzweig issued guidelines to his troops that were to fundamentally alter the nature of the campaign and hold out the hope of eventual victory. The guidelines can be taken as a 'bible' for successful relations with the local people during counter-insurgency and as such are reproduced here in full:

> If available; local division members should be brought together before entry into towns.
> Spare villages. No destructive rages; engage only the enemy.
> Always remember that the parents, brothers, and sisters of our fellow division members live in the vaillages.
> Destroy no houses.

Chop down no fruit trees.

Our doctors and dentists are to treat the civilian population whenever possible.

No shortsightedness toward the civilian population.

Those who carry on black marketeering and usurp the property of the people in the plundered homeland of the division will be sent to a concentration camp.

Remember, not: How many enemies have I killed? Rather: How many friends have I made?

This document is extraordinary and could have been transplanted into the most eminent anti-guerrilla warfare manuals of the past 60 years and more. If this approach had been adopted throughout Yugoslavia who knows what the Nazis could have achieved. At the very least they probably would have been able to fulfil Himmler's intent of withdrawing desperately needed German formations from the country and sending them to the ever-hungry Russian Front, and allowed mainly locally raised units to contain Tito. As it was, the opportunity was not taken and Phleps's response was the grandiose and ultimately futile Maypole offensive.

Unternehmen Maibaum (Operation Maypole) – offensive number 4

The arrival and advance of the SS-Handschar had changed the situation in Bosnia greatly. At the same time, Partisan forces in neighbouring Serbia to the east were also under increasing pressure from the Germans as the campaigning season got underway. Tito's plan was for the 16th Vojvodina and 17th East Bosnia divisions to cross the Drina River running north–south and move into Serbia to relieve other Partisan forces there that were under pressure from Axis attacks. This would severely weaken the communist force in north-eastern Bosnia but it was reckoned that with the SS-Handschar so active it was best to lie low anyway and more use could be made of available manpower in setting light to Serbia. The Germans, in the shape of *Heeresgruppe F* (Army Group F led by *Generalfeldmarschall* Maximilian Freiherr von Weichs), did foresee this move but they thought it was part of a much larger shift of forces whereby the entire III Bosnia Corps would cross the Drina. This meant the divisions would need to move east and concentrate at crossing points on the river, and this was considered a golden opportunity to bring firepower to bear and destroy the whole Corps. If this could be achieved then the Partisans would have suffered a major defeat and all of eastern Bosnia and western Serbia would be secure.

Phleps's plan – the Muslims operate outside their homeland

As the responsible Corps commander Phleps organised his troops to carry out this ambitious mission. The two primary formations to be engaged in the coming battle were to be Phleps's old division the SS-Prinz Eugen, and Sauberzweig's SS-Handschar. Croatian forces from the 369th were to be deployed as well but this was to be a largely Waffen-SS operation. The biggest decision made was that the battleground was going to be south of the River Spreca in the Stupari – Kladanj – Vlasenica area. This meant the Handschar was going to be leaving its designated 'home' area, having only advanced back into it some five weeks previously. Sauberzweig was extremely unhappy and complained personally to Himmler, but Phleps won the day and the Handschar turned to the south.

The plan was simple – hammer and anvil. The Handschar's role was two-pronged, firstly Raithel's Regiment 28 would drive south and take the major town of Tuzla. From there its two jäger battalions would split and take Kladanj in the west and Vlasenica in the east – the hammer. As Regiment 28 was moving into place the Handschar's second strike force of Hampel's Regiment 27 would move south, take Zvornik and form a hard blockade against the Drina (the piece missing from Signpost) to stop the Partisans crossing east into Serbia. They were to be the anvil against which the Partisans would be driven onto. Prinz Eugen's role mirrored that of Regiment 28, it was to strike north from Sokolac and Rogatica to meet Raithel's troops and complete the encirclement of III Bosnia Corps. It was an ambitious plan, good on paper but as with all operations in Yugoslavia difficult to achieve in practice.

Bosnia – the lie of the land

To truly understand the nature of military operations in Bosnia any student of warfare must start with the ground. Even in an age dominated by technology, the nature of the land itself still dictates combat to an overwhelming degree. When in the early 1990s, John Major, then Prime Minister, announced he was sending Britain's most potent military strike force, 16 Airmobile Brigade (now 16 Air assault Brigade), to Bosnia during its civil war, the first thing that every Brigade officer worth the name did was get hold of a map of Bosnia. The thing that struck us all was the mass of contour lines and contrasts. This meant a land of high mountains, steep ravines and crashing rivers. But little prepared us for the reality.

The areas we operated in were dirt poor; farms around Tomislavgrad (far to the south-west of the Handschar's zone) went dark when night fell as electricity was still a luxury. Even in an era of almost universal light pollution nightime was an experience of inky blackness largely forgotten in the West. Rastevic in the Serbian Krajina area of Bosnia was much the same despite being lower lying and more heavily settled. Agriculturally viable land was rare and tended to be in the bottom of mini-craters where topsoil had collected. Everywhere you looked was an almost moonscape horizon of rocks jutting menacingly out of the ground. There was no such thing as cross-country movement for vehicles, if you went off the few roads, even on motorbikes, you were asking for trouble and the result was often a puncture or worse. The ground tore at boots which wore out far quicker than in other theatres, and the weather was unpredictable. My tent mates and I woke up one morning at about 2am to look up at the stars as our canvas disappeared in a massive gust of wind that was followed by torrential rain that hurt your head it was so heavy. A few hours later we were desperately seeking shade as the sun came out and scorched us all. And of course any conversation about Bosnia can't be had without mentioning the big three: mountains, forests and rivers. They utterly dominate the country. The forests of Bosnia are sweeping, peaceful and dark. The rivers are deathly cold and incredibly fast-flowing for the most part, where they are forced to stream between walls of rock. Their constant efforts have carved out steep ravines that plunge down into darkness at the bottom of slither-thin valleys, and everywhere you look is the ubiquitous mountain. Climbing one just leads to another, and another. Large tracts of flat land are as rare as unicorns, this is a country of big gradients.

This was the environment for Maypole, an operation that ranked as one of the largest Wehrmacht anti-partisan offensives of the War. It would be no easy ride.

Maypole begins

On the morning of 23 April 1944, Regiment 28 began its advance south taking Tuzla on the first day before securing Stupari on the next. With Raithel's men cutting through the Partisan defences it was time for

Hampel to get in on the act and his assault kicked off on 25 April with a successful dash for Zvornik. They then set up a line on the Tuzla – Zvornik road to stop the Partisans breaking north, as well as extending their net south-east along the Drina.

Prinz Eugen also advanced swiftly against opposition from the 27th East Bosnia Division. Its men linked up with Regiment 28's lead elements at the village of Han Pijesak on the main Sokolac – Vlasenica road.

So far so good, but the Handschar did not have it all its own way. The Partisans were being hit on all sides by a coordinated assault but as ever, large numbers of them were able to escape through the net using the terrain as their greatest ally. Running was not their only option though and Raithel's Regiment were to feel the force of that at Sekovilci.

SS-Hauptsturmführer Heinz Driesner's I/28 (he had replaced Walter Bormann on 13 April) attacked Vlasenica itself and took the town after a fierce struggle, along with the neighbouring village of Sekovilci to the north-west on the Drinjaca River almost 30 kilometres away, which was occupied by a single company and the regimental headquarters. So far, as soon as a town or village was lost the Partisans had retreated into the countryside. Not at Vlasenica and Sekovilci. Although often loath to concentrate too many troops in one place for fear of being encircled and destroyed by superior Wehrmacht firepower, the Partisans also used their mobility to achieve a local advantage in numbers and hit back. The Italians never learnt to combat this tactic and suffered badly from counter-attacks and ambushes, and this was to be the Handschar's first experience of the same combat methodology.

With one of his six companies and his regimental commander miles away, Driesner was left with just five companies of jägers to hold Vlasenica against any counter-assault. Sure enough almost two entire communist divisions to the east who were yet to cross over the Drina, turned and hit Driesner's men hard. Simultaneously, another of III Bosnia Corps divisions surrounded Sekovilci, determined to annihilate the SS-Handschar men. For the first time since becoming operational the SS troopers were outnumbered and outgunned. The Partisans were liberally equipped with small arms and mortars and pressed home their attacks desperately. The fighting went on all afternoon and steadily grew in intensity. The German commanders were unsure what the strength of the enemy was and this, coupled with the horrendous terrain, slowed their response. The emergency dressing stations hurriedly set up in the two towns were soon full to overflowing with wounded men lying on straw and makeshift stretchers, while the harried medics and battalion doctors worked away up to their elbows in blood, with more men being brought in all the time.

Raithel realised towards evening that the entire battalion and regimental headquarters were now in danger of being exterminated and the Handschar could suffer a grave defeat. With a flexibility typical of the Wehrmacht he immediately ordered SS-Sturmbannführer Hans Hanke's II/28 to rush east from Kladanj and relieve their fellow jägers. This they did by late evening of the 28th, pushing the Partisans away from the town and giving them a bloody nose in the bargain. With Vlasenica now secure, Hanke's men dashed north-west the next morning to help their beleagured comrades encircled in Sekovilci. Somehow, the single company of jägers had managed to hold out against attack after attack, but by the time Hanke's men came roaring into the fight they were pretty much on their last legs. By the time they arrived II/28 had been in action almost non-stop for a week, the Partisans they met were in no mood to just fade away into the mountains, this time they stayed and fought. The battle went on for 48 hours. The garrison was relieved but soon they were almost all in danger of being encircled, as both sides struggled to achieve an advantage and deliver a knockout blow. The Handschar battalion threw everything into the fight:

> The battalion aid station is swamped. Our physician, Dr Nikolaus Frank, works without respite. The companies need reinforcement and ammunition desperately. The last reserves, the pioneer platoon and the pack animal tenders, have been thrown into the fighting.

SS tenacity won the day, and with the help of the newly-arrived Recce Battalion the Partisans were sent reeling back. Their attempt to overwhelm an isolated Handschar force had failed – this time. However there was ample warning for the division in the fighting at Vlasenica and Sekovilci. The need, dictated by the ground, to disperse forces and the problem with rapid regrouping and reinforcement meant that potential disaster was always a possibility. The key to avoiding it was steadfastness in defence of the sub-units under assault and the ability to regroup and quickly intervene with flying columns from the rest of the division. This saved the day during Maypole and led to the success of the operation, it was officially declared over on 6 May. The Partisans lost some 956 men killed and a further 96 taken prisoner. With a casualty rate of some 10 per cent the III Bosnia Corps had not only failed in its mission to move substantial forces across the Drina River to support their comrades in western Serbia, but had also been badly mauled itself. It would need several weeks to recoup and recover before it could again engage in large scale operations.

No rest yet – *Unternehmen Maiglöcken* (Operation May Bell)

The Partisans were widely scattered after Maypole but follow-up operations by Handschar Jagdkommandos identified a concentration of
several brigades in the Majevica mountains between Tuzla to the west,
and the River Drina in the east. Determined to build on the success of its
earlier actions, Sauberzweig resolved to launch a full divisional assault
and destroy the Partisans. Raithel's Regiment 28 would again take
a leading role and the tired jäger of the 1st and 2nd Battalions loaded
themselves up with ammunition and set off into the hills on 17 May
some eleven days after their last offensive finished. The fighting was
short and sharp with the Partisans being swept off the heights and
taking severe casualties into the bargain. A relief attempt by the ever-
present 16th Vojvodina Division was beaten back by the Handschar
and the divisional artillery was particularly active in pounding the
constricted Partisan units. By the end of 18 May it was all over. Those
Partisans that could, had slipped away and the rest were either dead on
the battlefield or prisoners of the jägers. For them Ustasha concentration
camps awaited, it was a grim fate.

The Handschar and the chetniks

May Bell was the first time that the Serb Chetniks operated in tandem
with the Handschar. This was pretty remarkable given that it was partly
the murderous Chetnik attacks on Muslim communities that had spurred
many men to volunteer for the Handschar in the first place. Hitherto,
the Serb royalists had kept themselves to themselves although they were
usually willing to fight the communists whenever they could. They had
shown no willingness to engage the well-armed and trained Handschar
in action since its arrival in the region in mid-March, but now their local
commander, Radivoj Kerovic, had decided on an approach of mutual
help when it suited the Chetniks. They were estimated to have some
13,000 men overall in north-eastern Bosnia, and so were potentially a
considerable force. By this stage in the War though, the Allies had abandoned them due to their collaboration with the Axis and thrown their
weight behind Tito. Their defeat at the Battle of the Neretva the previous year had effectively sealed their fate in the ongoing Yugoslav civil
war, with the initiative shifting inexorably to Tito and his JANL. Anglo-
American aid was by now flowing to the Partisans, while Mihailovic's
men languished in the hills, unwilling to fight the Germans and unable
to defeat the communists.

Rest and recovery

The end of May Bell was the end for the Handschar's first serious campaigning season. Following the close of the operation it returned to its home stamping-ground north of the Spreca River and was placed on garrison duty to recuperate. Casualaties had not been overly heavy, but neither had they been light. Several battalions were pretty hard-hit, especially Heinz Driesner's I/28, and needed to take in new recruits and get them up to speed. The Handschar's strength return at the end of May was a grand total of 19,136 men fit for duty. Sauberzweig reported the success of the situation as he saw it, although it hinted at darker tones:

> The territory between the Sava, Bosna, Spreca and Drina Rivers is now free of the Bolshevist terror…The enemy has been driven out with the heaviest losses. Scattered groups of defeated or expelled mobile enemy forces attempting to return shall be destroyed immediately. All local (communist) organisations have been eradicated through the elimination of all sponsors, organisers and commissars, among these many Jews.

The Handschar may have been out of the picture for a few weeks but the rest of the Corps was not, and away in western Bosnia preparations were well under way for what its planners hoped would be the decisive Axis offensive of the War in Yugoslavia.

Unternehmen Rösselsprung (Operation Knight's Move) – a last throw of the dice

Just one week after the Handschar went into recovery mode the Wehrmacht launched the boldest of its eventual seven major anti-Tito offensives to finally defeat the Partisans, Operation Knight's Move. Launched on 25 May the crux of the attack was nothing less than the capture, or assassination, of Josip Broz himself. As usual the Axis mobilised mechanised columns to advance into Partisan-held territory (again the SS-Prinz Eugen figured heavily), meeting and destroying communist units as they went, but the major departure for Knight's Move was the plan to land an entire parachute battalion at the site of Tito's Headquarters in the town of Drvar and capture him by *coup de main*.

The Germans had not attempted any serious parachute operations since the successful but bloody and costly invasion of Crete in 1941, and this was an imaginative but risky undertaking. The only battalion-sized drop carried out by the Germans in 1944 was also not a fallschirmjäger operation, but one mounted by the paras of the upstart Waffen-SS. SS-Sturmbannführer Rybka's SS Para Battalion 500 was the unit chosen to carry out the air assault. Originally established as a penal unit for Waffen-SS miscreants, the battalion had matured into an almost entirely volunteer outfit of the highest calibre. As with paras of almost every nationality, the men were highly motivated, aggressive, well-led but lightly armed. The SS troopers landed glider and parachute in Drvar itself and at the mouth of the cave outside the town where Tito actually worked. Bold they were but they were met by a resolute Partisan defence that recovered from the initial shock remarkably quickly. The result was predictable. The SS men fought with vigour and true élan but were massively outnumbered and outgunned. Tito's cave was never even reached and Drvar became the graveyard of SS Para Battalion 500. As Broz slipped away, via a back route out of the cave complex, more and more Partisan formations marched on Drvar, determined to wipe out Rybka and his men. The uneven battle lasted all day until spearheads of the Prinz Eugen finally arrived to relieve the beleaguered paras. They found a battlefield covered in dead paratroopers (of the original 600 troopers only some 200 were alive and unwounded at the end of the battle), while the only evidence of their quarry was a brand new Marshall's uniform that Tito had abandoned in his haste to get away. The gamble had failed, and with it, probably any chance of winning a decisive victory in Yugoslavia.

Overlord and Bagration

It was to be less than a fortnight before D-Day and less than a month before the Red Army's Operation Bagration against *Heeresgruppe Mitte* (Army Group Centre). These two vast undertakings would lead to the eventual destruction or decimation of four entire German armies and condemn the Third Reich to ignominious defeat. In Yugoslavia the result was a drying up of reinforcements and equipment that meant a shift from general offensives to an overwhelmingly rearguard stance. The Germans would not stop taking the fight to Tito but it was increasingly clear to all that their objective was now to only delay the inevitable and the conmbatants looked more and more to a post-Axis Yugoslavia and the final showdown in the civil war.

It would also mean that Wehrmacht commanders would cast their eyes again and again to the north-east as the incredibly powerful Red Army rolled out of Soviet Russia and drew ever closer to the Balkans.

A long summer

With Knight's Move a failure, as with Kursk the previous year on the Russian Front, the initiative in Yugoslavia was wrestled away from the Axis and was now firmly in the hands of the communists. With relish, Tito ordered a series of general offensives by almost all of the JANL across Yugoslavia. These attacks were to be carried out in force and were to be sustained. The message was clear; the days were gone when the Partisans were forever retreating in front of superior Axis forces, from now on they would begin to act more and more as a conventional army. The aim was to confine the Germans and their allies to major towns, to seriously disrupt communications, clear whole tracts of countryside and eliminate isolated and outlying garrisons. The country went up in flames almost overnight, and north-eastern Bosnia was no exception. The now-reconstituted III Bosnia Corps organised itself into three columns to advance north into the SS-Handschar's home area and defeat its Muslim enemy.

The ambitious plan called for Danilo Lekic's 16th Vojvodina Division to form the western prong of a trident formation and advance on Lopare. The centre prong, as it were, was to be formed from Milos Zekic's 38th East Bosnia Division moving to Priboj, and finally Marko Peric's 36th Vojvodina Division would be the furthest east, with its objective set as Krcina. If they were not stopped, then over half of the Handschar's hard-fought-for secure zone would be lost and the division would have essentially failed in its primary mission. All the Handschar's achievements since March would effectively be undone.

Sauberzweig's response – *Unternehmen Vollmond* (Operation Full Moon)

The Handschar got wind of the communist advance and initiated Operation Full Moon to defeat it. The plan called for the two jäger regiments, with artillery support, to act in concert by striking from the north and pinning the attacking Partisans to the Drina River to the east. There he could either flee into Serbia or be destroyed. Launched before dawn on 8 June, the hastily conceived operation went wrong from the start. Not for the first time, German intelligence failed to identify the whole picture and Sauberzweig had no clear idea of the forces ranged against him, in particular Danilo Lekic's 16th Vojvodina Division went almost undetected as it ghosted towards Lopare. The Handschar assault went awry and Hampel's men became separated and hopelessly interspersed with the Partisan spearheads. Taking advantage of German confusion, the two easterly divisions disdained anything other than heavy skirmishes with the jägers (and the odd spot of chetnik bashing) to press on towards their objectives and try to break up the entire Muslim division.

Slaughter at Lopare – the SS-Handschar's biggest ever defeat

In the midst of the chaos SS-Hauptsturmführer Heinz Driesner and his I/28 battalion took up position, as ordered, in the hills covering Lopare and its crossroads. A few kilometres to the east at Zajednice were Heinz Rudolph's artillerymen of the 7./AR 13 with their heavy 15cm guns, and to their rear in Brezovaca were their comrades of 6./AR 13. Communication between the sub-units was non-existant, the artillerymen had few small arms and were vulnerable to direct attack, and worst of all Driesner's men were mostly young and inexperienced having only just joined the division straight from training. His battalion had been battered in the fighting since March, as it fought under Walter Bormann, and to bring it up to strength whole drafts had been hurried in from the depots. The battalion had had no time to blood these youngsters and shake itself out ready for major combat. Driesner himself had no reason to believe that anything was amiss as he positioned his men in the afternoon of 8 June, and expected nothing more than a quiet night. What he did not know was that he and his battalion were but a few scant hours away from disaster and the biggest military defeat in the SS-Handschar's brief life.

The Partisans however, knew all about Driesner and his men and streamed towards them at a gallop. As the sun went down early that evening the hitherto unseen men of 16th Vojvodina Division mounted a full assault on the shocked jägers. The speed of the attack was such that Driesner had no time to call for artillery support from the two batteries in his area. Lekic's men had taken some beatings from the Handschar in the past few months but had got close at Vlasenica and Sekovilci to landing a real punch on them. This time they were determined not to lose their quarry and they set about Driesner's young jägers with a vengeance. Coordinated defence broke down almost immediately in the face of the savage assault and the battalion simply disintegrated. Survivors took to their heels and fled as the Partisans ran amok killing anyone who resisted. I/28 ceased to exist.

The defeat was compounded by Driesner's inability to even warn the rest of the division of the threat, and the 7th Battery paid the price as its 80 men were suddenly faced by over a thousand screaming Partisans still flushed with their success at Lopare. Incredibly, the gunners held out for four hours but with their small arms ammunition all gone and almost half their number dead they had no choice but to make a run for it, leaving all their equipment to the jubilant communists. Even the 6th Battery was attacked the following morning, but by that time Sauberzweig and Raithel knew what was going on and had reacted.

The Handschar counter-attacks

SS-Sturmbannführer Hans Hanke's II/28 was ordered south-east from Srebrenik in a desperate attempt to check Lekic's advance and try to regain the initiative. A few months before, the Partisan reaction to such a counter-attack would have been to put up a brief struggle and then melt away into the forests and hills. But times had changed and this time the Partisans stood their ground and fought ferociously. The four jäger companies were made to fight for every inch of territory and casualties were heavy. Hans König and his 9th Company actually found Driesner himself, who had managed to escape the debacle at Lopare and like so many of his men was wondering the area trying to avoid the rampaging Partisans. His ordeal was not over though, as a furious Raithel told him in no uncertain terms to either retake Lopare or face a court-martial; defeat was not going to be tolerated.

After snatching a precious few hours sleep the men of II/28 went back onto the offensive on the morning of 10 June as they attacked village after village on the way back to the killing grounds of Lopare and Zajednice. True to Waffen-SS doctrine, officers led from the front and as usual paid the price. The 10th Company saw its commander, Johann Eiden, cut down by machine-gun fire at Kameniti Brdo, and Heinz Driesner himself was killed leading an assault on Svetlika. Having held the Handschar all day, Lekic withdrew his men during the night of 10 June and left the bloodied jägers to enter the deserted streets of Lopare and Zajednice the following morning without a fight. The scenes they found shocked and dismayed even hardened veterans of the brutal Russian Front, and were to leave a lasting scar on the conciousness of the entire division. The 7th Battery's guns and vehicles, including their huge prime movers, were smoking wrecks and dead Handschar artillerymen lay strewn over the battlefield. Of Rudolph's original 80 men some 38 were found dead and a further 8 were missing. The dead had been viciously mutilated. Seeing comrades' corpses is one thing, but seeing them having been subjected to a sadists knife post-mortem is quite another. Thankfully, I never met any soldier during my own service who was ever anything less than horrified and disgusted by this practice that irregular forces sometimes seem to pride themselves on.

As for the Lopare battle ground, the carnage was absolute. The battalion had not suffered the same high percentage of casualties as Rudolph's men had, having been scattered so quickly, but dead jägers lay all over the position, surrounded by the detritus of defeat. Broken weapons (the Partisans had carried off any working ones), abandoned helmets and emptied kitbags and their contents lay strewn over the area alongside the battalion's burned-out vehicles and slaughtered pack animals. Small groups of survivors and individual stragglers started to come in or were found during the follow-up so that over 400 of I/28's complement were soon back with the division, but it would be a long time before most of them would be of any military use again.

The aftermath

The defeat at Lopare and Zajednice was not a killer blow for the SS-Handschar, but it was a huge setback. Prior to the Partisan advance, the secure zone of north-eastern Bosnia was relatively quiet and was a rare Axis success story in war-torn Yugoslavia. But the Partisan offensive took the division by surprise and the attack at Lopare was an accident waiting to happen. Vlasenica and Sekovilci were warnings of Partisan tactics. If they could achieve local superiority, and especially if they could neutralise the Handschar's heavy weaponry, then they would look to annihilate isolated units. In this case Driesner and his men, as well as Rudolph's, paid the price for the division pushing its luck just too far.

The effect on the Handschar was far reaching. With each jäger regiment being short handed at only two battalions a piece, the destruction of I/28 meant that a full quarter of its entire infantry strength was obliterated in a few hours. A Handschar officer said of Lopare that it 'haunted the entire division'. Losing Heinz Rudolph's four heavy guns and the majority of his skilled gunners was also a bitter blow. As a second tier anti-partisan formation the Handschar was not liberally equipped with such materiel and it relied on modern firepower to give it an edge over the JANL. The tide had indeed turned.

Full Moon ends

As resilient as ever, Sauberzweig scrambled to recover from the loss of I/28 and break up the Partisan offensive. Concentrating his remaining artillery and getting some limited armour support enabled the Handschar's one-eyed commander to stop the rampaging communists and push them back south over the Spreca River. This part of the offensive was a great success, as the harried Partisans suffered heavy losses during their retreat. It meant that on 12 June Sauberzweig could claim the III Bosnia Corps had been defeated in its attempt to infiltrate and conquer the secure zone, and had suffered some 1,586 men killed in just four days. This was a heavy blow and yet again the Handschar had proven its worth in combat against a strong and invigorated enemy. But the price paid was high. The division's own casualty list stood at 205 killed, 528 wounded and a further 89 missing. That was over 5% of the division's entire strength wiped off the roll in less than a week. Coupled with the news of the Allied landing in far-off Normandy there was a growing sense of unease in the ranks of the Handschar, as the Muslim members in particular began to foresee a German defeat. Slowly but surely, the rot was setting in and desertions started to increase.

Reorganisation and the SS-Kama

With the ending of Full Moon the Handschar went into full-on reorganisation mode. New recruits were drafted in to bolster numbers. Each of the two jäger regiments was expanded to three infantry battalions, some 500 Croatian volksdeutsche youngsters from the Reich Labour Service were brought in to form a 'stiffener' unit in the shape of *Einheit Hermann* (Unit Hermann – named after its commander Hermann Schifferdecker) and commanders who had proved themselves were promoted. But it was not the relaunch the division needed. The new battalions would struggle to fill their establishments from the start and new equipment was hard to find. Himmler's decision to form a second Bosnian Muslim SS division, the Kama, meant that a substantial cadre of the Handschar's best and bravest were stripped from the formation and sent to the new unit to form its *Stamm-Einheit* (for more details on the Kama see Chapter VII). The loss of so many experienced men, particularly NCOs and officers, dealt the Handschar a heavy blow. Key senior personnel also went, as Hellmuth Raithel handed over command of Regiment 28 to Hans Hanke, previously of his second battalion, as he was promoted to establish and lead the new Kama division.

The biggest change however was right at the very top. Karl-Gustav Sauberzweig, the *Schnellchen* himself, had run his course and Himmler now saw him leading the newly-created *IX Waffen-Gebirgs-Korps der SS (kroatisches)* – the 9th SS Mountain Corps, which would include the

Kama as well as the Handschar. At a small ceremony at Brcko on 19 June, Sauberzweig said goodbye to the division he had done so much to bring to life and make an effective fighting force. He left the Handschar in the hands of his erstwhile subordinate Desiderius Hampel who handed over his own Regiment 27 to SS-Obersturmbannführer der Reserve Hermann Peter.

The IX Waffen-Gebirgskorps der SS (kroatisches) – the 9th Waffen-SS Mountain Corps (Croatian)

Sauberzweig's new command was formally established on 29 May 1944 in Bacsalmas, Hungary, as part of Himmler's 'grand plan' for the Balkans' two territorial defence corps. Initially, just the Handschar and the Albanian Skanderbeg mountain divisions came under the new Corps, but in July it was decided to place the still-forming Kama in the Corps as well. Sauberzweig, now an SS-Obergruppenführer und General der Waffen-SS, was seen as the ideal choice to lead the new Corps.

Despite all of the huge handicaps he faced in getting the Corps off the ground, not least that fact that his three subordinate divisions were actually based in three separate countries hundreds of miles from each other, Sauberzweig managed a minor miracle in getting the formation operational. But the Corps struggled from its very inception.

No rest – a month of skirmishes

Even as this restructuring was going on the Partisans were flexing their growing muscles and continued to launch attacks into north-eastern Bosnia and harry the Handschar. Again and again, during the last two weeks of June and the first two weeks of July large bodies of Partisan fighters crossed into the area from the Spreca River to the south, the Sava River to the north and even from across the Drina River to the east. Each of these assaults had to be met and beaten back by the jägers who felt increasingly like men clutching sand. No sooner had one attack been stopped than another would start somewhere else. There was no let up and little hope of eventual victory, were the Mujos shedding their blood just to delay the inevitable? It was a question they were all asking themselves now in between firefights.

That is not to say the Handschar did not continue to fight well. A Partisan incursion at Doboj, north-west of Tuzla, by some 2,500 men was bloodily defeated by II/28 and a German Police Battalion resulting in

137 enemy being killed and a further 12 captured. II/28 only lost nine men in all with just two fatalites. The Handschar was not ready to go down just yet.

Offensive number 7 – *Unternehmen Fliegenfänger* (Operation Flypaper)

Not content with merely reacting to Partisan moves, Hampel decided to resume offensive operations to try and put the communists on the back-foot. Consequently he ordered the planning of Operation Flypaper to seize and destroy a Partisan airstrip in the Osmaci area that was being used for resupply by the Allies and to evacuate Partisan wounded to Italy for treatment. Operating with a chetnik battalion, the Handschar launched a limited attack on the area south-east of Tuzla on 14 June. The fighting lasted a single day, in which the Partisans lost 42 men killed against the Handschar's four men lost. The airstrip was destroyed and the communists withdrew from the area, but realistically, due to its impro-vised nature this was not a permanent solution, merely an inconvenience.

Hampel's next venture was altogether of a different magnitude. It had long been known that Sekovilci was acting as a magnet and supply base for Partisans across eastern Bosnia, and in a foretaste of the Vietcong two decades later, their chosen operational methodology was a series of caves and man-made tunnels hidden deep in the forests and hills. Out of sight of the prying eyes of Axis reconnaissance planes, the Partisans could rest and resupply in the myriad of underground tunnels that included rudimentary dressing stations, sleeping cells, ammunition bunkers and living quarters. The area was obviously heavily defended and the Partisans would be loath to give it up, as its loss would severely weaken their ability to mount operations north of the Spreca River. The objective lay outside the Handschar's secure zone, but Hampel and his men were well aware that as long as it remained a Partisan stronghold, their southern sector in particular was vulnerable to attack. So the attack was to go ahead.

Unternehmen Heiderose – Operation Wild Rose

Offensive Number 8 was envisaged as a three-pronged assault on the area, with the Handschar attacking from both the north (Regiment 28's II and III battalions) and the east (Regiment 27's I and III battalions along with a chetnik battalion). A battalion of the SS-Prinz Eugen would complete the order of battle as it advanced from the south to block any Partisan retreat in that direction.

The Handschar led the offensive, beginning their combined assault on 17 July, against fierce resistance. The terrain was extremely mountainous and the heavily-laden jägers struggled as much with the ground as with the stubborn Partisan fighters. The main JANL formation engaged was Marko Peric's 36th Vojvodina Division and it came under heavy pressure, having to give way against the weight of the Waffen-SS offensive. They lost Udrc on the 17th, Backovac on the 19th and finally Sekovilci itself on the same day. The response of III Bosnia Corps was to send the victors of Lopare, Danilo Lekic's 16th Vojvodina Division, from the north-west around Gracinica to try and link up with their comrades in the 36th and repel the SS troopers. This time though Lekic's men got short shrift and suffered heavy losses over several days of hard fighting. By 23 July the Partisans had had enough, having lost 947 men killed, they fled the area trying to avoid the Waffen-SS blocking teams.

Using specially selected search teams the Handschar then began a systematic operation to locate the hidden Partisan tunnels but inexplicably they found nothing. The entire operation looked increasingly like a costly diversion (the division had lost 24 men killed) until persistence paid off and the search teams found a series of tunnels that included a discarded map of further secret locations. The teams fanned out and soon made discovery after discovery, the bounty was huge. At the end of several days searching the haul of captured equipment included: 1 anti-tank gun, 2 mortars, 22 machine-guns, more than 800 rifles and nearly half-a-million rounds of ammunition. The Partisans had spent two years building the network of hidden bases and the Handschar had now found them, emptied them and then destroyed them, Wild Rose was a great success.

Unternehmen Hackfleisch – Operation Minced Meat

Within a fortnight the Handschar was in action again as Tito began to move large forces from Bosnia towards the Serbian border to support a general offensive into the country from Montenegro to the south. The Germans were determined to stop this and their response was to seek to encircle and destroy the mass of the Bosnian Partisan divisions being used in the offensive. This was another of the Germans preferred 'big battalions' offensives, and for the Handschar it meant all but II/27 of its gebirgsjäger sub-units would be involved in sweeping assaults against the likes of the 27th and 38th East Bosnian Divisions. Starting on 4 August the result of Minced Meat was the same as always – the communists took casualties and melted away from the aggressive Axis thrusts, only to reappear once the German columns had run their course. Some 227 Partisans were killed and a further 50 captured and dispatched to concentration camps, but the result was only temporary. Phleps and his fellow senior German officers were still fighting a conventional war against the most unconventional of foes.

No rest for the SS-Handschar

Operation Minced Meat damaged the Partisans, as did all the SS-Handschar's Bosnian offensives, but it was not the knock-out blow that the German commanders hoped for. As July became August it was increasingly clear that the flow of recruits to the communists was not ceasing and that equipment was now pouring in from Allied airplanes based over the Adriatic in Italy. The same could not be said for the Axis forces. At the same time the pace of activity became even more frenetic, as Tito's policy of continual attack on all fronts meant no rest for the occupiers and their local allies. Unlike the chetniks, the Partisans were constantly moving around their assigned areas, hitting the enemy at every opportunity and never giving them a moment's rest. A constant flow of reinforcements could have dealt with this modus operandi, but this was a luxury denied to the Wehrmacht.

For the SS-Handschar this last operation marked a decisive shift in their war. Minced Meat was officially the ninth offensive the Muslim SS men had carried out as they sought to dominate north-eastern Bosnia and defeat the Partisans. By the end of July 1944 they were no nearer this goal and were decidedly battle-weary. As their strength ebbed, that of their enemy continued to grow, from now onwards the division would be on the defensive and would never again initiate an offensive operation. Tito was winning.

August 1944 was a month of grind and grit for the SS-Handschar. In the heat of summer the Muslim jägers and their volksdeutsche and reichsdeutsche comrades marched from end to end of north-eastern Bosnia and beyond, fighting as they went, in a vain attempt to keep the Partisans out. Wherever they went they won, but it was always the same old story. As soon as they left the communists were back, in greater numbers than before, and in no time at all the Muslim SS men would have to come back and do it all over again. For example Osmaci, cleared of its makeshift airstrip in the middle of June had to be assaulted again in mid-August, and for a third time at the end of August. The Sekovilci area, scene of so much fighting in Wild Rose, was the focus of more heavy fighting from 28–31 August. This time the communists lost 121 men killed, while the Handschar suffered 18 fatalities. Even now, the Muslim troopers were killing Partisans at the rate of 10–1, but it was not enough. Just as with the Ostheer facing the Red Army to the north-east, the SS-Handschar was being gradually burnt out. The division had been in combat almost continuously for six months and in that time had lost over 10% of its strength through combat and desertion. This may not seem particularly high, but as ever figures do not tell the whole story. The losses were concentrated amongst the fighting troops rather than the divisional supporting elements, and so in the jäger battalions almost one man in four who crossed the Sava back in spring was now gone.

September 1944 – the beginning of the end

On 1 August, hundreds of miles to the north on a hot summer's day in Warsaw, a young Polish patriot, whose *nom de guerre* was 'Mark', was leading his company of resistance fighters to a pre-arranged jumping-off point in the city when they came across a German patrol.

> There was a moment when we watched each other with absolute clarity. The Germans were obviously calculating the possible gains and losses, whether to challenge us or whether to pretend that they hadn't seen this group of youngsters wearing half-concealed uniforms and carrying sub-machine guns under their coats…We threw our grenades into their lorry.
> (From Norman Davies, *Rising '44 The Battle for Warsaw*, Pan, 2003)

The Warsaw Rising had begun and the map of Europe was about to be changed for the next 50 years. From June 23 onwards and the launch of Operation Bagration, the Soviets had been storming west under the command of the half-Polish Marshal Konstantin Rokossovsky. Released from the Gulag on Stalin's personal orders, Rokossovsky had first smashed Busch's *Heeresgruppe Mitte* (Army Group Centre) in Belorussia before sweeping across eastern Poland right up to the very gates of the Polish capital itself. There, on the right bank of the mighty Vistula River the Red Army behemoth paused for breath. Since the German defeat at Kursk the previous summer the Soviets had been advancing west at an average of some 5.3 kilometres a day, if they continued at that pace then Berlin would fall to Stalin on 11 December 1944 – the War would really be over by Christmas. The nationalist Poles of the Home Army seized their chance to claim their own city, as the Parisians would do weeks later, so that they could be masters in their own house. At this moment, with victory within his grasp, Stalin made a momentous decision. The Red Army would stay where it was on the Vistula and would instead turn its attention south towards the Balkans and the Third Reich's client states in Eastern Europe. Stalin knew Nazi Germany was beaten, the real battle for him now was who would take the victors share of the spoils. If the War ended before the Soviet Union could occupy Hungary, Rumania, Bulgaria, Yugoslavia and maybe even Greece, then Stalin feared being denied what he saw as Russia's just desserts for their enormous sacrifices. As for the Western Allies they were still bogged down in the Normandy bocage. The Wehrmacht may have been losing 2,000 men a day to the relentless Allied pressure, and especially its crushing airpower, but they were not beaten yet and were still further away from Berlin than the Russians were.

The other factor was Poland itself. Stalin had already invaded the country twice, firstly back in the 1920 war when his incompetence had caused him to be denounced by Trotsky, and secondly in 1939 in conjunction with Hitler his then-ally, and he had no intention of losing it this time. In 1939 he had applied his customary genocidal tactics to Poland's leadership and slaughtered up to 5,000 captured Polish Army officers in the forests of Katyn, and now those who had escaped his, and the Gestapo's massacres, were in revolt in Warsaw. Far better to let them be exterminated by the Nazis to remove them as possible opposition – this was Soviet realpolitik. Rokossovsky's plan to break-out from the Soviet bridgeheads across the Vistula and head to Berlin was turned down, and instead Red Army attention swung south. Marshal Tolbukin was tasked to conquer all in his path, and this included Yugoslavia.

As the Red Army stormed its way across Bulgaria, Rumania and down towards the very borders of Serbia, it was increasingly clear to every Muslim in the SS-Handschar that it was only a matter of time before the Wehrmacht had to abandon Bosnia and head home, the question was, what then for the Muslims wearing the feared sig runes?

The South is lost

On 4 September Tito ordered yet another general offensive by his divisions in north-eastern Bosnia. That old nemesis of the Handschar, the III Bosnia Corps, rallied its troops and attacked. The garrison at Srebrnik was the first to bear the brunt, losing four men in a night's fighting. They were not the last, as village after village came under attack from the Partisans. As usual, aggressive Waffen-SS counter-attacks were sent in, the I/28 hitting the communists at Dobosnica on the 6th, and then Slatna on the 10th, while II/28 seized Mededa the same day, but it was a losing battle. The whole first week of September the Allied airforces flew massed air attacks against key transport and supply routes across the Balkans to hamper the ongoing German withdrawal from Greece and the Aegean. Road and rail links were badly hit and vital supplies disrupted. Even the chetniks got in on the act, turning against their former allies and attacking the base at Dragalijevac, just south of the Sava River. Supply columns were also ambushed as the Serbian guerrillas sought to capture materiel to aid their future fight against the communists.

Exhausted, and with desertion now becoming endemic, at the end of the second week of September the SS-Handschar withdrew northwards to Brcko on the Sava River. Having lost more than 2,000 men to desertion since the 1 September the division was in crisis. Disintegration was now a definite possibility as its Bosnian members saw the writing on the wall and either took their weapons and headed home to defend their families, or even worse joined the Partisans. Offered an amnesty by Tito, several hundred ended up in the ranks of III Bosnia Corps armed with German weapons fighting against their old comrades, the irony was complete. As for the SS-Handschar's homeland, which it had fought so hard to protect, the southern half of the secure zone was left in the hands of the 12th Ustasha Brigade, based at Tuzla, while the Muslim SS regrouped to the north. On 17 September the entire brigade deserted en masse to the Partisans of the 38th East Bosnia Division. Tuzla and the entire southern half of the region from the Spreca River north was now lost to the Axis forever.

Auftrag Sauberzweig – the Sauberzweig Proposal

Recognising the gravity of the situation, Hampel met with Sauberzweig and the two of them devised some radical alternatives for the future to be presented to Himmler for his decision. Basically the choices, as far as the two Waffen-SS officers could see, were either to strengthen the Handschar by 'importing' at least 2,000 trained Germans into the ranks to make the division fully one-third German, and releasing from duty all the Bosnians who were not prepared to fight on any front outside of Bosnia. Or, the nuclear option was to disband the division all together, release the Bosnians to the Ustasha and use the division's weapons and German personnel as replacements for now-forming Waffen-SS formations in Hungary. By now these reichsdeutsche and volksdeutsche numbered some 279 officers, 1,611 NCOs and 4,125 men, and the Waffen-SS could ill-afford not to make use of almost 6,000 experienced fighters. At the same time Sauberzweig was only too aware that the recruiting and training of the SS-Kama in Hungary was not going well. Unsurprisingly, Bosnians were unwilling to come forward, leave their homeland and throw in their lot with what was now clearly the losing side. The Schnellchen reasoned that a contingent of Mujos would volunteer to stay on if given the choice, and if combined with the German cadres from the Handschar and Kama there would be enough men to form a viable fighting force. Himmler did not agree.

When Sauberzweig presented him with the plans on 18 September the Reichsführer blew his top. The problem, as far as the he saw it, was one of a lack of strong leadership. The Handschar was not to be dissolved and the Bosnians were not to be released, instead they were to be filled with renewed 'National Socialist vigour' to continue the fight. Both the Handschar and the Kama would remain divisions, although at a lower establishment than before, and the Handschar was also to lose four of its key sub-units who would come under Himmler's control via Sauberzweig's IX Waffen-Gebirgskorps der SS (kroatisches). These were the Handschar's Recce, Panzerjäger and Pioneer Battalions as well as its Artillery Regiment. This effectively reduced the division to a purely infantry force with hugely reduced firepower. Without these changes the division could not beat the Partsians, so in the new structure it was going to be touch and go if they could even hold their own. By this stage, the division contained 18,520 men of which 6,015 were Germans, ethnic or otherwise.

Phleps dies in the north

Even as Sauberzweig was being shouted-down by an out-of-touch Himmler, events were running out of control for an increasingly enfeebled Wehrmacht. Rumania had switched sides in late August and taken her armed forces with her, they were now dying on German guns instead of Soviet ones. In the ensuing scramble, and with petrified volksdeutsche communities taking to the roads, Artur Phleps was dispatched north to try and conjure a defensive line out of the shambles in his native Rumania. Amazingly the Red Army was held long enough for the Germans to salvage something from the wreckage of their southern wing, but it cost Phleps his life. On 21 September as he went forward to see the situation himself, he was captured by a Soviet patrol and killed in the confusion of a subsequent air raid. A paranoid Himmler even suspected he had deserted before his death in action was confirmed. The dominant Waffen-SS figure in Yugoslavia during the War and the architect of the unsuccessful 'big battalions' strategy was now dead. It is fair to say his demise was no loss to the Muslim SS of whom Artur Phleps was no friend.

Janja, Vukosvaci and defending the North

As September gave way to October the Red Army was getting ever closer to Bosnia as it entered northern Serbia and began to fight its way south through the rapidly thrown together German lines. For the Germans, the spectre of disaster was now looming. If the Soviets could break through German lines and reach the Adriatic then the entire southern wing of the Wehrmacht would be trapped in a 'super-Stalingrad' encompassing Heeresegruppe's E and F in Greece, southern Yugoslavia, Albania and those troops still fighting in Rumania. All of the Balkans would be in Soviet hands and the Red Army could literally stroll into Austria and Vienna. It was vital the Red Army was held and the escape corridor to the north-west through Belgrade and Vinkovci was held open. This necessity was to be dominant in German planning in Yugoslavia for the remainder of the War.

For the Partisans the goal was equally clear, advance north and try to link up with the Soviets. Tito, despite being a fervent communist, was no Stalinist and feared a Red Army 'liberation' of his country. As far as he was concerned it was far better for the JANL to free as much of the country as possible itself, move north and greet the Russians with the job done rather than try to get them out once they were ensconced in Belgrade, Sarajevo and Zagreb. So with the majority of German forces facing the Soviet threat to the north it was left to a relative few units to try and hold off the Partisans advancing from the south, of which the Handschar was one.

The first big test was at Janja, just west of the Drina River, when the newly-arrived Partisan 28th Slavonia Division launched an all-out assault on the company-sized garrison of the Handschar base there at 0500hrs on 3 October. With the Handschar men hard-pressed, Corps threw in the division's Recce Battalion – its commander Heinrich Brichze was killed in the fighting – and III/27 as well as all the heavy firepower of 3./AR 13. The battle lasted throughout the day and night before slackening off over the next few days. The action was fierce and casualties were heavy, but the Handschar staved off possible defeat and scattered the attacking Partisans. Sauberzweig hoped that his beleaguered troops would soon be reinforced by the Kama as it left Hungary and returned to northern Bosnia, but this hope was soon dashed as the stuttering new division was swept up into the fighting in Hungary (see the Chapter VII on the SS-Kama). The Handschar was alone and would remain so.

Despite the dire nature of the situation, local successes were still possible, none more so than on 9 October when Hans König, a typically aggressive Waffen-SS leader if ever there was one, carried out a masterly company ambush on the Partisan's experienced 17th Majevica Brigade at Vukosavci. Using mortars and heavy machine-guns he surprised the well-armed and confident Partisans with a storm of fire and steel before taking them on with the bayonet. The entire Brigade was crushed and wiped out as an effective fighting force. Sixty-seven communists were killed and the survivors were scattered as they abandoned all their equipment to flight. But victories like these were getting rarer and commanders like the aggressive König could not be everywhere, although he would go on to battalion command and be awarded the coveted German Cross in Gold for bravery.

Leaving Bosnia – disaster for the SS-Handschar

Up until now the Germans had mostly kept their word and the Handschar had stayed in north-eastern Bosnia where it could defend the lives and homes of its members' families. But in mid-October the situation against the Red Army became so perilous that there was no choice but to transfer the Handschar to the north into Croatia proper to help hold the line. Division, Corps and Army Commands knew that such a move would probably mean mass desertions and the end of the SS-Handschar as a Muslim SS formation, but there was no choice, it had to be done. The Division was formed into two marching columns on 16 October and led north across the Sava, leaving Bosnia behind. The desertions started immediately. Regiment 27 lost an incredible 642 men in a couple of days as the Muslim troopers simply picked up their weapons and headed home. They all remembered what had happened in 1943 when they had gone to train and their communities were left to the tender mercies of the Partisans, Ustasha and chetniks, and there was no way the Mujos would repeat that experience. Ripping off their distinctive Handschar collar tabs the men either surrendered to the Partisans (and ended up fighting their old German comrades), any available local Muslim militia or just sat at home with their guns on their laps waiting for the inevitable retribution. SS-Oberscharführer Beger, a doctor of science recently posted to the Division in the Brcko bridgehead due to his knowledge of Islam, said of the situation:

> ...they deserted with all of their equipment. The reason that they gave
> for their desertion was that they were needed to defend their (Bosnian)

homeland, and taking them away went against all the promises they had been given. (Letter to the author from Bruno Beger PhD, dated 9 November 2006)

In fact the unit was so weakened that it was referred to now as the *'Waffenverband Handschar'* and not as a division. Desertions were not just single men either, whole sub-units upped and walked, or even drove. The so-called élite Divisional Staff Security Company of 101 men mutinied en masse on the urging of the Divisional Imam Abdulah Muhasilovic, and took its vehicles, small-arms, four machine-guns and even three 20 mm anti-aircraft guns with it. Muhasilovoc, who had spoken so passionately at the divisional Bajram festivities back in October 1943, citing the need to defend their Bosnian homeland, could now no longer see a future with the Germans, the Muslims would have to look to themselves. As if to emphasise the new reality, Belgrade fell to Tito and Tolbukin's 3rd Ukrainian Front of the Red Army on 20 October, and with it went all of Serbia.

Himmler finally wakes up – *Unternehmen Herbstlaub*

With the division breaking up before his eyes Himmler at last recognised the truth of the situation and ordered a wholesale reorganisation codenamed *Herbstlaub* – Autumn Leaves. The Bosnians (there were still some 10,000 of them in the division) were to be disarmed, apart from the minority who were considered to be unswervingly loyal, and their weapons distributed to German units. The ex-SS men were to be formed into labour battalions or sent as Hiwis to other regular formations, although it was suspected that many would simply melt away and head home. More reliable units like the Heer's 1st Mountain Division would have to take over their sectors of the front on the Drina River and near Zagreb as well as the Brcko bridgehead in the south.

On the morning of 25 October 1944 the delicate operation to take weapons away from men who hitherto had been fighting for Nazi Germany for over seven months began. Remarkably the whole series of actions concluded with no recorded instances of trouble. The effect on the Handschar was dramatic. Almost overnight it went from being a Muslim-dominated division to one where Islamic soldiers barely made up half its strength. This percentage would fall further as the War entered its final, bloody phase.

Sauberzweig's Corps disappears

With the dissolution of the infant SS-Kama, and the drastic paring down of the SS-Handschar, there was clearly no further need for the still-forming IX Waffen-Gebirgskorps der SS (kroatisches). Following on from the Kama's fate, the Skanderbeg was dispatched in November, so that in a little more than three months the Corps was reduced from three to just the one division, the SS-Handschar itself. The Corps's future was destined to be a bloody one.

The Corps fights in Budapest

In these changed circumstances Sauberzweig was succeeded in December by the policeman, and now senior Waffen-SS officer in Hungary, SS-Obergruppenführer und General der Polizei Karl von Pfeffer-Wildenbruch. While still nominally controlling the Handschar, the Corps was reinforced with the addition of the Waffen-SS's two cavalry divisions, the Florian Geyer and the Maria Theresia. These hitherto rear area anti-partisan divisions were now transferred to frontline duties as the Ostheer reeled under hammer blows from the Red Army. Along with two Army divisions transferred in (the exhausted 13th Panzer Division and the formidable 60th Panzergrenadier Division Feldherrnhalle), the 9th Corps went on to fight in Hungary before becoming bottled up in Budapest when it was encircled. When the city fell in February 1945, the Corps and all of its constituent divisions were wiped out with only 785 men surviving the breakout from the doomed city and reaching the safety of German lines.

As for Sauberzweig himself, on leaving the Corps he was summoned to Berlin for debriefing and another dressing down by Himmler. Placed on 'official leave' he watched as Germany's fortunes fell even further over the winter of 1944–45. With the Wehrmacht nearing collapse in early 1945 he was recalled to the Heer and discarded his Waffen-SS uniform. He was given command of a Corps in Heeresgruppe H in northern Germany based around Wismar (the area where the Flemings of the SS-Langemarck Division ended up – see *Hitler's Flemish Lions*). Here he awaited the arrival of the Anglo-Americans from the west with his dilapidated force.

The Muslims' last chapter – *Kampfgruppe Hanke* – Battlegroup Hanke

For the Muslim SS jägers still serving, their final hurrah was to be on the mighty Danube, the artery of the Balkans. When the Soviets secured some bridgeheads over the river in late October the Germans saw disaster writ large. The river was the last great natural barrier barring the Red

Army from sweeping up to the very gates of ancient Vienna itself, and if the Red Army footholds were not destroyed the end would be very nearly in sight. At 0915hrs on 9 November the orders were passed down to the Handschar: head into Hungary and attack. Here, the Handschar was to fight alongside the barely-trained Hungarian volksdeustche of Gustav Lombard's 31st SS Division, the successor unit to its sister formation the SS-Kama and where most of its cadre personnel and equipment had ended up. To fight this battle the division underwent yet another reorganisation. SS-Sturmbannführer Hans Hanke, the Russian Front veteran and former commander of the Handschar's Signals Battalion, took command of the most battle-worthy elements of the division and headed north. His battlegroup comprised three jäger battalions; the I/27, I/28 and II/28, a company or so of Pioneers and the artillery of III/AR 13. Not the most impressive force with which to throw the veterans of General Scharochin's 57th Army back over the Danube, but the attempt had to be made. Sent by train direct to the front at Batina, Hanke's 1,200 men set up hasty defensive positions in the gently sloping vineyards surrounding the city. In conjunction with a smiliar assault at the Apatin bridgehead the Handschar men attacked the Soviets in a bid to extinguish their positions on the western bank of the river. Supported by the Luftwaffe, a rare event indeed, the German forces succeeded in driving in the Russians and almost pushing them back at both Apatin and Batina on 12 November, but it was not quite enough. By 20 November the Red Army had slung pontoon bridges over the river and were flooding troops and equipment forward, the Germans could not hope to counter the sheer weight of the Soviet reinforcements and were soon fighting for their lives. The aggressive Hans König, now commanding I/28 as a lowly SS-Obersturmführer, typified the Handschar's predicament:

> After König's battalion withstood five days of the most difficult defensive fighting against a vastly superior foe and sustained bloody losses, the enemy broke through positions situated to the west of the battalion's sector after the last company commander was killed. In spite of the hopelessness of the situation, König personally led eleven of his men in a counter-attack and threw the enemy back. The foe answered with the fire of their heavy weapons on the breakthrough point, killing ten of the men and seriously wounding another. König, himself wounded, held the position single-handedly with hand grenades and ammunition brought forward by his messenger … He held the enemy long enough for his shattered battalion to consolidate and re-organise in a new position 100 metres behind the breakthrough point. (Citation for German Cross in Gold in Personnel file of Hans König, Berlin Document Centre)

But bravery alone was not enough, and on the night of 21 November a fresh Soviet assault by the newly-arrived 113th Rifle Division swept aside the remnants of Kampfgruppe Hanke. As the survivors were bowled back to the town of Hercegszollos they had time to count their losses, and they were grievous indeed. Of the 1,200 men Hanke had led to the Danube, only some 200 were left standing after little more than a single week's combat.

By now the Handschar was reduced to a strength of 12,793, and was no longer a Muslim SS formation but a rump of volksdeutsche and reichs-deutsche personnel with a few Muslims left in the ranks, as a reminder of its past. This is not to denigrate what these remaining Muslim jägers did, and would still do, alongside their German comrades, but the Handschar was no longer Islamic and so for the sake of this history its last few months are more of general interest rather than as a history of Himmler's Muslim standard bearers.

The Waffenverband Handschar fights on

The Handschar limped on over the winter, first being assigned to the *Margarethestellung* (Margarethe Position) defensive line stretching south from Lake Balaton in Hungary to the Croatian border, where it was involved in bitter fighting into the new year and well into February 1945. It then took part in Nazi Germany's final offensive in the East, *Unternehmen Frühlingserwachen* – Operation Spring Awakening – in Hungary. In the last hurrah of the formerly mighty Sixth SS Panzer Army, Sepp Dietrich led his dwindling band of men east again as they slammed into the shocked Russians on 6 March. The Handschar, part of Second Panzer Army, played a minor part in the offensive, although for the most part it stayed where it was and fended off local Red Army counter-attacks. Despite some initial successes the days of the all-conquering Nazi blitzkrieg were truly over and Spring Awakening soon ground to a halt in the rain and mud of the Magyar Plain. By 15 March the last ever German offensive of the War was finished.

As for the SS-Handschar, its strength return of 24 March 1945 was as follows, 9,062 troops on duty, 3,770 of whom were combat ready, heavy weapons totalled just 10 heavy anti-tank guns. According to the OKH reports the division was officially rated as a III on the Heer's battlewor-thiness scale; I being excellent and capable of full offensive action, down to IV being poor and of very limited combat value. To put this grading in context the only division in Austria at the time that rated higher than a III was the élite Heer 1st Gebirgsjäger Division with over 12,000 men still on strength and classed as a II i.e. capable of limited offensive action. By comparison the SS Das Reich and Reichsführer-SS divisions were both classed as IIIs.

By this time the Red Army was the most powerful military force on the Continent and a true juggernaut. After shrugging off Spring Awakening, it launched its own offensive on 29 March and poured westwards. The Handschar, along with all the other German units in the Ostheer's southern wing retreated in a desperate attempt to out-pace the Soviet spearheads and avoid encirclement. Every position the exhausted Germans reached was soon either outflanked or rolled over by the Soviet armies, who were now the true masters of mobile warfare. The Wehrmacht was condemned to continual scrambling retreats west to try and survive. Throughout the week following the opening of the attack, the SS-Handschar continued to fight, taking heavy casualties in men and materiel without ever being able to halt the Soviets. By 6 April the Red Army was over the border of the Third Reich in their sector in the Ostmark – the former Austria, the end was truly in sight.

By this time the division included the hastily called-up Volkssturm (German Home Guard – even though many of these elderly men were actually ethnic Slovenians and so rather loath to die at this stage for *Volk, Vaterland und Führer*) militiamen, several hundred anti-communist Hungarians and even 165 Italians. There were still Muslims in the unit at this late stage, one company commander in I/27 wrote of how his men's imam was wounded by Soviet mortar fire in a counter-attack on 8 April north-east of Pettau (now named Petj).

The division actually fired its last shots of the War at Kiesmanndorff on 19 April when Regiment 28 repulsed a Soviet attack.

The Knight's Cross

In belated recognition of the Division's valour during this period it was announced on 3 May that five of its members were to be awarded that most coveted of German medals, the Knight's Cross. These were the only Knight's Crosses ever given to members of Muslim SS units, although all four recipients were Germans and not Muslims. The list was as follows, SS-Standartenführer Desiderius Hampel, SS-Obersturmbannführer Hans Hanke, SS-Sturmbannführer Karl Liecke, SS-Sturmbannführer Albert Stenwedel and SS-Hauptsturmführer Helmut Kinz. These awards were added to the five German Crosses in Gold and one in Silver that the Divison also earned during its short service life.

It was relieved from the line on 5 May and pulled back west to Kellersdorf on 7 May with a view to heading even further west and sur-rendering to the Anglo-Americans at the War's end. When the news of the Reich's capitulation came over the radio the following morning events went into overdrive as peace dawned.

'Enjoy the War while you can, because the peace will be hell!'

Gallows humour, but for the men wearing the dreaded sig runes this veterans' saying was all too true. Few had any illusions as to the fate that awaited them if they fell into the hands of the Red Army, and for the Handschar survivors, that went for Tito's Partisans too. Their only hope was that the western Allies would be more lenient and they might survive the peace, but for the Divisions' remaining Muslims their only thought was of Bosnia. Led by their imams the few hardy souls left in the ranks went to their German commanders and asked to be freed from their oaths and allowed to strike for home. Officers like Hans Hanke were des-perate to save their men and begged them not to go as they knew all too well what awaited them back south of the Sava River – a Partisan firing squad – but to no avail. Bidding farewell to the comrades they had fought alongside for fourteen bloody months, the last of Heinrich Himmler's Muslim SS men slung their weapons over their shoulders and headed east to try and make it back home to their mountains and villages.

Postscript on the mutiny

So the SS-Handschar did fight, often with some distinction, particularly during its early months, but the scar of the mutiny in France will forever hang over it, the question is should it?

What is clear is that the mutiny should be seen in the context of an event like the Texel Island revolt of 6 April 1945, where the entire 1,200 men of the Heer's 822nd Georgian (i.e. Christian) Battalion based on the Island just off the coast of the Netherlands rose up in revolt and proceeded to massacre most of their 400 strong German cadre staff and comrades. The Battalion's German Commanding Officer, a Major Breitner, somehow managed to escape the slaughter and alert the Wehrmacht higher command on the mainland. A force was hurriedly put together and the Island assaulted to suppress the mutiny, but it took a whole week of bitter fighting and cost the lives of hundreds of men. In comparison, the SS-Handschar event was little more than a small-scale incident, tragic, but not of great magnitude.

VI

Albanian Muslims – The History of the 21st SS Mountain Division 'Skanderbeg' (21. Waffen-Gebirgs Division der SS Skanderbeg (albanische Nr.1))

Although the raising, training and combat record of the SS-Handschar as a Balkan Muslim Waffen-SS formation was a decidedly mixed affair, Himmler himself saw enough positives in the experience to develop an overarching strategy for future Balkan Muslim SS expansion and deployment. His plan was to meet the growing communist Partisan threat in Yugoslavia, and to a lesser extent in Greater Albania, with the establishment of two local Muslim territorial corps that would play a far greater role than first envisaged in defending their own regions against Tito and his expanding multi-ethnic JANL in particular. This would then negate the need to find ever more German troops from the hard-pressed Waffen-SS and Heer to combat the guerrillas, and would also act as a protective barrier for Nazi Germany's raw materials sites in Yugoslavia, such as the vital bauxite mines, and her vulnerable volksdeutsche communities. In a letter to the SS-Prinz Eugen's commander at the time, SS-Obergruppenführer Artur Phleps, Himmler said:

> My goal is clear, the creation of two territorial corps, one in Bosnia, the other in Albania. These two corps, with the Division 'Prinz Eugen', as an army of five SS mountain divisions ... are the goal for 1944.

The Bosnian Muslim SS-Handschar, and the soon-to-be-recruited SS-Kama, would form the envisaged Bosnian corps with further divisons to be raised from Yugoslavia's southern Muslim neighbour, the little-known country of Greater Albania.

Italian Albania

This tiny country, dominated by its ancient mountains and forests and with a people still very clan orientated in structure, had only declared its independence from the Ottoman Empire in 1912, after the First Balkan War, but was then annexed with little bloodshed by the Italians in March 1939 some six months before general war broke out in Europe with the Nazi invasion of Poland. The sovereign King Zog had been duly deposed by the conquerors after 11 years as ruler and the Italian aristocrat, the Duke of Spoleto enthroned instead, although he would never visit his new kingdom.

The Italians had then used Albania as the launching pad for their ill-fated invasion of Greece in the winter of 1940 that had led to disaster as the outnumbered Greeks promptly routed the Italian attackers and swept into Albania itself. Forced to rely on German help to stave off further humiliation, Mussolini was very keen that Italy undeservedly gain from the resultant conquest of Yugoslavia by the Wehrmacht in the spring of 1941. Italy was duly rewarded with the historically symbolic Yugoslav province of Kosovo.

Kosovo – ethnically Albanian, historically Serb

Sitting on Albania's north-eastern border the region of Kosovo is one of the great fault lines in the Balkan maelstrom. Originally a Serb province it came to symbolise that people's constant battle for survival after the cataclysmic Battle of Kosovo on June 23 1389. At that time the Serb ruler, Prince Lazar, had gathered an army to face the invading Ottoman Turks of the Sultan Murad. At Gazi Mestan outside the capital Pristina the two armies met, and the result was disaster for the Serbs who were utterly annihilated with Lazar himself being killed in the fighting. Kosovo became a Turkish *vilayet* (province) and so began a long process of islamicisation, as ethnic Muslim Albanians migrated north to the region even as the indigenous Serbs moved out. The result was that by the end of the nineteenth-century the majority of the province's million-plus population was Albanian. But no matter the demographics, for the Serbs, Kosovo was the cradle of their nation and its history. A comparison for England would be if Sussex and the ancient battlefield of Hastings were annexed by France due to overwhelming French migration – the result of that idea can be imagined!

In 1931 King Zog had already made a weak play for some sort of overlordship in Kosovo by creating his nephew and heir to the throne the

'Prince of Kosova' (Kosova is the Albanian name for Kosovo), though this farcical attempt at laying a claim to the territory disappeared with Zog's kingship in 1939. The Germans of course had no historical scruples and were not going to pander to Serb nationalism. They duly ceded Kosovo to Italian Albania to form 'Greater Albania'.

'Greater Albania'

Although initially quiet and submissive as elsewhere in the Balkans, the launching of Operation Barbarossa in June that year was the trigger for the local Albanian communists to rise up and vigorously resist their erstwhile conquerors. The Italians, with what little military capability they had focused in North Africa, Russia and to a lesser extent their other possessions in the former Yugoslavia, had little to give in Albania. The result was the usual picture for Axis-controlled territory in the East, of the occupation forces controlling the towns and cities with the countryside more or less given up to the power of the resistance movement, in this case Enver Hoxha's Communists. However the fighting was only intermittent and not at anything like the levels seen in neighbouring Yugoslavia, but the capitulation of Italy in September 1943 had radically altered the picture with the resistance movment able to grab large amounts of weapons and materiel that the Italians had simply abandoned.

As elsewhere across the Balkans, the Germans had reacted incredibly quickly to the Italian surrender in Albania and prevented the wholesale takeover of the country by the Partisans. German paratroops, the famed *Fallschirmjäger*, had seized the capital Tirana and were joined by the élite 1st *Gebirgsjäger* (Mountain) Division, the 100th Jäger Division from Greece and the 297th Infantry Division from over the border in Serbia. But now more than ever the overall situation was of stalemate, as the Wehrmacht did not have the military strength to win a decisive local victory. Himmler saw the answer in eventually raising a full local Albanian SS corps that would in effect take over the defence of the entire country and allow the Wehrmacht to use its troops elsewhere where they were sorely needed.

He was strongly supported in this move by local nationalists who were keen to safeguard Albanians from possible Serb reprisals after several years of persecution under the local Italian-backed administration. There was also a powerful racist element in Albanian nationalism that wanted to create an 'ethnically-pure' Greater Albania free from Christian Serbs, Jews and gypsies (the Roma). Needless to say, Himmler was sympathetic to such a view. With Nazi approval, the old nineteenth-century nationalist movement, the League of Prizren, was resurrected as the Second League of Prizren on 16 September 1943 by Dzafer Deva following Italy's defection to the Allies. The League incorporated a range of extreme nationalist groupings, foremost among them was Deva's own organisation the *Balli Kombetar* (the BK – National Union), and was headed by Bedri Pejani of the BK. Under the auspices of the League, local militia bands from the BK and the *Vulnetara* (another nationalist paramilitary organisation) terrorized all non-Albanians. More than 10,000 Serb families living in Kosovo fled north into Serbia proper in the winter of 1943–44 in an attempt to escape the ensuing violence. Bedri Pejani went further in the spring of 1944 when he wrote directly to Himmler on 19 March calling for the creation of Albanian military units to be formed in the Wehrmacht:

> Excellency, the Central Committee of the Second Albanian League of Prizren has authorised me to inform you that only your Excellency is united with the Second Albanian League, that you should form this army, which will be able to safeguard the borders of Kosovo and liberate the surrounding regions.

Establishment and organisation

With Himmler now firmly in favour of the idea, and with strong local backing from the League and a host of clan militias and paramilitary groups, the decision was made in Berlin to begin the process of raising a first ethnic Albanian SS division. On Himmler's order the head of the *SS-Führungshauptamt* (the SS-Main Operations Office), SS-Obergruppenführer und General der Waffen-SS Hans Jüttner, sanctioned the establishment of this most unusual Waffen-SS formation on 17 April 1944. The division was to be mustered in the northern Pac-Pristina-Prizren region, with recruitment from Albania proper as well as Kosovo.

Georg Castriota – Iskander Bey

As ever in the detail-obsessed world of the SS much thought was put to the administrative and organisational minutiae of the new formation. This included special uniform dispensations, collar tabs, armshields, cuff titles, and of course the biggest decision of them all – the division's honour title. The vast majority of the Waffen-SS's field divisions (in fact 29 out of an eventual 38) bore honour names and the Albanians would have one too. The honorific 'Skanderbeg' was chosen for the Division with reference to the greatest of all Albanian national heroes, Iskander Bey (Skanderbeg in German).

Iskander Bey had been born Georg Castriota in 1403, son of the Albanian ruler John Castriota, in the era of Ottoman Turkish rule just over fourteen years after their victory in Kosovo. Like so many of his fellow country-men, young Georg had found favour and fortune serving the Empire when he and his three brothers had been conscripted into the Ottoman's Janissary Corps in 1421. The Janissaries were primarily recruited from the Balkan Christian lands as children, before being trained and equipped as the élite of the Turkish Army. Membership of the corps could bring great advancement if the individual survived the privations of pretty-much constant war on behalf of the Empire. Whilst all three of his brothers were killed in service, Georg was the lucky one in his family, rising to the rank of General and becoming an important imperial official, hence the title of 'Bey'. However, having married back into the Albanian aristocracy he returned home and turned against his former patrons to lead an uprising in the 1440s. An impressive commander and improviser he used a ruse to take the Ottoman mountain stronghold of Kruje and then used it as his base to attack the Turks with the support of the seafaring Venetians and Neapolitans. Unable to win a decisive victory against his hugely-power-ful foe, the rebellion managed to rumble on for years. Castriota did fail in his ultimate aim of liberating Albania from Turkish rule, but he did suc-ceed in becoming the acknowledged Captain-General of Albania and in sowing the seeds of future independence, before his death in 1468 at the ripe old age of 65. His name, Iskander Bey, was a derivation of the eastern name for neighbouring Macedonia's Alexander the Great, and Castriota became venerated by Albanians as their great folk hero. A large lake in the region is also named in his honour.

On a related note Alexander's sunburst emblem was appropriated by the Albanian's sister division, the Bosnian Muslim SS-Kama, as their collar patch. It was obviously thought that any association to such a mil-itary genius as Alexander was useful.

The *Stamm-Einheit* – the cadre unit

D-Day was still over a month away, as was the Soviet's summer offen-sive, Operation Bagration, but even without this knowledge it was plain to the SS authorities that they would have precious little time to recruit and train the new division before it would be needed on the Wehrmacht's hard-pressed order of battle.

Naturally, to build the division and get it combat effective in as short a time as possible it was essential to use an experienced cadre (in Wehrmacht terms the *Stamm-Einheit*) that would act as the 'frame' around which the new recruits could be moulded. The winter battles in Russia, both Lake Ladoga in the north around Leningrad and the vicious encirclements at Cherkassy-Korsun and Kamanets-Podolsk in the Ukraine, had left the Waffen-SS battered and bloody. Major parts of the order of battle, including the Leibstandarte, Das Reich, Wiking and Hitlerjugend, were either being rebuilt or were in the process of formation themselves. There was no chance that the Skanderbeg would rate so highly as to get a cadre from these formations. As it was Jüttner's *SS-Führungshauptamt* turned to the only available source of trained manpower in the region, the SS-Handschar.

This was a classic case of robbing Peter to pay Paul, as the Handschar itself had only recently become fully operational in its homeland that spring. It was also struggling to fill key vacancies at NCO and officer level and it was exactly these grades and specialists that were needed to act as the backbone of the Skanderbeg. In essence, strengthening the Skanderbeg would correspondingly weaken the Handschar. But needs must and so it was decided to transfer all serving ethnic Albanians from the Handschar as well as numbers of reichsdeustche and volksdeutsche veterans, principally from the SS-Prinz Eugen Division. By an order of 1 May 1944 the entire complement of the 1st Battalion of the Handschar's 28th Mountain Infantry Regiment (I/28), composed primarily of Kosovan Albanians, was transferred en masse to the new Division and taken by rail from Bosnia to Pristina. These ethnic Albanians had first been drummed up by the SS in August and September of the previous year to fill the ranks of the Handschar which, of course, was having its own recruitment problems. The drive was obstructed at the time by the Germans own Plenipotentiary to the Albanian Government, Hermann Neubacher, who argued that the move threatened Albanian sovereignty, and his calls were echoed by von Ribbentrop's Foreign Office. Berger, as resourceful as ever, calmed the situation by writing to both offices saying that:

> ...when the division returned to Croatia, additional volunteers would be recruited, and the Albanians would be returned to their homeland, where they would form the cadre for an Albanian division.

As ever, Berger was thinking ahead and anticipating his master's next wish.

The 1st Battalion was commanded by a Reich German officer, SS-Hauptsturmführer der Reserve Walter Bormann, who had led the sub-unit since its formation on 1 August 1943. Although lacking in military experience, and criticised for this by his regimental commander, Bormann was determined to do well and had worked hard with his men to get them up to standard. The proof of that effort had been seen at the division's blooding at the crossing of the Sava River back in mid-March and the subsequent fighting during Unternehmen Osterei (Operation Easter Egg) in April, when the Battalion had distinguished itself with the successful assault on the Partisan-held Majevica heights. The Battalion was partially understrength however, with only 18 officers and 127 NCOs out of a proposed establishment of 31 and 199 respectively, although it was only about 50 rankers down at a total of some 1,340. But it was experienced officers and NCOs the new division desperately needed. With the move to the Skanderbeg by him and his men their places were filled in the Handschar by new recruits and Heinz Driesner, and this gaping hole in experience led in part to the disaster at Lopare later that year.

It must be remembered that the Waffen-SS was always intended to be an all-volunteer praetorian guard for the Nazi regime, with incredibly high standards for entry, but this was not going to be the case for the Skanderbeg. After all, even back in 1942 the very first Balkan Waffen-SS formation, the SS-Prinz Eugen Division, was recruited partially through conscription in its volksdeutsche homelands. Recruitment in Greater Albania was also meant to be on a voluntary basis, but from the start there was an element of compulsion. Albania had its own local civil government (under German tutelage of course) and this administration was required to submit the names of eligible young men directly to the divisional recruiting teams who were tasked with selecting suitable candidates and inducting them. In this way, a potential 11,398 recruits were initially identified with 9,275 of these judged suitable for drafting. Of this cohort only some 6,491 ethnic Albanians were finally accepted into the SS-Skanderbeg with the majority of the other 2,784 rejected on medical grounds.

Two-thirds of the men were from Kosovo, in particular the western Metohija basin territory, and most of them were from the Bektashi and Sunni sects of Islam. This recruitment picture created a serious imbalance in the make-up of the new division that was caused primarily by two factors and would have dire consequences in the future. Firstly, due to Kosovo's mixed ethnic composition the local Albanians felt that their communities were under threat from their Serb neighbors, who usually either supported the royalist chetniks or the communist Partisans.

In order to protect their homes and families the Kosovo Albanians joined the Skanderbeg in large numbers as they felt it would give them access to modern German weapons and training. Secondly, the Albanian government itself was keen to shield its own population as much as possible from the German recruiting effort and was prepared to sacrifice its ethnic Kosovan cousins if necessary. The net result was that the Skanderbeg tended to have the feel and outlook of a 'frontier' force overwhelmingly concerned with looking after its own, rather than fighting communism in general. From the start Orthodox Christian Serbs and Jews were looked upon as potential enemies and targets of persecution. As recently as June 1942 the Albanian Prime Minister, Mustafa Kruja, had told a meeting of Kosovo's Albanian leaders:

> We should endeavour to ensure that the Serb population of Kosovo area be cleansed and all Serbs who had been living there for centuries should be termed colonialists and sent to concentration camps in Albania. The Serb settlers should be killed.

This was a truly frightening backdrop to the raising of the Skanderbeg for the minority Serbs and Jews in Greater Albania. However, in a strange twist the division would have a somewhat mixed heritage as several hundred Albanian Catholics were also recruited, although they tended to be submerged in the greater mass of Muslim soldiery.

Himmler himself, as the architect of the Skanderbeg, was happy with the recruitment from northern 'Greater Albania' as it conformed to his racial ideals. During their occupation the Italians had carried out spurious 'anthropological research' that sought to show the Ghegs of the north (in the south Albanians were from the Tosk tribe) were actually Aryans, this was music to the Reichsführer's ears.

Overall, the numbers of men coming forward for the division, be they actual volunteers or 'government-recommended', were disappointingly low. As with all Waffen-SS divisons, the Skanderbeg was intended to have an establishment of as close to 20,000 men as possible. Even the traditionally much smaller German Army divisions were still running at a manpower rate of around 12,000 men in 1944, so the Skanderbeg was from the start a 'mini-division' and the picture only got worse over time as desertion became a distinct problem. The issue of desertion was a new phenomenon for the Waffen-SS who were much more used to dealing with highly motivated recruits and had little or no experience of less-than-eager grenadiers. But whereas the Skanderbeg did indeed have numbers of dedicated Albanians, it also had large numbers of 'fellow-travellers' who were only keen to serve if the advantages of doing so were clear. For many erstwhile recruits the thought of combat against hardened Partisan fighters was not viewed with relish. The end result was that even as recruiting was going on there was a steady leakage of men to desertion, so that by the end of July the Division had actually shrunk to just over 6,000 effectives.

Command and control

If the choice of cadre was important to the new formation, the choice of commander was equally so, and the decision was taken to entrust the fledgling Division to a man with a wealth of experience in dealing with non-German troops, the 48-year-old Austrian SS-Brigadeführer Josef Fitzhum. Fitzhum had begun his service with foreign volunteers in 1942 when he had taken over command of the Flemish SS-Legion Flandern from the wounded Michael Lippert and the dead Hans von Lettow-Vorbeck (for more information see *Hitler's Flemish Lions*), and had then gone on to command the Flemings' sister unit, the Dutch SS-Legion Niederlande. Arriving in Pristina, Fitzhum went about organising his new division and preparing it for combat. His first task was to establish a suitable order of battle (the unit orbat) and staff it as best as possible. The structure was set-up as follows:

Order of Battle for the 21st SS Mountain Division 'Skanderbeg'

With limited numbers the usual Waffen-SS mountain division structure of two regiments rather than three was opted for, with three mountain rifle battalions in each. The Division would also have integral battalions of reconnaissance troops, artillery, combat engineer and anti-tank gunners as well as the normal roster of logistics and supporting sub-units.

Divisionsstab (Divisional Headquarters Staff) – SS-Brigadeführer Josef Fitzhum (formerly the commander of SS-Legion Flandern)
Waffen-Gebirgsjäger-Regiment der SS 50 (albanische Nr.1)
50th SS Mountain Infantry Regiment intended to comprise three rifle battalions, the I/50, II/50 and III/50.

Waffen-Gebirgsjäger-Regiment der SS 51 (albanische Nr.2)
51st SS Mountain Infantry Regiment comprising three rifle battalions, the I/51, II/51 and III/51.

Waffen-Gebirgs-Artillerie-Regiment der SS 21 (21st SS Mountain Artillery Regiment)

SS-(Gebirgs) Aufklärungs-Abteilung 21 (21st SS Mountain Reconnaisance Battalion)

SS-(Gebirgs) Panzerjäger-Abteilung 21 (21st SS Mountain Anti-tank Battalion)

SS-Gebirgs-Pionier-Bataillon 21 (21st SS Mountain Assault Engineer Battalion)

SS-Sturmgeschütz-Abteilung Skanderbeg (SS self-propelled assault gun battalion)

SS-Nachrichten-Abteilung 21 (21st SS Signals Battalion)

SS-Sanitäts-Abteilung 21 (21st SS Medical Battalion of doctors, medics and vets for the Division's horses)

SS-Verwaltungs-Abteilung 21 (21st SS Divisional Administrative Battalion responsible for all logistics)

SS-Nachschub-Abteilung 21 (21st SS Supply Battalion)

SS-Feldersatz-Bataillon 21 (21st SS Replacement Battalion designed to act as a depot unit training and preparing men to go to the Division as replacements)

This was a restricted and truncated structure and even then it could not be met due to the paucity of recruits, cadre personnel and equipment. Both of the Waffen-Gebirgsjäger-Regiments struggled to raise their complements and so in practice reduced their establishment down from three battalions to just two and a headquarters, much like the Handschar. The Signals battalion fared little better, only managing to hit a strength of three companies, two of mountain telephone and one of mountain radio, though on the plus side much of it was motorised. Where the division especially fell down was in weight of punching power. The artillery regiment was meant to comprise four battalions, mainly smaller and portable mountain guns but also a longer range element for heavy fire support. The regiment needed a lot of equipment, both guns and prime movers, as well as a host of skilled specialists to man the weapons systems. The Skanderbeg had neither, and the result was the artillery sub-unit was woefully small and nowhere near a four battalion complement. The same was true for the anti-tank battalion which struggled to fill its equipment quota, in the end the unit was only able to form one motorised company of towed PAK 35/36 guns. These were obsolete 37mm pieces with an effective range of only 600m. However they were pretty well suited for anti-Partisan fighting, being light at only 430kg (946lb) and therefore easily manoeuvred around by their three-man crew. The other fictitous part of the formation was the planned-for armoured component of the division. Along with the artillery it was this unit that could have provided the Albanians with a real shock action element and given them an indisputable advantage over their erstwhile Partisan enemies, however in Nazi Germany's shrinking empire in the summer of 1944 it was not deemed a priority to equip an Albanian SS mountain division with self-propelled assault guns and the sub-unit was never formed.

Atrocity number 1

As the division was being formed the Balkans and Eastern Europe were very much in the grip of Adolf Eichmann's drive to implement the Nazis' Final Solution. Inspired and led by Germans from Eichmann's office and the wider SS apparatus, but utilising local troops and militias wherever possible, hundreds of thousands of Jews were rounded up, driven onto waiting railway cattle trucks and transported to their deaths in the Project Reinhardt extermination camps of Auschwitz-Birkenau and Treblinka among others. Hundreds of years of Jewish communities and traditions in Greece, Rumania and Hungary were wiped out and Greater Albania was to be no different. Pristina was the home of the majority of Kosovo's tiny Jewish community of around 200 and a pogrom was organised by the local authorities for 14 May 1944. Even though this was less than a month after the division's inception in mid-April and only two weeks after a cadre was transferred from the SS-Handschar it was decided to use the fledgling unit in the planned anti-Jewish sweep. On the day itself, Skanderbeg soldiers marched from their barracks into Pristina and raided the homes of local Jews, looting them of anything of value and beating up all who resisted. Driven from their homes and businesses by the rifle butts of the Skanderbeg men, Pristina's small number of Jews were herded like livestock to the railway station where sure enough the ubiquitous trains were waiting. Loaded on and locked in they were deported to almost certain extermination in the Nazis' Belsen concentration camp to the north.

Fitzhum leaves

This 'action' was the last that Josef Fitzhum would be involved in as Divisional Commander as he was replaced in June 1944 by the Prinz Eugen veteran SS-Standartenführer August Schmidhuber. Schmidhuber's time in command was to be an unhappy one for all concerned.

Fighting the Partisans

Raised ostensibly to fight the growing threat from Tito and his expanding army, the Skanderbeg was allowed next to no time to become established, with only a few weeks elapsing after the Pristina pogrom before they were thrown into action at the beginning of June in the Djakovica region of northern Kosovo. The Albanians fought against Partisan bands in the Mokra Gora to the north-west of Pac and near Hadzovici and Algina Reci. But with the majority of the division, less its German and Handschar cadre, having received less than two months training in total and with equipment and troop numbers woefully short, it was difficult to see what the Skanderbeg was expected to achieve. Unsurprisingly, the Albanians did not fight well and numbers of men began to desert from the start; they were also prone to committing atrocities against their traditional Serb enemies. For this the SS hierarchy must take overwhelming responsibility. The two key features of any military training programme are to impart technical knowledge and discipline. The latter probably being more important. Without it any unit is little more than a rabble of men with weapons who are as likely to turn to extreme violence as they are to just run away. In combat situations such men are entirely unpredictable and innocent civilians usually bear the brunt of their often bloodthirsty behaviour.

However, with the Anglo-American invasion of Normandy on 6 June Germany was now fighting on two major fronts and was in desperate need of every man it could get hold of. As such, the Skanderbeg was to get no more training time and was again plunged into battle in *Unternehmen Draufgänger* (Operation Daredevil), the German Army's latest attempt to destroy Tito's growing power. The operation was launched in July with the aim of surrounding and eliminating Partisan forces in tiny Montenegro, bordering Greater Albania to the north-west. Again, their efforts did not meet with much success and the rank and file were unhappy about being sent outside their home areas. As with the Bosnians of the Handschar, the Skanderbeg Albanians overwhelmingly enlisted to protect their homes and families (and in Skanderbeg's case to rid Greater Albania of Serbs in particular) and were simply not interested in fighting a wider war against Nazi Germany's multitude of enemies. Following the ending of Draufgänger they were sent back to guard the chromium mines near Kosovo, but they were less than successful, as the Partisans virtually overran the area, with the Skanderbeg putting up only limited resistance. Indeed, many volunteers just deserted, with one of the two mountain infantry regiments alone reported as losing 1,000 men.

Following this debacle *Generaloberst* Alexander Löhr's *Heeresgruppe E* (Army Group E), under whose command the Skanderbeg ultimately came in theatre, reported to OKW that the division had absolutely 'no military value'. In an attempt to rejuvenate the tottering formation, SS-Standartenführer August Schmidhuber was replaced after less than three months in command by SS-Obersturmbannführer Alfred Graaf who took over in August 1944. He would remain in command of the division for the rest of its short life. It was not to be a long term command appointment.

The end of the SS-Skanderbeg

Unable to hold its ground against an increasingly strident Partisan threat, the SS-Skanderbeg retreated to its home region of Kosovo and fell apart over the course of the late summer and early autumn of 1944. After its failures in Monetenegro and at the chromium mines, no further equipment was forthcoming from an exasperated Wehrmacht and the ethnic Albanians voted with their feet and drifted away home. This was exactly the time that the hard-pressed Wehrmacht needed all the help it could get. Nazi Germany's erstwhile allies, Rumania and Bulgaria, were desperate to save themselves from impending immolation by a rampant Red Army and were intent on switching sides and thus destabilising the entire southern wing of the German Eastern Front. In August and September that year, Tito saw his chance of joining up with the advancing Soviets and turncoat Rumanians and Bulgarians, and directed his forces east into Serbia to effect the link-up. Luckily for the Germans, the SS-Prinz Eugen and the 1st Gebirgsjäger Division were on hand to stop the JANL advance and even deal the Partisans a heavy blow, but every man with a weapon was needed by the Germans, including even the deteriorating SS-Skanderbeg who deployed as many troops as it could muster in the early stages of the battle. It was to be the last fight of the old Skanderbeg.

At the beginning of October 1944 the division was reported as being down to 4,900 men, of whom only 1,500 were fit for combat. Of these, the majority were German cadre personnel, either volksdeutsche or reichsdeutsche, with only some 500 combat-ready troops being ethnic Albanians. In desperation some 3,800 unemployed Kriegsmarine sailors based in the Aegean but with no ships to crew, were drafted into the division to up the numbers.The division was moved to garrison Skopje, the capital of Macedonia, and positioned to meet a renewed threat from the Red Army to the east. Here the bemused ex-sailors were given some limited infantry training, but OKH realised that it was finished as a fighting formation. Having suffered over 3,500 desertions from its meagre ranks during its lifetime, and with little equipment, no appreciable combat record and dark tales of atrocity surrounding its conduct, time was called on Himmler's Albanian SS division on 1 November 1944 after little more than six months in existence. The 21st SS Mountain Division 'Skanderbeg', was officially disbanded in Pristina and the remaining Albanian Muslims were released from service.

'Skanderbeg' lives on

This, though, was not the end either for an SS unit operating under the name of 'Skanderbeg', or indeed for several hundred ethnic Albanians from the unit who remained true to the Nazis and continued to fight for them as SS-Skanderbeg men.

Firstly, the name lived on, as the reichsdeutsche and volksdeutsche personnel (including the ex-sailors), were formed into SS-Kampfgruppe Skanderbeg, still under Graaf's command, and transferred from Pristina North to the Kraljevo district in Yugoslavia. With the Germans hurriedly evacuating Greece and retreating north-west, SS-KG Skanderbeg was used along with any other units to try and keep the vital escape route from Skopje via Mitrovica, Kraljevo and Uzice to Sarajevo open. Without it, all of Army Group E was lost. The Skanderbeg was involved in bitter fighting in the Uzice-Rogacica region, east of Sarajevo near Podromanija and also fought in the Vardar River valley in Macedonia with the Prinz Eugen. Alongside its better known stable mate, it then retreated northwards into the Janja-Bijeljina area via Kosovska Mitrovica in Kosovo and then the Sava River district near Brcko in Bosnia (the Handschar's old secure zone), where its remnants were fully absorbed into the Prinz Eugen in December 1944, with the SS-Freiwilligen Gebirgsjäger Regiment 14 given the honorific 'Skanderbeg' in memory of its sister formation. There were still a handful of ethnic Albanians serving in the Regiment at the time, though numbers were only in the dozens, but these men continued to fight both the Red Army and Tito's Partisans through to February 1945, before finally retreating west to Austria at the end of the War. Although there were reports that a handful even appeared on the Oder Front of all places, in the vicinity of the last gasp 32nd SS-Freiwilligen Grenadier Division 30 Januar where they were crushed by the Soviet juggernaut. This is certainly where the ex-Skanderbeg divisional train sub-units ended up, as they were found a new home along with some of the bewildered former Kriegsmarine men.

The last SS-Skanderbeg men in Albania

Back in Albania, several hundred SS-Skanderbeg Albanians also refused to give up the fight when the division was disbanded at the beginning of November. In an effort to delay the advancing Red Army, an attempt was made by various German special forces agencies, including the Brandenburg's Mil D section and the Abwehr's *Sonderkommando Albanien* (Special commando Albania), to establish weapons caches and supply dumps for pro-Axis Albanian tribal chieftains. Small groups of SS-Skanderbeg volunteers, mainly Kosovan Albanians, were also left behind to provide these tribal militias with some trained military muscle so they could hamper the advance of the Red Army. These disparate units kept up radio communications with the retreating Wehrmacht for some time, but one by one they went silent as they were either wiped out in the confused fighting or gave up the uneven struggle and went home.

Wehrmacht Muslims in Albania

The SS-Skanderbeg were not the only Muslims wearing German uniform in Albania in the autumn of 1944. There was also a battalion of Turkmen who had been relocated there from the Russian Front as part of Hitler's orders to disperse the Osttruppen away from the East. Unhappy at being sent away from fighting their Red Army enemies the Turkmen promptly mutinied in September 1944, murdered their German cadre officers and defected en masse to the resistance. This presaged the 1st East Mussulman SS-Regiment mass desertion in Slovakia by some three months.

Postscript – revolt in Kosovo

As the Germans retreated out of Albania and Yugoslavia to the north-west in late 1944 Tito was extremely keen to reverse the 1941 dismemberment of his country and reunite all its constituent parts into a new communist-ruled whole. Regardless of the fact that Enver Hoxha was a fellow communist, Tito was especially determined to take back Albanian Kosovo. Its place in the Serb national conciousness being so hugely symbolic. The Partisans invaded the province hoping and expecting to be greeted with open arms by the local people and treated as welcome liberators. It was a rude shock for Tito's men when they were met, on the whole, by at best sullen resentment, and at worst outright hostility. The murder by local resistors of a Partisan sentry caused outrage among the JANL forces who resorted to vicious reprisal more reminiscent of the Nazis and the Ustasha than supposed 'national heroes'. The JANL rounded up 300 innocent local Kosovan Albanian men and shot them as a warning to the rest of the populace. The effect was instantaneous. Led by former SS-Skanderbeg men the entire province rose in revolt and heavy fighting was reported in Gjilan, Drenica and Trepca. These were not small-scale skirmishes either. In the largest battle near Presovo, some 1,500 Partisans were killed or wounded when the entire Partisan 17th Brigade was overrun and annihilated and several other units were severely mauled. More Yugoslav troops were sent in to flood the province and martial law was declared. Eventually, Tito's men got the upper hand, but guerillas (many of them ex-SS-Skanderbeg soldiers) were still carrying out attacks as late as the 1950s.

Given the Skanderbeg's performance in Montenegro and at the chromium mines, it is hard to come to any other conclusion but that as a military formation the division was useless. Large numbers of ethnic Albanians did not come forward to man it and the tide of war was against Germany when the decision to raise the unit was made. Equipment was scarce, and most of all, training time was not allocated, resulting in many Skanderbeg soldiers being in effect, little more than militia rather than members of a Waffen-SS élite. Worst of all, the division was without doubt guilty of multiple atrocities, including taking part in the Pristina pogrom and numerous small unit actions – particularly against Serbs – that left villages burned to the ground and hundreds if not thousands of innocent civilians butchered. The SS authorities must accept the lion's share of blame for these crimes. Nevertheless, the SS-Skanderbeg did have an effect out of all proportion to its military achievements or limited longevity, as many of its members continued to carry the torch of ethnic Albanian nationalism far after the ending of the War in 1945. This was especially true of Kosovo, the home of the majority of Skanderbeg men. German training (limited though it was), arms caches and support for independence helped fan the flames of racial tension in the region for decades – this was the true legacy of the SS-Skanderbeg.

Uniforms and insignia

The SS-Skanderbeg wore standard Wehrmacht uniform, as used by the Waffen-SS, although they did not wear the ubiquitous Waffen-SS camouflage and stayed with field grey instead. As a mountain division the troopers wore the SS-type edelweiss badge on the upper right arm and the side of their caps. On the opposite left arm, the SS-Skanderbeg sported a national shield just under the Nazi eagle, as indeed did most of the foreign Waffen-SS formations. In Skanderbeg's case, the national shield was a black double-headed Albanian eagle with yellow eyes on a red background. Further to this, members of the division wore a silver-grey machine-woven BeVo-style cuffband with the inscription 'Skanderbeg'. A collar patch was produced for the division that depicted Iskander Beg's famed goat-crested helmet but there is no evidence of it either being produced in large quantities or worn at all. As with its sister Bosnian Muslim formations, the Skanderbeg was distinguished from its Waffen-SS brethren by its unusual headgear. Muslim members of the formation wore the same fez as the Bosnian Muslims in the Handschar and Kama, field grey for service use and red for 'walking out' and ceremonial. When serving with the Handschar, Himmler suggested that the Albanians of I/28 should wear a distinctive white cap, as with the old Austro-Hungarian Albanian Legion's so-called *Albanerfez*. This was never implemented officially, even though a small number of the battalion's members did wear an extremely rare traditional Albanian conical fez made in white lamb's wool, with the SS eagle and death's head on the front.

VII

The Last Gasp in the Balkans –
The 23rd SS Mountain Division 'Kama'
(23. Waffen-Gebirgs Division der SS Kama
(kroatische Nr.2))

The war in the summer of 1944

By the late spring of 1944 Nazi Germany was exhausted, having been at war for over four-and-a-half years. *Reichsminister* Albert Speer's economic reforms had transformed German war production so that at no time was she producing more weapons and equipment, whilst her armies were still in control of a vast empire that stretched from central Russia in the east to the Channel coast in the west. But behind this facade, there were huge cracks appearing in Hitler's vaunted Thousand Year Reich.

The disasters at Stalingrad and Tunisia had seen entire German field armies wiped out for the first time since the defeat at Jena by Napoleon in 1806. Mussolini's Fascist Italy was out of the War and already half-liberated by the Anglo-Americans. Back on the home front, Germany's once-beautiful cities were being pounded to dust by the might of the RAF by night and the USAAF by day. The Allies were yet to land in France but everyone knew it was just a matter of time, and the threat in the East was very real, as the shambolic Red Army of 1941 was replaced in 1944 with a military juggernaut of unprecedented power.

The Wehrmacht was still an impressive force overall, but the U-boats of the Kriegsmarine were dying in a lost battle in the Atlantic, while the majority of the surface fleet were more or less at the bottom of the sea. The once-dominant Luftwaffe was now outnumbered on every front and being shot out of the sky in outdated planes using outdated tactics. In the West it was hardly ever seen, while in the East it was losing the air to a resurgent Red Airforce. As for the Army, the famed Heer, it was still a technically and tactically advanced force of great power but at every level it was haemorrhaging and its vital offensive capability was a shadow of even its 1943 self.

Hitler and OKW knew the summer campaigning season of 1944 would bring further challenges and were desperately trying to prepare for the inevitable onslaught. The Eastern Front was now no longer the sole driver in German strategic thinking, as all eyes turned to France and the invasion fleet waiting in England's ports. But equally, Nazi Germany's leadership fully expected the Soviets to launch a major offensive in the East and were struggling to raise adequate troops to face it when it came. Men and equipment were stripped from the homeland and the occupied territories, and although this was relatively easy in the West where resistance was still pretty low-key, further east this was asking for trouble.

Himmler was keen to play his part, and expand his own power base at the same time of course. He now saw the opportunity to create new formations from non-Germans that would be able to take over anti-partisan duties, in particular, from German formations that could then be more usefully employed in the frontline in the East. With this in mind he turned yet again to the Balkans and the indigenous Muslims. The Handschar was performing creditably and so, in Himmler's view, it was time to go once again to the well and recruit another Bosnian Muslim Waffen-SS division. But on the ground in Yugoslavia, it was clear to all but the most naïve, that the writing was on the wall for Nazi Germany and its allies. Tito's Partisan JANL was now an army, well-equipped and supplied by the Allies by airdrop, that controlled large tracts of the countryside and increasingly, the local Axis forces were on the defensive.

Establishment

It was to counter this growing threat that the second of the Bosnian Muslim Waffen-SS divisions, the Kama, was to be born. Himmler took the idea of forming another Muslim SS division to Hitler who, desperate for more manpower for the West and East, immediately agreed, as a drowning man clutches at straws. Approval was swift and the SS bureaucracy went into action with Jüttner's SS-Führungs Hauptamt issuing the establishment order on 28 May 1944, stating that the new division was to be officially combat ready by the end of the year. To raise, train and equip a new division in six months was a challenge at any time, but given that the formation was to be composed of non-Germans and that the year was 1944 and not 1941, it was a tall order indeed.

Responsibility for recruitment, as ever with the non-German Waffen-SS, sat with Gottlob Berger, who threw himself into the push with his customary enthusiasm. A stream of orders was issued from his Berlin office, but from the start things did not go as planned. The division was authorised to a reduced strength of around 19,000 men, but as its already-established sister formation, the Handschar, was having great difficulty reaching and maintaining its strength it was unlikely that the Kama would fill this quota. The initial plan called for the majority of the division to be formed from the Bosnian and Croatian Muslim communities, but was also realistic enough to state that the recruitment of Catholics to make up the numbers was to be encouraged as well.

The Stamm-Einheit – the Handschar cadre

As with all of the Muslim SS divisions, there was to be a spine of non-Muslim officers and soldiers (either reichsdeutsche or local volksdeutsche) in the formation, mainly filling command and specialist roles. This element would be crucial. If the new division was to have any chance of becoming operational by the end of 1944, it was going to need a relatively large injection of combat veterans and a ready stock of weapons and equipment so that training could start immediately.

Incredibly, the former at least, was forthcoming. The Handschar, even though it was still striving to establish and maintain operational effectiveness, was ordered to hand over its entire Aufklärungs-Abteilung (the Reconnaisance Battalion trained as in most units even up to today as an élite within a formation), as well as three NCOs from every company, and divisional staff elements including the Kama's first divisional commander appointed on 1 July, the 38 year old SS-Standartenführer Hellmuth Raithel (at the time the commander of the Handschar's Regiment 28). In total, the Handschar handed over 1,350 men, including 54 officers, 187 NCOs and 1,137 enlisted men. It must be remembered that this was only one month after the Handschar had given up its Kosovan Albanian 1st Battalion from the 28th Mountain Infantry Regiment (I/28) to the still-forming 21st SS Skanderbeg Division. In just four weeks the senior Balkan Muslim Waffen-SS formation had lost 72 officers, 314 NCOs and 2,427 men in total, a hammer blow for any division, let alone one with so little experience and reinforcement to fall back on. This was not all though, the second phase of the cadre plan called for the Handschar to hand over to the Kama an entire cavalry squadron, one artillery battery from each of its artillery battalions as well as specialist signallers, doctors and vets, in effect, an entire regiment in strength.

Order of battle for the 23rd SS Mountain Division 'Kama'

The orbat – order of battle – for the new Division was as follows:

Divisional Commander	SS-Standartenführer Hellmuth Raithel (ex-Handschar regimental commander)
Ia (Divisional Operations Officer)	SS-Hauptsturmführer Otto Reuter (began his service in the 2nd SS Panzer Division Das Reich before serving in the Handschar and after his short stint in the Kama went on to be promoted to SS-Sturmbannführer and transferred to the 31st SS Division as their Operations Officer)
IIa (Divisional Adjutant)	SS-Obersturmführer Georg Kuhnert (went on to same post in the 31st SS Division)
IIb OO (Divisional Orderly Officer)	SS-Obersturmführer Robert Meyer (both he his colleague SS-Untersturmführer Friedrich Knox went on to same post in the 31st)
IIb (Quartermaster)	SS-Hauptsturmführer Ernst-Friedrich Fritscher (also went on to the 31st)
IVb (Divisional Medical Officer)	SS-Sturmbannführer Dr Karl Matz (also commander of SS-Sanitäts-Abteilung 23 medical battalion of doctors, medics and two companies of vets for the division's horses, he served in the Handschar beforehand and went on to the same post in the 31st)

- Waffen-Gebirgsjäger-Regiment der SS 55 (kroatische Nr.3) – SS Mountain Rifle Regiment 55 (Croatian no.3)

Commander	SS-Obersturmbannführer Holzinger (this regiment's reichsdeutsche and

volksdeutsche cadre went on to form the basis for the SS-Freiwilligen Grenadier Regiment 78 in the 31st Division).

I/55 – 1st Battalion
Commander

SS-Sturmbannführer Kurt Praefke

II/55 – 2nd Battalion
Commander

SS-Obersturmbannführer Walter Domes (a volksdeutsche from Moravia who had been transferred from the Slovakian Army on 21 August 1944 where he was a decorated regimental commander serving on the Russian Front)

III/55 – 3rd Battalion
Commander

SS-Obersturmbannführer Robert Schneider (went on to regimental command in the 31st)

- Waffen-Gebirgsjäger-Regiment der SS 56 (kroatische Nr.4) – SS Mountain Rifle Regiment 56 (Croatian no.4)

Commander

SS-Sturmbannführer Joseph 'Sepp' Syr (originally an NCO in the pre-War Reichswehr and then the Heer at the beginning of the War, he transferred to the SS Cavalry and achieved officer rank before going on to fight with the Ukrainian 14th Waffen Grenadier Division der SS Galizien and the Handschar Division before joining the Kama, and finally went on to regimental command in the 31st)

I/55 – 1st Battalion
Commander

SS-Sturmbannführer Heinrich Albrecht (graduate of Braunschweig SS-Officer Academy back in 1935 and a highly experienced officer)

II/55 – 2nd Battalion
Commander   SS-Hauptsturmführer Ewald
                                   Schumacher (ex-10th SS Panzer
                                   Division Frundsberg veteran)

III/55 – 3rd Battalion
Commander   unknown

Each of the two Mountain Rifle Regiments was meant to comprise
a Headquarters and an unrealistic four jäger battalions but this
was quickly reduced down to three as in the Handschar and the
Skanderbeg, but even this couldn't be filled.

- Waffen-Gebirgs-Artillerie-Regiment der SS 23- SS Mountain
  Artillery Regiment 23

Commander   SS-Sturmbannführer Karl-
                                   Friedrich Dehnen (an
                                   ex-instructor from SS-Artillery
                                   School II, he was replaced at the
                                   end of September just before
                                   the Kama's dissolution by SS-
                                   Sturmbannführer Hans Zeysing
                                   an ex-SS anti-aircraft officer
                                   – both went on to serve in the
                                   31st Division)

I/AR 23 – 1st Battalion
Commander   SS-Hauptsturmführer Josef
                                   Mailhammer (ex-4th SS
                                   Panzergrenadier Division SS-
                                   Polizei veteran)

II/AR 23 – 2nd Battalion
Commander   unfilled as the sub-unit was
                                   never formed (this post was
                                   held in the 31st Division by
                                   the Kama's former artillery
                                   regimental commander SS-
                                   Sturmbannführer Karl-Friedrich
                                   Dehnen)

III/AR 23 and IV/AR 23 – both the 3rd and 4th Battalions were
never activated

SS-Aufklärungs-Abteilung 23 – SS Reconnaisance Battalion 23
Commander   SS-Sturmbannführer Syr (cadre
                                   of ex-Handschar men, Syr was
                                   quickly moved up to command

of the Waffen-Gebirgsjäger-Regiment der SS 56 (kroatische Nr.4) see above, and replaced by SS-Hauptsturmführer Ludwig Zeitz. The reconnaissance battalion had a heavy anti-tank platoon that was equipped with three of the excellent towed 75mm Panzerabwehrkanone 40 guns – anti-tank PAK 40. With a range against tanks of 2000m and against infantry of 7500m, this high velocity gun gave the unit at least a modicum of punching power.)

SS-Panzerjäger-Abteilung 23 – SS Anti-tank Battalion 23

Commander   SS-Sturmbannführer Richard Landwehr (ex-2nd SS Panzer Division Das Reich and 7th SS-Freiwilligen Mountain Division Prinz Eugen veteran. Unbelievably given the circumstances the intent was to have a fully self-propelled anti-tank battalion as envisaged alos for the Skanderbeg, but this didn't materialise given the supply situation and the division's disbandment.)

SS-Flak-Abteilung 23 – SS Anti-aircraft Battalion 23 (this sub-unit was never formed and no commander was appointed)

SS-Gebirgs-Pionier-Bataillon 23 – SS Mountain Assault Engineer Battalion 23

Commander   SS-Sturmbannführer Hermann Otto

A highly trained and well-equipped sub-unit in any Wehrmact formation this Battalion was composed of three companies plus a headquarters, they were mainly men from the Handschar although Otto himself was a former instructor from the SS-Pioneer School at Hradischko in Bohemia and prior to that served in both the 3rd SS Panzer Division Totenkopf and the 6th SS Mountain Division Nord.

SS-Gebirgs-Nachrichten-Abteilung 23 – SS Mountain Signals
Battalion 23

Commander   SS-Sturmbannführer Albert
                                             Reimann

Signals battalion charged with all communications in the formation. Intended to have a full organisation table, in reality hardly any
of its component units were either manned or equipped, at best it
had a handful of 1-man crewed Stoewer AW2 communication cars.

SS-Nachschub-Abteilung 23 – SS Divisional Supply Battalion 23

Commander   SS-Hauptsturmführer
                                             Wilhelm Morisse (these men
                                             were divisional supply troops
                                             responsible for all logistics,
                                             Morisse himself survived the
                                             War only to die in Soviet
                                             captivity afterwards)

SS-Verwaltungs-Abteilung 23 – SS Administrative Battalion 23

Commander   unknown

(administrative battalion for the division)

SS-Feldersatz-Bataillon 23 - SS Field Replacement Battalion 23

Commander   SS-Hauptsturmführer
                                             Grünwald

The replacement battalion was designed to act as a depot unit for the
Division; training and preparing men to go to the Kama as replacements.
Grünwald himself was a decorated veteran who commanded a cadre of
often wounded instructors who were convalescing, prior to return to their
units. The bulk of the manpower were volksdeustche from the Balkans.
Initially formed as the replacement battalion with a Headquarters and
four jäger companies for the Handschar, the Battalion was then used as a
shared resource for both divisions, before finally becoming a part of the
Army's 9th Mountain Division, formerly Kampfgruppe Semmering/
Raithel, as it was thrown into battle in Austria in March 1945 where it
fought until the surrender of Nazi Germany, itself surrendering to the
Americans at Liezen on the river Enns.

Kama also had its own police unit of *Feldgendarmerie* ('chaindogs' as
they were not affectionately known by the troops, due to the metal disc
they wore around their necks to denote their status), established on the
basis of the German SS Field Police Training and Replacement Company
of the SS Motor Vehicle Training and Replacement Battalion Weimar-
Buchenwald. This sub-unit then went on to form the same unit in the
31st Division.

Honour title

Unlike other formations there was no debate about an honour title for the Division. There was no attempt to pick a suitable historical figure as with 'Skanderbeg' for the Albanians, or a geographical area such as 'Wallonien' for the Belgian Walloons. Instead, the new Division was named after a traditional Balkan Muslim weapon, in this case the *kama* which was a short Turkish sword or fighting knife usually about 20cm long and commonly carried by shepherds guarding their flocks in the hills.

Uniforms and insignia

As always with SS bureaucracy, much time and energy was spent on the minutiae of uniforms and unit designation. The division was to wear standard Wehrmacht field-grey with camouflage SS smocks, and in essence, was to look very similar to the Handschar. Headgear was to be Islamic, with Muslim personnel wearing the field grey fez or the red fez for 'walking out' or ceremonial occasions. German members of the division, both reichs and volksdeutcshe, were encouraged to wear the fez to show solidarity with their Islamic comrades, but were also allowed to wear the standard SS field cap if they wished.

The divisional emblem was intended to be a collar patch bearing a 16-point sunburst emblem which was the ancient symbol of Alexander the Great (previously in the frame for the Skanderbeg), and although this was designed, there is no evidence of it ever being worn or even produced in large numbers. A plain black collar patch, the standard SS sig runes or whatever troops already had were mostly worn during the Division's short history. Being a mountain division the troopers wore the SS-type edelweiss badge on the upper right arm and the side of their caps, and on the opposite left arm they sported the red and white checkerboard shield of Croatia as a national shield just under the Nazi eagle. Members of the division also wore a silver-grey machine-woven BeVo-style cuffband with the inscription 'Kama'.

The well drys up

With a commander appointed and a cadre identified, the Kama was originally allocated the Handschar's secure zone in north-eastern Bosnia, bounded by the Save-Bosna-Speca-Drina Rivers as its establishment base, but all was not well. The ever-threatened invasion of France had been launched with D-Day on 6 June and the Red Army's mighty Operation Bagration had steamrollered into Army Group Centre on 22 June. Nazi Germany's facade was fatally shattered, as was any belief among Germany's allies and fellow-travellers that anything but defeat awaited them. With literally tens of thousands of German soldiers being killed every week and mountains of precious equipment being lost, the fate of a second-tier anti-partisan Muslim SS division in far-off Yugoslavia fell massively down the OKH priority list. First call on personnel and every kind of weapon and supply was obviously given to the two major battle zones, with the OKW trying to throw the Anglo-Americans back into the Channel in the west and desperately stitching together a viable frontline in the east before all of Belorussia was overrun.

In such circumstances, there was hardly likely to be an avalanche of willing volunteers to wear the uniform of the losing side. Coupled with that, prospective recruits were also worried about leaving their homes and families undefended in the face of the growing power of Tito's vengeful communist Partisans. This was prescient, as on 24 June the formation's assembly area was switched from Bosnia to the ethnic German inhabited Batschka (Bacska or Backa) region of southern Hungary (formerly part of the Vojvodina region of Yugoslavia, along with the Banat and Baranja areas, which had been annexed by Hungary after the invasion of Yugoslavia in 1941 and its subsequent dismemberment). This decision was made to avoid interference from Tito's Partisans in the training of the Kama. The local populace was friendly, being mainly volksdeutsche and Hungarian Csangos who had been resettled there from Rumanian Bukovina, ceded to the Soviet Union in 1941 before Barbarossa was launched. This area had earlier been used to form the volksdeutsche-manned 18th SS-Freiwilligen Panzergrenadier Division Horst Wessel. The two recruiting depots were in Sombor and Bogojevo, with the mountain infantry regiments based between Sombor and Vrbas (*Werbass* in German and designated as the headquarters town of the Kama and incidentally later on for the 31st SS-Freiwilligen-Grenadier-Division). The heavy weapons subunits, including the proposed artillery regiment, were located near the town of Kula.

SS-Untersturmfuhrer Hans Villier, who had earlier served in the SS Cavalry Brigade in Russia, was transferred to command a platoon in the Divisional Signals Battalion in the Kama. Shortly after his arrival in the Batschka he observed the following incidents:

> On one occasion my Muslims entered a village and shot all the pigs! The Hungarian farmers were furious. I too was angry and raised hell with

them about it. Ali, my interpreter, told me that this was normal, and that pigs were dirty animals anyway.

And secondly;

> There was a Muslim festival that was celebrated by firing shots into the air. I wanted to use blank ammunition and prohibited the use of live rounds for this purpose. The Muslims ignored my order and used live rounds anyway, whereupon I too became 'live' and nearly came to blows with them.
>
> Late that night I awoke to find Ali seated near me with his dagger drawn. At first I was startled and thought he was going to kill me, until he told me he was there for my protection, as many of his comrades were quite angry at me. (From Rudolf Pencz, *For the Homeland! The History of the 31st Waffen-SS Volunteer Grenadier Division*, Helion, 2002)

The issue of Islam and religious fervour was a factor in the division; indeed, Fredo Gensicke, a reichsdeutsche SS sergeant transferred as part of the cadre to the Kama on 20 July 1944 said of his new Muslim charges:

> There were forever complications with the Bosnian soldiers ... On the other hand, there were those Muslims so fanatical in their religion that one could get a knife stuck in the back if you would twist your head around, forcing the tassel on the fez hat to move around.

Cultural differences were not the only issues facing the new division as it struggled to form. Even though its assembly area had been moved, specifically to negate interference from Tito and his Partisans, the Kama could not escape their growing influence. Heinz Hummel, a platoon leader in the pioneer battalion, wrote:

> There were a number of shady characters among the Muslims. Several of the ethnic Germans believed that these individuals were actually partisans who had volunteered for the Division simply to receive military training, and would desert back to the partisan ranks after the return to Bosnia ... I bunked with two NCOs, Werner Rauner from Thuringia and a Muslim ... One day he [the Muslim NCO] took leave of us; he had received a furlough. His last words were that he would not be returning. We took this as a joke. In fact, we never saw him again. (From Rudolf Pencz, *For the Homeland! The History of the 31st Waffen-SS Volunteer Grenadier Division*, Helion, 2002)

Overall, the move north-east was not a popular one for the Muslim soldiery as it took them away from their home villages and left recruits feeling they were abandoning their families in a time of great need. These views from the soldiers went straight back to their communities in the hills and valleys of Bosnia and the flow of volunteers effectively stopped. Berger himself travelled to Novi Dori in Croatia to meet local government officials on 13 August to work out possible solutions. Following the meeting, the ever-practical Gruppenführer wrote to Himmler on 17 August 1944 laying out the issues:

> ...the induction of 10,000 Croatian citizens of the Islamic faith not possible, for such a number of reliable youngsters simply not available, and thus Catholic Croatians will be accepted.

Berger's plan now changed drastically so that it retained its overall strategy to encourage volunteers, targeting in particular on the membership of existing Muslim local defence militias, but now there was to be conscription as well. All able-bodied Muslim men from the birth years of 1926 and 1927 were sent conscription notices ordering them to report for medical examination and induction. The vast majority simply ignored the order or went into temporary hiding to avoid it. Some even joined the Partisans rather than join the Kama. It was a disaster.

At the end of June 1944, a month after its official establishment, the Kama stood at a total of only 2,199 men, with almost 1,400 of these being former Handschar soldiers. As summer turned into autumn things did not get much better, despite the best efforts of the SS recruiters, so that at its peak on 10 September 1944 the entire 23rd SS Mountain Division 'Kama' could muster just 126 officers, 374 NCOs and 3,293 men, for a less than grand total of 3,739 men in all, not even a quarter of its authorised strength.

Rumania switches sides

As the attempt to create a second Balkan Muslim Waffen-SS division was failing, the now punch-drunk Ostheer was being dealt another shattering blow. Somehow, in the wake of the disaster of Army Group Centre's destruction, the Germans had managed to cobble together a frontline in the east. But no sooner had they achieved invaluable breathing space than the front in the south was sundered by the defection of Rumania from the Axis on 23 August 1944. After losing hundreds of thousands of men, Rumania's military losses during the War amounted to a staggering 519,822 men killed. After three years of slaughter on the Eastern Front the Rumanian King Carol had had enough and in a last throw of the dice he attempted to save his nation from further disaster by abandoning Nazi Germany and throwing in his lot with Stalin's Soviet Union. Ultimately, this gamble was to be in vain, as he was soon deposed and his country condemned to decades of Communist repression directed from Moscow.

However that was in the future, at the time, the result was that an entire German Army Group was now trapped in enemy territory and the whole Carpathian Front was shattered. The Germans scrabbled to try and retrieve something from the wreckage, as Rumania's volte-face threatened a 'super-Stalingrad' in the south, with the Red Army having a clear line of sight right through to the eastern borders of Serbia and the Adriatic Sea beyond. A successful thrust there could cut-off all the remaining Axis forces in Rumania, Greece, the Aegean and southern Yugoslavia – disaster loomed for the Ostheer. Crucially for Germany, the loss of Rumania also meant the loss of its vital oilfields at Ploesti and with it Nazi Germany's most significant source of oil, as now, the very lifeblood of a war effort. From now on every drop of petrol, diesel and aviation fuel was precious for the Germans. Its growing scarcity would mean that in the last six months of the War the Wehrmacht increasingly became a horse-drawn and footborne force more reminiscent of the nineteenth than the twentieth century.

The death throes of the Kama

Back in rural Rumania, desperate German troops flooded west to Hungary to avoid entrapment and destruction at the hands of their former Rumanian allies and their new Soviet friends. With the situation swiftly deteriorating, every man was needed to try and patch together a frontline and so Kama was ordered to be combat-ready by 24 September and not the end of December. The ex-Handschar men and the German cadre were, of course, ready to go, but even though the couple of thousand Muslim 'volunteers' had undergone some intense work since their arrival in the Batschka in late-June it was clear that their basic military training was not even complete. Contrast the three-and-a-half months the Kama was given to become operational, with the 12 months that the 12th SS Panzer Division Hitlerjugend was given from mid-summer 1943 until their committment in Normandy after D-Day. True, the Hitlerjugend was an armoured formation and as such the degree of technical training needed was far higher than for a simple infantry division such as the Kama, but even so, trying to get the Division ready by the end of September was a pipe dream. A modern British Army infantry soldier will undergo a minimum of six months training before being posted to their battalion, and there they will be surrounded by a host of experienced men from whom they will then learn a far deeper understanding of their profession. Three-and-a-half months of training will produce nothing more than enthusiastic militia at best.

Bizarrely at this incredibly late stage, it was decided to change the leadership of the Kama, and on 28 September 1944 SS-Standartenführer Hellmuth Raithel was replaced by SS-Brigadeführer Gustav Lombard. Lombard was an experienced officer who had commanded a Waffen-SS cavalry regiment in the 8th SS Cavalry Division Florian Geyer in Russia, his command of the Kama would last less than a week.

Eventually, even the fantasists in Berlin had to face up to the stark reality of the how unprepared the Kama were. Following the passing of the September deadline, with the Division woefully understrength, equipment almost non-existent and now even the divisional training areas under threat from the Red Army, the order was given on 1 October 1944 to disband the unit. The 23rd SS Mountain Division 'Kama' had been in existence for just four months.

The SS-Kama splits up

With Rumania's defection in August, the Red Army was able to swiftly advance through the entire country right up to the borders of Hungary and Yugoslavia as the Ostheer's southern wing literally dissolved overnight. Desperate to form a new defensive line on the Rumanian-Hungarian and Rumanian-Yugoslav borders, the OKW stripped men and material from the Balkans and sent them to the north-east. The Handschar, as already covered, was caught up in this process and so was the Kama. For the Handschar, it presaged mass desertions among the remaining Muslim soldiery who were not interested in fighting the Red Army, and for the Kama it meant their disbandment.

The mass of the Muslim rank and file, and the few Catholic Croatians enrolled, were given transport and reporting orders that would take them back south-west to Bosnia and effectively convert them into a sort of local SS militia under the Handschar depot umbrella. Sent on their way the vast majority clearly realised their future no longer lay with the Waffen-SS and Nazi Germany and did not turn up at the Handschar's headquarters back in Bosnia. Keeping their weapons, and throwing away their telltale uniforms, the half-trained recruits went home and prepared to defend their families and homes from the now-inevitable Partisan retribution.

With Soviet Marshall Rodin Malinovsky's 2nd Ukrainian Front all set to cross the River Tisa (also called *Tisza* and *Theiss* in German) into southern Hungary on October 4 1944, the ex-Handschar men and the ethnic German cadre from the Kama were grouped into three distinct formations for dispatch to the front and combat with the Red Army. Malinovsky's advance may have been seen as little more than a large scale diversion for the incredibly-powerful Soviets, but for the weakened Germans a major effort was required to halt it, and every soldier available was needed.

Firstly, the ex-Handschar men were returned to their parent unit as it came up from Bosnia and became part of the Handschar's *Kampfgruppe Hanke*. The majority of the volksdeutsche and reichsdeutsche personnel, including most of the command element, were designated as the cadre for yet another new division, the Hungarian volksdeutsche 31st SS Freiwilligen-Grenadier-Division. Indeed, the run-off from the Kama to the 31st was almost seemless in many cases with commanders keeping their positions and simply swapping Muslim recruits in fezs for bewildered volksdeutsche teenagers and middle-aged farmers and artisans whose Magyar was far better than their German. There would be a somewhat symbiotic relationship between the Handschar, the Kama, the Skanderbeg and the 31st for the closing stages of the War, with much intermingling of manpower (particularly cadre personnel), equipment, logistics and base locations. The Waffen-SS Kama personnel at the Sombor assembly centre for instance, were transferred en masse to form the 13th Company of the new 31st Division's 80th Grenadier Regiment on the former's dissolution. Gustav Lombard himself went straight from commanding the Kama to the same appointment in the 31st. Last but not least some men from the Kama were grouped into *Kampfgruppe Syr* (led by SS-Sturmbannführer Josep 'Sepp' Syr), and sent straight to the frontline on the River Tisa. It was this element that is most intriguing in terms of discovering if the SS Kama did any fighting at all during its brief lifetime.

The SS Kama – a combat record?

Although the Kama experiment was a clear failure and one that no-one came out of with any glory, the issue of the Division having any sort of combat record has been controversial ever since. After all, the very essence of the creation of the Kama was as a fighting force not a propaganda tool, so did all the effort, time and resources used in establishing the division lead to any success on the battlefield?

There is no mention of the Kama in the OKW War Diary, the official record of all Wehrmacht engagements during the War, and this would indicate that the division never saw combat as a whole during its minis-cule lifespan, however some reports indicate that Bosnian Muslims from the Kama did indeed see action in October 1944 with Kampfgruppe Syr in Hungary. Syr's command was a true hotchpotch of men and sub-units from the Kama, with the mainstay undoubtedly being ethnic Germans, but it would seem that a certain number of Muslims from the division voluntarily stayed to fight on with their German comrades. A telegram, dated 7 October 1944, from SS-Obergruppenführer Karl von Pfeffer-Wildenbruch the *Befehlshaber der Waffen-SS Ungarn* (Senior Waffen-SS Commander in Hungary) states:

> …combat-ready parts of Division Lombard [author's note: the just form-ing 31st SS Freiwilligen-Grenadier-Division], including the Muslims of the Kama Division (2,600 men) deployed on the Theiss to protect the Batschka.

Further to this on 9 October a further telegram from the same source reads:

> …the combat-ready parts of SS-Oberführer Lombard's new division, together with the Bosnians of the Kama are to be thrown into the battle.

This would indicate that at SS headquarters in Hungary at least, there was a clear belief that Muslims from the SS Kama were still serving. If this was the case then they were too few in number to make any differ-ence to the outcome. At most, there may have been a couple of hundred Muslim Bosnians who stayed on in Hungary and were then caught up in the Soviet forestorm of that October, and just like their fellow Waffen-SS men in the 31st they were annihilated in bitter fighting.

Aftermath of the SS-Kama

Never an organisation to dwell on the past, the SS hurriedly moved on from the Kama fiasco and soon, even the divisional number 23 was reassigned to another formation, the newly-established but much more reliable Dutch 23rd SS-Freiwilligen Panzergrenadier Division Nederland. The Dutch would bring a great deal more glory to the Waffen-SS divi-sional roster during their short lifespan than their erstwhile Bosnian Muslim colleagues of the Kama.

As an interesting postscript, the Division's first commander, Hellmuth Raithel, was charged with war crimes by Tito's new Yugoslav government after the War but was never apprehended by the authorities. Avoiding extradition back to the Balkans from Germany he eventually died in 1990 aged 84.

Much has been made by historians and commentators since the War of this seemingly laughable attempt to form a second Muslim division from the apparent flotsam of a Third Reich nearing cataclysm. Reasons for its failure have focused on the relative administrative chaos prevailing at the time and misguided recruitment policies, but by far the biggest hypothesis generally advanced for the Kama disaster, is lack of committment by the Waffen-SS itself. But this view simply does not chime with the facts. The vast majority of the core of the Kama division, i.e. its command and cadre elements were not washed up retreads from paramilitary rear area police formations or old men chased out of comfortable desk jobs in the Nazi empire, but rather they were in the main Russian Front combat veterans who had served in some of the Waffen-SS's most venerated formations. There were veterans from the Das Reich, Totenkopf, SS-Polizei, Prinz Eugen and Frundsberg among others and these men would have been welcomed back into their parent formations if they were made available. They were not because the Waffen-SS had decided to invest them as a resource in the SS-Kama. If nothing else, this proves that the drive to establish the Kama was a serious one on the part of the Waffen-SS, at a time when every experienced soldier was desperately needed at the front, and that the experience of the Handschar had not put off the authorities in Berlin. Militarily useless the SS-Kama may have been, but a sideshow given no resourcing she was not.

VIII

Himmler's Muslim Brigades

The Waffen-Gebirgs Brigade der SS (Tatar Nr. 1) – The 1st SS Tartar Mountain Brigade

This unit was formed in May 1944 when Himmler ordered the establishment of a Tartar mountain regiment to be assembled in Hungary. Initially called the *Waffen-Gebirgs Jäger Regiment der SS (Tatar Nr.1)* (1st SS Tartar Mountain Rifle Regiment), the cadre, the Stamm-Einheit, were 200 German police unit members who were transferred en bloc to the SS. The majority of the manpower was to be formed with the merging of several Crimean Tartar *Schutzmannschaft* (Schuma for short) security battalions who had retreated westwards with the Germans after their Crimean homeland was abandoned to the advancing Red Army. Initially comprising two full-strength battalions of four infantry companies each, plus a headquarters company, the unit was renamed as the 1st SS Tartar Mountain Brigade and placed under the control of the Higher SS and Police Leader of Hungary for its establishment phase and for further intensive combat training. However, the Waffen-SS bureaucracy did not share Himmler's apparent belief in the fighting qualities of the Tartars, particularly as their homeland was now lost to the enemy, and the police authorities were unwilling to hand over their members to the tender mercies of such a unit. The result was organisational inertia and obstruction that delayed the formation of the unit so that it was not until almost five months later in September that it came onto the Wehrmacht Order of Battle. Even then, the Brigade was not really fit for operations with the main issue being a huge shortfall in equipment. This was also a key issue for its fellow Muslim SS units raised at the same time, the Albanian Skanderbeg and the Turkmen of the East Musselmann Regiment.

By December 1944 the Brigade did muster a pretty impressive paper strength of 3,518 men under the command of SS-Standartenführer Fortenbacher but the reality on the ground was an ill-trained unit lacking in even the basics of soldiering such as boots and uniforms, let alone modern weapons. With the worsening situation on the Eastern Front the decision was made to focus on more battleworthy formations and the attempt to set up the unit was abandoned. The Brigade was disbanded in January 1945 and thereafter its members were transferred en masse to the *Osttürkischer Waffen-Verbände der SS*.

The Osttürkischer Waffen-Verbände der SS – East Turkic SS Armed Detachments

The winter of 1944–45 was a time of woe for the Wehrmacht in the east. The defeats of the summer and autumn of 1944 had hemorrhaged men and equipment from the Ostheer, and vast tracts of territory had been lost too. By 1945, the Balkan Muslim Waffen-SS divisions had been gutted by desertion and had released from service more or less the majority of their remaining Islamic soldiery. Some were still fighting with the Germans, but they were the exception and not the rule.

The ex-Soviets in the Muslim Waffen-SS were in no better shape. The Turkmen of the 1st East Mussulman SS-Regiment were in disarray in Slovakia and falling apart, and the experiment of the 1st SS Tartar Mountain Brigade had conspicuously failed. It was time for a rethink in Berlin as to the future of the Muslim Waffen-SS.

The *SS Waffen-Gruppe* – Muslim SS Armed Groups

After all the organisational shenaningans of 1944 endured by the Turkmen and their fellow Muslims, in the last act of their War they returned to the unit concept that the Ostheer had first come up with back in 1942, that of the holding units such as the 162nd Division, which would act as the basis for fighting and support formations. Thus, born in January 1945 was the *Osttürkischer Waffen-Verbände der SS* – the East Turkic Armed SS Detachments – and their stablemates the *Kaukasischer Waffen-Verbände der SS* – the Caucasian Armed SS Detachments. Indeed Himmler went even further back in an attempt to salvage the situation and resurrected the old national Legion idea from 1942.

The 3rd Battalion of the East Mussulman SS-Regiment was renamed the *SS Waffen-Gruppe 'Idel-Ural'* based as it was on Volga Tartars, and reinforced by men from the disbanded 1st SS Tartar Mountain Brigade. The sub-unit was quite strong having two rifle battalions, each of five companies with a regimental headquarters. Inexplicably the SS-Hauptamt thought that the incompetent SS-Standartenführer Harun al-Raschid Bey would make a good commander for the unit, although this was probably more of a needs must situation, as in the new year of 1945 Nazi Germany did not have a surfeit of capable officers. Through the offices of the Haj Amin al-Husseini the Germans did manage to win over a distinguished Tartar poet, Musa Dzhalil, to support the new formation. Dzhalil agreed to join the 'Idel-Ural Tartar National Committee' (formed explicitly to achieve the establishment of a Muslim state on the banks of the Volga). Unsurprisingly, Dzhalil soon realised his mistake and tried to back out after having second thoughts. His reward was to be court martialled on very dubious legal grounds by the Germans, and after being found guilty, he was shot.

The second sub-unit set up was the *SS Waffen-Gruppe 'Krim'*, which was mainly based on the Crimean Tartars from the 1st SS Tartar Mountain Brigade and a handful of eligible men from the East Mussulman SS-Regiment. It too had two battalions of five companies each.

Last but not least, the bulk of the men from the East Mussulman 1st and 2nd Battalions, being ethnic Turkmen, were rebadged as *SS Waffen-Gruppe 'Turkistan'*. The same establishment of ten companies organised in two battalions with a headquarters staff was used.

Perhaps the biggest change was visited on the very numerous Azeris, of whom the Waffen-SS found themselves with almost 3,000 in various sub-ubits. Those who had somehow slipped into the East Turkic SS Armed Detachments or were still in the East Mussulman SS-Regiment were weeded out and re-christened the *SS Waffen-Gruppe 'Aserbeidschan'*. Under their ethnic Azeri commander, Waffen-Obersturmführer Kerrar Alesgerli, they were then reassigned to the East Turkic's sister formation the Caucasian Armed SS Detachments. This Waffen-SS unit was primarily made up of Christians organised into SS Waffen-Gruppes *'Armenien'*, *'Georgien'*, *'Nordkaukasus'* and now also *'Aserbeidschan'*.

Himmler's hope was that these parent units would gain experience at the front and then act as the cadre for the creation of several Muslim SS divisions including the grandly titled *Mussulmanischen SS-Division Neu-Turkistan* – the Mussulman SS-Division New Turkistan. The majority of men for these fantastical divisions were to come from Turkic German Army Osttruppen, Hilfswillige, ex-POWs and Muslim labourers working across the shrinking Nazi Third Reich. Even for Himmler this was utterly delusional. But in those last bloody months of the War every manner of weird and wonderful scheme seemed entirely appropriate. Over half-a-dozen Waffen-SS divisions were created, mainly being of regimental size (if that), composed from the dregs of the manpower barrel and equipped with little more than small-arms. Himmler's SS empire was in flames and there was nothing the Muslim SS could do to stop it.

What was true, was that in purely numerical terms the East Turkic sub-units were quite strong. After all, the French SS-Charlemagne Division had only four grenadier battalions when it went into combat, and even the classic SS divisions such as the Leibstandarte had only six grenadier battalions on establishment. So theoretically, the six rifle battalions of the East Turkic SS Armed Detachments could have constituted a division. In reality however, a fighting division is not made up solely of riflemen but of a host of supporting and specialist sub-units, as well as the crucial command and control elements that will coordinate and lead it into battle; this the Muslim SS riflemen did not have.

The East Turkic SS Armed Detachments commander

Despite the growing chaos of imminent defeat, the bureucracy of the Nazi state carried on, as all bureaucracies tend to do. The new formations needed an overall commander, someone with the requisite qualities and a special knowledge of Islam, and that person was SS-Hauptsturmführer Dr Reiner Olzscha. Olzscha, a practicing physician before the War, was himself an interesting figure who had carried out a fairly large scale scientific study into cholera in Russia in 1938 and whose interests had broadened to include the Turkmen of the southern Soviet Union. He and a fellow-writer, Georg Cleinow, had co-authored a book in 1942 entitled *Turkistan: the political and economic problems in central Asia*. Olzscha was no novice in serving with the foreign legions of the Waffen-SS having previously served on the headquarters staff of the 3rd Battalion of the Dutch SS-Freiwilligen Legion Niederlande.

There is a lack of clarity around Olzscha's appointment and its longevity. It seems he was in command in Slovakia during the early set-up phase but this was not a match made in heaven. As the East Mussulman SS-Regiment was gradually dissolved and men and equipment (what little there was) transferred over to the new formation, it must have been a difficult time command-wise, as officers with more rank and experience than Olzscha, arrived to find themselves taking up relatively junior appointments. This was the case for the

'Idel-Ural's commander, SS-Standartenführer Harun al-Raschid Bey, who was a full three ranks above Olzscha. The unease of the relationship between the two officers can only be guessed at, but it was not to be a problem for long, as Olzscha was quickly replaced by SS-Hauptsturmführer Fürst (still an incredibly junior officer to command what was almost a division, in terms of manpower). However it was clear that there were real problems between the cadre staff and the mass of the Islamic soldiery. The officers viewed their men as second-class members of the Waffen-SS, and in return the Muslim rank and file felt like neglected cannon-fodder. The SS authorities' answer was to draft in some experts in Islamic and Asian affairs to try and build bridges between the Muslims and their commanding cadre. One of these experts was a former Handschar NCO, SS-Oberscharführer Beger:

> I was attached to the *Osttürkischer WaffenVerbänd* from 15 March 1945 in northern Italy. They thought my knowledge of the peoples of inner Asia would help improve the bad climate between the troops and the cadre personnel...My time with them ended when I was taken prisoner by the Americans on 27 April 1945. (Letter to the author from Bruno Beger PhD, dated 9 November 2006)

Under Fürst's command in March 1945 the Muslim SS men were placed in the rear of Eighth Army at the front, as a reserve north-west of Modrovka and west of Backov. They would see no further action. Vienna was to their south-west and as the whole German war effort collapsed around them the Muslims decided to try and save themselves from Soviet vengeance by heading west.

Uniforms and insignia

Along with a common base of standard Wehrmacht field grey M36 and M40 uniforms, the wide array of ethnic Muslim legions and units that served in the Ostheer received a multiplicity of insignia denoting their origins and status. These special insignia included arm badges showing mosques and the Arabic phrase *'Biz Alla Bilen'*, which the Nazis believed was the Arabic equivalent of their own *'Gott mit uns'*. However, not only is the translation wrong, it should read *'Allah biz bilen'*, but Arabic is not a commonly understood language for the Turkic peoples, for whom Kazakh, Kirgiz, Turkmen, Uzbek or Tajik would have been more relevant.

For the formation of the Ostturkischer Waffen-Verbände der SS, a special collar patch sporting a white wolf's head – a traditional Turkic device – was designed and produced, although it was not universally worn due to the hectic conditions of the time. A cuff title was also produced that bore the unique distinction among the ranks of the Waffen-SS of not being silver on black but pale grey on a lime green backing, the reasons for which are not clear.

IX

'Free India' – Indian Muslims in the Waffen-SS

Muslims from the sub-continent

After Indonesia, modern-day Indian is home to the second largest population of Muslims in the world. At the time of the Second World War, the British Raj, encompassing as it did, both modern-day Pakistan and Bangladesh as well as India itself, was the largest home to Muslims on the planet. Traditionally, the British-led Indian Army had recruited heavily from the Muslim peoples of northern India and this meant that come the advent of the Second World War there were a very high number of British-uniformed Muslim soldiers available for service. The vast majority fought for the Allies with great distinction, combating both the Japanese in the Far East, the Italians, and later Rommel's Afrika Korps in the deserts of North Africa. But the string of British defeats in the Far East in 1942 saw thousands of Indian Army soldiers become prisoners of the Japanese. The same was true, although to a far lesser extent, in the desert, as the Italian Army took a considerable number of Indian soldiers prisoner.

The Italians' response to this was to set up three camps to try and 'turn' the prisoners (and other local North African Muslims) into willing allies; Centro A for all Arab groups and North African nationalities except Tunisians, Centro I for Indians and Centro T for Tunisians. The men were kitted out with Italian tropical uniforms and weaponry, with the Indian contingent (approximately battalion-size) sporting an armshield in the national colours of orange/white/green. However like almost all Italian military ventures during the War it was a disaster, with the Indian soldiers refusing to serve under Italian officers, whom they held in very low regard. The battalion was quickly disbanded and the idea shelved. The Arabs and Tunisians did not fare much better, although it would seem that some did go on to fight with the Germans in the 845th German-Arab Battalion (see Chapter III).

Subhas Chandra Bose

The Germans made no such recruitment attempts until the situation was radically altered by the arrival in Nazi Germany of a figure in the spring of 1941 who still arouses controversy today. That individual was a rather portly, bespectacled lawyer called Subhas Chandra Bose, also known as the *Netaji*. Prior to the War, the Indian independence movement was already powerful and influential with a cohort of national leaders dedicated to ending British hegemony. Mahatma Gandhi, Pandit Nehru and Muhammed Jinna are by far the most famous, but at the time the Calcutta lawyer Subhas Chandra Bose was also a leading light. Like his more well-known contemporaries in the Congress Party, Nehru and Gandhi, Bose was a middle-class Indian Hindu educated in the pseudo-British public school system set up in India after the Mutiny of 1857. Born in 1897 into the prosperous urban middle-class in predominantly Muslim Bengal, he had also proved himself a firebrand having been arrested no fewer than eleven times by the British authorities in an attempt to stop his agitation. This was all pretty much par for the course, but where Bose did differ from his fellow political leaders was in not agreeing with Gandhi's non-violent approach, indeed he advocated violence as the only way to secure India's freedom. The War then was his opportunity.

Bose in Berlin

With Chamberlain's declaration of war, Bose recognised an opportunity to enlist the active support of Nazi Germany as a powerful ally in the struggle for independence. Travelling through Afghanistan and the Soviet Union he reached Berlin on 3 April 1941, coincidentally enough, at the same moment as the Iraqi revolt that the Nazis tried to support. With Nazi support, Bose established a 'Free India Centre' from where he broadcast anti-British announcements and published propaganda material. By the end of the year he was rewarded by being given official recognition by Germany as the 'government-in-exile' of a free India. At first, the relationship between the Indian radical and the Nazi regime went well, until on 22 June of that year the Wehrmacht launched Barbarossa. The invasion of the Soviet Union went down spectacularly badly with Bose, who like most of his fellow Indian independence leaders was a socialist and great admirer of communism. But he was now stuck and had to come to some sort of accommodation with the Nazis if he was to see them support his dream of a 'free India.' Realising he could do little to change Nazi policy he ploughed on with wooing the regime and proposed establishing a fighting force as the nucleus of a future independent Indian Army. It took a couple of months of negotiation to convince the Germans of the viability and useage of such a unit, but finally on 26 August 1942 the *Legion Freies Indien* – Free Indian Legion, was formally created.

The Free India Legion

Bose's ambitious plan was for a massive force of over 100,000 men, armed and equipped by the Germans, and recruited from the thousands of prisoners captured by Rommel in the desert. As such, it was the Heer that first thought the idea worth backing and they arranged for the Netaji, and his entourage of eight confidants from India, to tour the camps and exhort his listeners to turn their backs on their British comrades-in-arms and join him in the struggle for freedom. One of his earliest recruits, Barwant Singh (who became a lieutenant in the Legion), said of Bose's arrival in his POW camp:

> He was introduced to us as a leader from our country who wanted to talk to us. He wanted 500 volunteers who would be trained in Germany and then parachuted into India. Everyone raised their hands. Thousands of us volunteered.

While recruitment was not exactly stellar there were enough volunteers, some 3,000 in total, to form a three-battalion regiment, the officially entitled *Infanterie-Regiment 950 (indische)* – the 950th Indian Infantry Regiment. Each battalion was four companies strong and was equipped with small-arms, although its only heavy weapons were a paltry six obsolete light anti-tank guns grouped in one company. This was mainly due to German doubt about their new allies potential fighting role, as well as general shortages of heavy equipment in the Reich. As with British India's religious makeup the unit was formed of Muslims as well as Hindus and Sikhs. The Germans did not distinguish between Hindu, Sikh and Muslim volunteers during the recruitment of the Legion, but records indicate that two-thirds of the regiment were Muslim. Hindi was the official language of command but the all-German officer cadre had difficulty mastering it and not all of the recruits spoke it anyway, so in effect the most commonly used language was actually English. Bose's plan was to use the Legion to strike southwards from the Caucasus, through Afghanistan and on to India, where it would lead a national rebellion against the British, but it soon became clear that the Heer itself was more intent on utilising the Regiment for its propaganda value rather than as a serious attempt to man combat units with Indian soldiers. This, and the failure of von Kleist's offensive into the Caucasus in autumn of 1942, was a serious blow for Bose, who realised that his plan to use Nazi Germany to help free India was a washout.

Bose heads for Tokyo

Bose was still determined to use the Axis to further his cause, but as he could not get the help he wanted in Berlin he decided to head east and throw in his lot with the Japanese. Without telling his men, Bose boarded a submarine in February 1943 and sailed for Tokyo Bay. The effect on the Legion was devastating. Without his leadership, morale plummeted, disaffection spread and in no time at all the unit became dysfunctional.

The Legion heads for France

Officially still a German Army formation, following its training the regiment was posted first to occupied Holland and then on to the Bay of Biscay to carry out light garrison and coastal defence duties. But with the launch of Operation Overlord and the invasion of France in June 1944 the picture changed dramatically as resistance became much more widespread and the Indians were involved in local skirmishes with an increasingly active French resistance movement. However, they were operationally ineffectual and ended up being left pretty much to their own devices as the Germans in France concentrated on their life and death struggle with the Anglo-Americans in Normandy.

The Indian Waffen-SS

With the German Army unconcerned about the future of its Indian regiment, Himmler intervened and the unit was transferred en masse to the Waffen-SS on 8 August 1944 and renamed as the *Indische Freiwilligen*

Legion der Waffen-SS, an infantry-heavy unit with a strength of some 2,300 men, 81 motor vehicles and 700 horses. Their new commander was SS-Oberführer Heinz Bertling, and for the first time he was joined by a cadre of Indian officers made up of ex-senior NCOs who had passed a shortened officer training course. Bertling was a former Foreign Ministry official who was deeply unimpressed by his new posting and paid it very little attention from the start. Military life went on though, and the transfer initiated a reorganisation of the regiment resulting in the following order of battle being formalised:

Commander SS-Oberführer Heinz Bertling (from 8 August 1944 to 8 May 1945)
I Bataillon (infantry battalion)
II Bataillon
III Batallion
13. Infanteriegeschütz-Kompanie (infantry-gun company)
14. Panzerjäger-Kompanie (anti-tank gun company)
15. Pionier-Kompanie (combat engineer company)

Interestingly, the Legion was the only ever foreign Waffen-SS unit to be recruited not to fight against the Soviet Union. The ideological struggle against Bolshevism that was so much a part of the Waffen-SS's make-up was entirely absent from the takeover of the Indian Legion. It was never envisaged to switch the unit to the Eastern Front, and just as with the much more effective 17th SS-Panzergrenadier Division Götz von Berlichingen, the Waffen-SS used the Indians solely to face the western Allies. The experiment was a disaster from start to finish. With the post-Falaise collapse of German forces in France, the Indians were ordered back to Germany on 15 August just a week after becoming Waffen-SS 'stormtroopers'. Like everyone else, they pelted hell for leather for the border, losing a lot of precious equipment and even a few men in the process, as they fought running skirmishes with local guerillas and even a few advanced Free French forces. Along the way they seemed to display disturbing signs of ill-discipline and barbarity, with accusations of atrocities. According to a former resistance fighter, Henri Gendreaux, the SS-Legion retreated through his home town of Ruffec in the Poitou-Charente region and behaved appallingly:

I do remember several cases of rape. A lady and her two daughters were raped and in another case they even shot dead a little two-year-old girl. (From Mike Thomson's BBC interview with Rudolf Hartog for the 'Hitler's Secret Indian Army' programme, 2004.)

Gendreaux's claims are unsubstantiated, and it is pretty hard to believe that ex-British soldiers committed these acts, which were entirely absent from their fellow Indians' behaviour in all other theatres of the War in which they fought. But given the reputation of the Waffen-SS it is not a wholly impossible scenario either.

On arrival back in Germany the Waffen-SS attempted to turn the Legion into a proper fighting unit, however the project misfired from the start, especially as all the Indian's heavy equipment was pretty much immediately requisitioned for use by the newly-created Hungarian volksdeutsche 18th SS-Panzergrenadier Division Horst Wessel. Without adequate weaponry it proved impossible to deploy the Legion, so that even by March 1945 as the Red Army neared Berlin, the Legion had still not done any real fighting, and when Hitler was informed by an SS liaison officer, SS-Sturmbannführer Johannes Göhler, that the unit was away from the front resting and refitting, Hitler exploded with sarcasm:

> As I see it, units in rest and rehabilitation are those who have been engaged in heavy fighting and therefore require refreshing. Your units are always refreshing and never fighting. (From George H. Stein, *The Waffen-SS, Hitler's Elite Guard At War 1939–1945*, Cornell University, 1966)

Hitler had more to say of his Indian 'revolutionaries' at a conference in the Führer Bunker during the night of 23/24 March, when he held forth with his views on many of Himmler's eastern units in particular. As regards the Indians he said:

> The Indian Legion is a joke. There are Indians that can't kill a louse, and would prefer to allow themselves to be devoured. They certainly aren't going to kill any Englishmen ... I imagine that if one were to use the Indians to turn prayer wheels or something like that they would be the most indefatigable soldiers in the world. But it would be ridiculous to commit them to a real blood struggle ... The whole business is nonsense. If one has a surplus of weapons, one can permit oneself such amusements for propaganda purposes. But if one has no such surplus it is simply not justifiable. (From George H. Stein, *The Waffen-SS, Hitler's Elite Guard At War 1939–1945*, Cornell University, 1966)

With Nazi collapse imminent the Legion tried to escape into neutral Switzerland, but this was blocked, so eventually they surrendered to the Americans and Free French. Their German translator, Private Rudolf Hartog (he was Heer and not Waffen-SS), said:

The last day we were together an armoured tank appeared. I thought, my goodness, what can I do? I'm finished, but he only wanted to collect the Indians. We embraced each other and cried. You see that was the end. (From Mike Thomson's BBC interview with Rudolf Hartog for the Hitler's Secret Indian Army, programme, 2004)

The British and the Indian SS – what to do?

Handed over to the British, the quandary was now what to do with these most bizarre of renegades. After almost a year in POW camps they were shipped back to India and held in jail pending a final decision as to what to do. The British did put three of their most senior, though still pretty junior, officers on trial in Delhi but there was an outcry in the army and outbreaks of unrest. Wary of creating martyrs and further fuelling an already difficult situation on the sub-continent, the British opted not to make an example of the men and they were all quietly released and sent on their way. By that time it was in no-one's interest to wreak vengeance on these most ineffectual of all Hitler's Waffen-SS men. Indeed, all evidence of the Legion was placed under wraps and labelled 'Secret', with the relevant papers not slated for release until 2021. When Barwant Singh was finally tracked down by a BBC team intent on making a documentary of the story he said: 'In front of my eyes I can see how we all looked, how we would all sing and how we all talked about what eventually would happen to us all.'

Postscript – Bose and the Indian National Army

As for Bose himself he attempted to fulfil his ambition with the help of the Japanese Empire. On arrival in Tokyo he offered his services in raising an 'Indian National Army' (INA) of fully three divisions, made up of former POWs. As in the west, Bose toured the prison camps and recruited freely. Unsurprisingly, given the appalling treatment meted out by the Japanese to captured enemy soldiers, he was pretty successful, as many men were desperate to escape the inhuman conditions they were held under. But his men were regarded as traitors by the rest of the loyal Indian Army, and when these units were deployed at the front some time later after having been equipped by the Japanese Army and received partial re-training, they proved themselves less than steadfast in combat. But there was no denying it was a substantial movement and that it, just as with its 'cousins' in the Waffen-SS Indian Legion, gave the British serious problems about what to do following the end of hostilities. Bose himself dissolved the INA on 17 August 1945 with the words: 'The roads to Delhi are many and Delhi still remains our goal.' Bose's end was as controversial as his life. He was killed in an air crash in Taiwan on 18 August 1945 in the closing days of the War, but rumours abounded that he had not died there but in the Soviet Union, where he had returned to drum up support for his moribund movement. His ashes were buried in a Buddhist temple in Tokyo, but little real information about the manner of his death was forthcoming, and neither Taiwan or the USA said they had any record of the crash, so fuelling the conspiracy theorists.

The controversy ground on but was finally settled in January 2008 with the release of confidential Indian Government files and reports that confirmed Taiwan as the crash site. The key report, dated 29 September 1945, was of an interview with one of Bose's closest aides who accompanied his leader on the doomed flight but survived the accident, Habib ur Rahman. Rahman stated that soon after take-off from Taihoku (now Taiwan's capital Taipei) the aircraft vibrated violently and then burst into flames, 'The seat Bose occupied in the aircraft was beside a petrol tank; at the time of the crash the tank exploded, spreading the burning fuel on Bose's clothing.' Even in India today his legacy lives on with a 'Netaji Research Bureau' based in Chennai (Calcutta) headed by his 77 year-old nephew, Krishna Bose.

The SS Muslims of India

Overall, the Waffen-SS never made any concerted effort to turn the Indians into a viable military unit, and it remains unclear as to what they thought they would get out of the ill-starred venture. Muslims did indeed make up the majority of the Legion but they were never seen by the SS in the same way as their co-religionists in either the Balkan Muslim or Turkic formations. The Indian Legion was a futile and ultimately empty gesture that did nothing to enhance the reputation of the Waffen-SS or contribute to the Nazi War effort.

Uniform and insignia

When the original Heer unit was created, the Indians wore standard Wehrmacht field grey with an armshield in the national colours on their right upper arm depicting a leaping tiger and crowned by the title

'Freies Indien'. Turbans were also worn as required by the different religious groups. On transferring to the Waffen-SS no major changes were instituted. A stylized tiger head collar patch was designed but never manufactured let alone worn. The same could not be said for medals, of which Bose himself instituted a vast array that he spread around like confetti. Despite the Legion's conspicuous lack of combat time, almost half its members were personally decorated by Bose, although for what can only be guessed at.

X

Peace and Retribution

Stalin's revenge

The greatest number of Muslims who had served with Hitler's armies came from the lands of the Soviet Union, and as the curtain fell on Nazi Germany's War effort, tens of thousands of these men found themselves far from home in Europe with a vengeful Red Army all to close. Their numbers were large; the OKH's own statistical department, based on September 1944 ration returns, said there were 13,000 Azeri Hiwis with another 4,795 in pioneer and transport units and 21 Azeri construction companies serving in the Heer alone. There were also 15 Volga Tartar construction companies, and an incredible 111 of Turkmen. A further 20,000 Turkmen were organised into 5 pioneer battalions.

Most of them, along with their non-Muslim Waffen-SS comrades, knew all too well what fate awaited them if they surrendered to the Soviets, so made every effort possible to hand themselves in to the western Allies and hopefully survive.

The 8,500 men of the *Kaukasischer Waffen-Verbände der SS* (the Caucasian Armed SS Detachments) were transferred from the Neuhammer training camp (where its reserve/training battalion the *Turkistanische Ersatz Abteilung* stayed) to the town of Paluzza (near Tolmezza) in northern Italy in January 1945. There, they continued work-up training right to the War's end. Being mainly Christians from Armenia and Georgia, and having not fired a shot in anger for many months, the unit's commander SS-Standartenführer Arved Theuermann, considered the men to be relatively safe from reprisal and approached the advancing British forces and surrendered the entire unit pretty much intact. The Muslim Azeris in Theuermann's command were definitely the lucky ones.

Their comrades in the Osttürkischer Waffen-Verbände der SS (the East Turkic Armed SS Detachments) who were almost all Islamic soldiers, were not so fortunate. They too were in Italy come the end of the conflict, having fled south-west from Slovakia before the Red Army to reach Merate in northern Italy, some 20 kilometres north of Milan in Lombardy, by March 1945. From here, the Turkmen of SS Waffen-Gruppe 'Turkistan' (formerly the 1st and 2nd Battalions of the East Mussulman SS-Regiment) were sent to Carpi in Modena on garrison duty. Back in Merate with German resistance collapsing, the commander of the SS Waffen-Gruppe Idel-Ural, the incompetent and previously sacked SS-Standartenführer Harun al-Raschid Bey (formerly Wilhelm Hintersatz), met the leader of the local partisans and agreed to surrender his Tartars to them on condition they were treated humanely.

The decision to surrender to partisans rather than the oncoming Americans was motivated by an irrational fear on the Tartars behalf that the GIs would mistake them (with their Asiatic features) for Japanese and so would proceed to mow them down with tanks. So, according to the agreement on 26 April the Tartars laid down their arms and some 150 were promptly shot by the partisans at Col Di Nesse. They were then handed over to the Americans of the 1st US Tank Division anyway who did not mistake them for Japanese and did not shoot them out of hand. The end result was much the same though, as with so many of Stalin's former subjects. The agreements, made by the Big Three political leaders at Yalta the year before, came into effect and the Tartars as Soviet citizens were sent back to the tender mercies of the waiting NKVD. Many were shot within minutes of being handed over and the remainder were shipped to the infamous gulags of Asiatic Russia, to be worked to death in slave labour camps like Vorkuta and Kolyma.

The Muslims of the Waffen-SS were not the only Islamic volunteers to suffer. The Heer mother-unit that started it all back in 1941, the famed 162nd Division, was stationed in the beautiful northern Italian city of Rimini when peace came. The whole division surrendered to the British, who promptly shipped them to the border where the Soviet rail wagons were waiting. Their fate echoed that of the Tartars.

The exile of the nations

It was not only the volunteers themselves who were to suffer Stalin's wrath, back in Moscow, the Georgian supremo and his sadistic NKVD boss,

Lavrenti Beria, had devoted considerable time and thought to what they were going to do with the lands and peoples they retook from the retreating Ostheer. For the Muslim populations of the south a time of horror awaited them. Condemned as traitors by Stalin, the Chechens, Ingush, Balkars, Karachais and Crimean Tartars were all to be internally exiled. With the Germans pushed out of the Soviet Union and back towards their own borders it was time for the Soviet Union's terror machine to kick into gear. No excuses were accepted. It did not matter that 50,000 Chechens were serving in the Red Army, far more than were with the Wehrmacht. One-quarter of the entire population were to die. Divisions of special NKVD troops appeared in the south and began to implement Beria's plans. With a murderous efficiency that echoed the Nazis' Final Solution, entire Muslim populations were rounded up and transported in cattle trains to the almost-uninhabitable wastes of Soviet central Asia and Siberia. They were told they would never return to their ancestral homelands. Provided with no shelter and little food on arrival, they died like flies. There are few accurate records, in fact very few records at all of the casualties but conservative estimates place the numbers who perished in the hundreds of thousands. Whole generations were wiped out by starvation and disease. For the Crimean Tartars, for instance, half a million of them were sent east to Uzbekistan and the casualty rate was 50 per cent. As a nation they were destroyed.

With Kruschev's elevation to power on Stalin's death, a wholesale programme of de-Stalinization was instituted and the case of the Muslim peoples was re-examined. It was decreed that they had been punished enough and they were allowed to return to their old communities in the Caucasus. All that is, except the Crimean Tartars, who even Kruschev viewed as being now beyond the pale, given their wartime record of considerably more than 20,000 men who fought willingly for Germany. For the Tartars, banishment was to be permanent and even today their former homes in the Crimea are empty and silent. Over 600 years of Muslim history and culture in the Crimea were wiped out in less than a decade.

Tito and the communists in Yugoslavia

Yugoslavia's suffering in the War was immense. The country was conquered in just twelve days and the dead in the short-lived invasion only numbered in their thousands, but by the end of the War just four years later the Triune Kingdom had lost one in ten of its entire populace, 1.7m people gone. All of Yugoslavia's multiple ethnic groups were decimated.

The slaughter was particularly brutal in Pavelic's Croatia where the barbarity of the Ustasha seemingly knew no bounds. They even went so far as to establish their own series of concentration camps (the only system set up by an Axis state outside the Third Reich itself), including the infamous Jasenovac to the north-west of Banja Luka. Jasenovac was not a Reinhardt-type extermination camp like Treblinka or Auschwitz-Birkenau, but was still a place of misery, torture and mass murder. Most of the 200,000 people exterminated at Jasenovac were Serbs, although many of Yugoslavia's Jews and Roma died there too. Those Jews and Roma that Jasenovac did not claim were sent north to their deaths in the Nazi camps. In all over 60,000 Yugoslav Jews were murdered, along with 26,000 Roma, in what their own community called the *Porajmos*. Before the War, Belgrade had a Jewish community that numbered some 12,000. By the end of the War only 1,115 were still alive, the majority of the rest were murdered in Jasenovac.

A ray of hope

But among the settling of old scores and the stoking of ethnic hatreds there were glimmers of humanity. On the Avenue of the Righteous Among the Nations at Yad Vashem, the memorial to the victims of the Holocaust in Jerusalem, stand dozens of small plaques commemorating those who risked their own lives to help save Jewish lives during the War. Oskar Schindler is remembered there, as is the Swedish diplomat Raoul Wallenberg, and tucked away in the green borders is one plaque dedicated to the Muslim Hardaga family from Bosnia. Mustafa, Zejneba, Izet and Bachriya Hardaga and their friend Ahmed Sadik helped hide Jews from the rampaging Ustasha and the SS. Facing great danger, the entire family saved the lives of dozens of Jewish men, women and children who otherwise would have been taken away to their deaths in the concentration camps. Honoured by the Israeli state after the War the Hardaga family eventually emigrated from Bosnia to Israel and converted to Judaism.

The SS-Handschar and atrocities

What is clear is that the war in Yugoslavia was characterised as much by unspeakable brutality as it was by selfless heroism. What is also clear is that atrocities were not the preserve of any one side, all indulged in them to some degree. The Geneva Convention was disregarded to the detriment of all, and the result was an evil in Yugoslav society that lives on today in the various successor countries.

The most obvious case was that of the Ustasha who revelled in atrocity, but although they were among the very worst offenders they were far from alone. At the time, the greatest impediment to Tito's freedom of movement from 1943 onwards, as his army grew, was the fate of his several thousand wounded. Bitter experience had taught the Partisans that to leave their wounded behind was in effect to condemn them to death. That was not to say every wounded Partisan or prisoner was automatically executed by Axis personnel, but it was a lucky one that survived. The result was that all movement had to be carried out with the fate of the columns of wounded in mind. Things were no better on the other side of the coin. Without POW camps the Partisans could not keep prisoners, so to fall into their hands was a death sentence. Royalist chetniks, Croat Ustasha or Waffen-SS, all shared the same fate when taken by Tito's men. When Axis soldiers found their comrades murdered and mutilated it did little to persuade them to act leniently the next time a Partisan put his or her hands up. For civilians, to be caught in the middle was to be in the line of fire. As far as all sides were concerned there was no such thing as non-combatants.

The SS-Kama may have contributed some manpower to combating the Red Army, but was never operational in Yugoslavia so does not concern us here. As for the Albanians of SS-Skanderbeg, their record is covered in their own chapter. But what of the SS-Handschar, in the midst of all this horror did it keep its hands clean?

The Division has consistently been tarred with an unenviable record of brutality. The accepted view is that it was one of the more bloodstained Waffen-SS formations and that from its inception it showed an immediate proclivity for murder. A host of crimes has been attributed to the Unit with little in the way of contradictory evidence. But when the reality is that any survivors keep their heads down and avoid drawing attention to their service there is likely to be little said in the way of defence.

Some allegations do not stand up to scrutiny. The otherwise extremely reliable Yugoslav historian, Vladimir Dedijer, wrote of the Koritska Gorge massacre of over 150 defenceless Serb villagers in June 1941, claiming that along with the Ustasha the SS-Handschar were responsible for carrying out the atrocity. Clearly this can not be true as the Handschar was not even established until 1943. He states that a member of the division, a Muharem Glavinic from the neighbouring village of Kljuc, signed the order to attack Koritska. Glavinic was apparently a Muslim and it may well be that Dedijer is confusing a local Muslim militia with the SS-Handschar. It is even possible that some of the perpetrators of Koritska Gorge ended up in the Handschar, but this is all conjecture. What is incontrovertible is that the Koritska Gorge massacre did actually occur, but the SS-Handschar was not responsible for it.

Trial in Tito's Yugoslavia

Following the end of the War the new Yugoslav Government did all in its power to bring those it considered to be war criminals to justice. Any it had itself captured, if they survived the event, were sent to trial and strenuous efforts were made to locate and extradite back any others from the teeming POW camps in Europe.

The Muslim members who had survived did everything they could to hide their wartime service, rightly fearing judicial vengeance. One ex-Handschar man, Ibrahim Alimabegovic said of his own escape: 'When the British came, they took people's medals etc and checked under our arms for the SS blood type tattoos. I didn't have one...'

Alimabegovic was not sent back and lived. Many did not. Unsurprisingly the Partisans did not keep any records of what they did to prisoners in the chaos of victory, but it seems that large numbers of Waffen-SS personnel in particular were shot out of hand more or less as soon as they were captured. There were at least three recorded instances of mass executions; one at Maibor on the Drava River, another near to the town of Raamanders, and a further one at an unnamed location. Exact details are sketchy, but it would seem that hundreds of survivors of the SS-Handschar and Prinz Eugen were butchered at these sites in retribution for their wartime records.

The SS-Handschar personnel who were not handed over by the Anglo-Americans to the Partisans were placed in camps, where Tito's officers then appeared and began to trawl through them to identify those they wished to extradite and try on Yugoslav soil. The list was long and consisted of many of the Division's leaders. Co-operative as ever, the British allowed the extraditions to go ahead and the men were sent east to an uncertain fate. Their trial was held en masse before a military court in Sarajevo on 22 August 1947. Defended by three attorneys; two civilian and one military, the total of 38 defendants were charged with numerous crimes including the murder of over 5,000 civilians in Bosnia. The trial took just eight days to conclude and all were unsurprisingly found guilty as charged. The majority, 28 in all, were given prison terms ranging from five years to life, but ten (all of them Germans) were handed the death sentence. On 17 July 1948, Rolf Baumeister, Walter Eipel, Kurt Lutkemuller, Bruno Lutjens, Heinz Masannek, Josef Palmke, Wilhelm Schmidt, Willi Schreer, Erich Schwerin and Kurt Weber were shot. Their comrade Wilhelm Mann later died in prison and Hermann Behrends was executed by firing squad in Belgrade on 4 December 1948.

Missing from this list though were the really big fish, the top commanders of the Handschar, specifically Karl-Gustav Sauberzweig, Desiderius Hampel and Hellmuth Raithel.

Desiderius Hampel had no illusions about his fate if sent back to Yugoslavia, so after having surrendered to the Allies and put in a make-shift POW camp he lost no time in escaping when security was lax and promptly disappeared. Being a Croatian volksdeustche, going home was out of the question and he had to start a new life in the West. Evading arrest and extradition for decades he eventually died peacefully in Graz, Austria in 1981.

As for Raithel, he too knew what the sentence of a Yugoslav court would be and again he went to ground as soon as the War ended. Despite efforts to locate him over the years the former Handschar regimental commander, and first and only divisional commander of the SS-Kama, was never apprehended or tried and died of old age nine years after his compatriot Hampel in 1990.

Sauberzweig, the *Schnellchen* himself, was not so lucky. Surrendering his Corps to the British in northern Germany he was placed in Internment Camp No.6, formerly Neuengamme concentration camp, where many senior German officers were held awaiting investigation of their wartime activities. The new Yugoslav Government found out about his presence there and successfully applied to have him extradited back to face charges as a war criminal. In order to avoid this, the night before the Yugoslavs were due to arrive and collect him he took cyanide (the suspicion was that he was supplied this by one of the British officers guarding him) and died on 20 October 1946. When a Yugoslav Army officer dutifully arrived the following day to escort the prisoner he was dismayed to be told of his sui-cide only hours before. Rather foolishly the communist officer demanded to see the body as proof. The affronted British officer in charge snarled back; 'For you, the word of a British officer will have to suffice!' This did not go down well with the Yugoslav, who stormed back to Belgrade and reported that the the the man who had led the SS-Handschar division for most of its short life had cheated the executioner and taken his own life.

The end of the War in Europe was, despite the utter joy of it, an often grim time riddled with events and actions of mind-numbing hypocrisy, none more so than the appalling maltreatment of so many prisoners and their families (and occasionally, as with the Cossacks, of whole peoples) as the British and Americans handed them over en masse into the blood-stained hands of Stalin's murder machine. If a British officer did supply Sauberzweig with a cyanide capsule perhaps he was mindful of acts performed by the British in the recent past that sometimes were less than glorious. After all, it was Air Vice-Marshal Sir Arthur 'Bomber' Harris himself, Commander-in-Chief of the RAF's Bomber Command from February 1942 and architect of the area bombing strategy against Germany, who said before the War; 'The only thing the Arab understands is the heavy hand.' Harris had learned his trade fighting insurgents in British-dominated pre-war Iraq where whole villages were bombed to obliteration as either punishment or to smoke out the terrorists. Brutality, unfortunately, is part and parcel of war.

Nuremburg and the Waffen-SS

Officially at least, ever since the War, the Waffen SS has lived under the cloud of the Nuremburg Tribunal's verdict on it as an organisation, which states:

> The SS was utilised for purposes which were criminal under the Charter involving the persecution and extermination of the Jews, brutalities and killings in concentration camps, excesses in the administration of the occupied territories, the administration of the slave labour program and the mistreatment and murder of prisoners-of-war … The Tribunal declares to be criminal…those persons who had been officially accepted as members of the SS as emunerated in the preceding paragraph (members of the Allgemeine SS, members of the Waffen-SS, members of the SS Totenkopf Verbände…)

The meaning was clear. If you were joined to the Waffen-SS you were not simply 'just another soldier', but a war criminal regardless of your personal actions. Membership of the organisation was enough to be condemned.

Alfred Rosenberg's fate

As with the vast majority of Nazi Germany's highest leadership, who did not commit suicide, Alfred Rosenberg was tried at Nuremburg for his part in the horrendous crimes of the regime. At the hearings he claimed to be ignorant of the Holocaust, despite the fact that his close colleague Leibbrandt and his deputy, Alfred Meyer, were both present at the infamous Wannsee Conference that set the wheels of mass extermination in motion. His defence did not hold up and he was convicted of conspiracy to commit crimes against peace, of planning, initiating and waging wars of aggression, war crimes and crimes against humanity. He was sentenced to death and executed with other condemned co-defendants at Nuremberg on the morning of 16 October 1946. The man born on the same day as him, 12 January 1893, was also due for execution that day but Hermann Goering had cheated the hangman by taking poison the previous night. When Rosenberg was standing on the gallows he was asked if he had any last words. His response was 'No.'

XI

Legacy

The aftermath of the Second World War was characterised by joy and relief among the victors, and utter misery among the vanquished. As the horrors of Hitler's regime were obliterated, its links with Islam were buried in a welter of blood as Stalin and Tito's terror machines went into top gear to exact vengeance. But was it purely a marriage of convenience and nothing more? For the Bosnians of the Handschar their main motivator was a desperation to protect their embattled communities, while their co-religionists in the Caucasus yearned for independence from Moscow's iron grip. It was clear that Islam and Nazism had little in common philosophically, and although tens of thousands of Muslims had fought in the Wehrmacht it was obviously not due to a feeling of kinship between their faith and the hate-filled creed of Adolf Hitler. But, just like a virus, contact with the evil of Nazism infected some people and communities it touched to the detriment of all. This was most profoundly felt in Bosnia and the Middle East.

Bosnia's President was an SS-Handschar recruiter

The early nineties in Europe were scarred by wars in the Balkans. With Tito's death it became apparent that Yugoslavia was a failed concept and that the different ethnic groups in the country were in effect nationalities, who yearned for their own homelands. While Slovenia gained its independence at the cost of a handful of dead and wounded, the same was not true for neighbouring Croatia. But even the pitched Croatian battles around Vukovar and the Serb-dominated Krajina, were nothing compared to the slaughter and barbarity of the subsequent Bosnian war. Yet again, Bosnia-Herzegovina suffered from its mixed ethnic composition and the world had a tragic new phrase added to its lexicon, 'ethnic cleansing'.

The Serb and Croat communities were supported by their racial cousins across the borders to carve out 'ethnically pure' areas and fight savage campaigns against their neighbours. Caught in the middle, just as in the Second World War, were the province's Muslims. As the largest community in the region, when given the chance to vote they elected a fellow Muslim as President, Alija Izetbegovic, in 1990. To the outside world, at the time Izetbegovic portayed an image of himself as a respected and slightly other-worldly scholar who had been thrust into the political spotlight, much as the poet and playwright Vaclav Havel had been in the Czech Republic following its Velvet Revolution. The reality though was very different. In Bosnia itself Izetbegovic was a divisive figure whose election caused genuine fear among the Orthodox Serb and Catholic Croat minorities. One young Bosnian Serb girl who had watched her aunt and three cousins raped and murdered by Muslim militia in 1941 spoke of wanting 'to kill every Turk there is.' Incidents like this are remembered in the Balkans, and come Izetbegovic's election that young girl was a grandmother whose entire family had been brought in the knowledge of that atrocity amongst others.

Izetbegovic was born in 1925 in Bosanski Samac in northern Bosnia. The Izetbegovic family were minor aristocrats in the Ottoman Empire (*beys*) and had lived in Belgrade until the Muslim exodus from the city in 1868. Settling in Bosanski Samac, Izetbegovic's grandfather became the town's mayor and was instrumental in saving the lives of 40 local Serbs threatened with murder in the backlash following the assassination of Archduke Franz Ferdinand in 1914 in Sarajevo. Young Alija became a strong advocate of his faith and at the tender age of 16 following the German invasion he founded the *Al Hidayya* organisation (the Muslim Youth Society) which was associated with the militant 'Young Muslims'. He became a full member of the Young Muslims on 5 March 1943. For Izetbegovic, the ideas emanating from the prestigous Al Azhar University in Cairo were very exciting, and this may have influenced his willingness to be involved in the Mufti's (an ex-Al Azhar student himself) drive to support the raising of the Handschar. It was this involvement in the recruiting effort for Handschar men that condemned Izetbegovic in the eyes of Christian Bosnians. He may never have worn the SS sig runes himself but as far as the Serbs in particular, were concerned he may as well have. Following the end of the war he was arrested, tried and convicted of collaboration on 15 June 1946 by the Yugoslav Supreme Court and sentenced to three years imprisonment and a further two years deprivation of civil rights. Upon release Izetbegovic continued his agitation while studying law at Sarajevo

University, and went on to write the inflammatory *Islamic Declaration: A Program for the Islamization of Muslims and the Muslim Peoples* of 1970 that accused the West of wanting to 'keep Muslim nations spiritually weak and materially and politically dependent.' This text, banned in Yugoslavia until general publication in 1990 following Izetbegovic's election, saw him recognised by Saudi Arabia's King Fahd as Islamic Figure of the Year in 2001 but stirred up nothing but fear of Islamic insurrection in Bosnia's Serbs and Croats. For them he was a dangerous Islamic supremacist and their actions were nothing more than a necessity to avoid an Izetbegovic inspired pogrom of which they would be the victims.

This then was the backdrop to the War and the brutality that followed. For many Croats and Serbs, the mentality was 'get them before they get us' and pre-emptive violence was the order of the day. They did not need to look back into centuries of history but simply ask their parents who had been witnesses to and survivors of the civil war of Pavelic's regime. The butchery of Srebrenica, Gorazde and Zepa was born in the Waffen-SS recruiting offices for the Handschar and Kama. For the Christian Bosnians a clear thread ran through from the days of the SS-Handschar and SS-Kama through to Izetbegovic's troops and the extremist Islamic mujihadeen they fought alongside.

Post-war Arab links to Nazism

The horrors of Bosnia were bad enough, but the legacy of Islam's links with the Nazis has been most keenly felt in the Middle East. It was, and remains, the vexed question of land that sits at the heart of much of the hostility in the region. Jewish immigration to Palestine and the creation of the state of Israel was the trigger for the current round of hostility, but Nazism has helped instill deep rooted religious anti-semitism into the conflict. The Mufti and his predominantly Iraqi entourage were the bridge for this process that helped infect Arab nationalism with virulent anti-Jewish sentiment. Recognition of these links was clearly widespread in Nazi Germany and the exile process seen for militant Arabs was now put into reverse. The exodus of Nazi war criminals after the fall of the Third Reich saw many Latin American countries willingly play host to some of Hitler's most notorious and brutal henchmen. But it was not just sympathetic right wing regimes such as Argentina's Peronist government that welcomed fleeing Nazis, but also governments in the Arab world. King Farouk (and later the man who deposed him Gamal Abdal Nasser) in Egypt was a leading proponent in enticing Nazi war criminals to bring their grisly 'expertise' to help them against their political left, and later on the newly-born state of Israel. Men like SS-Gruppenführer Alois Moser, who was involved in the extermination of the Ukraine's Jews, and SS-Obersturmbannführer Eugen Eichberger a former battalion commander in Oskar Dirlewanger's Sonderkommando, found a warm welcome in Egypt and set about transforming the country's security apparatus and military establishments. Those with experience in the Balkans were welcomed too, such as Joachim Däumling, the ex-Gestapo chief of Düsseldorf, who served in Croatia alongside the genocidal Ustasha.

The distinguished academic, Dr Matthias Küntzel, a research associate at the Vidal Sasson International Centre for the Study of Antisemitism at the Hebrew University of Jeruslaem, wrote in the *Jewish Political Studies Review* in the spring of 2005:

> Anti-Semitism based on the notion of a Jewish world conspiracy is not rooted in Islamic tradition, but, rather, in European ideological models. The decisive transfer of this ideology to the Muslim world took place between 1937 and 1945 under the impact of Nazi propaganda.
>
> Although Islamism is an independent, anti-Semitic, anti-modern mass movement, its main early promoters, the Muslim Brotherhood in Egypt and the Mufti and the Qassamites in Palestine, were supported financially and ideologically by agencies of the German National Socialist Government.

When Küntzel was invited to the University of Leeds to lecture on the topic in 2007 there were protest letters written by the University's Islamic students' society that caused it to be cancelled by the authorities on 'security grounds'.

The end of Judaism in Egypt and Iraq

In Egypt and Iraq especially, this swing to the Right and its embrace of virulent anti-semitism has had, and still does today, extremely grave consequences. The Jewish population of Egypt for instance was 75,000 in 1948 but from then on suffered official state persecution reminiscent of the infamous Nazi Nuremburg Laws of the 1930s. In 1956, some 4,000 Jews were summarily expelled after having their property expropriated by the State, in 1957 all Egyptian Jews not in 'continuous residence' since 1900 were deprived of citizenship; 1960 saw a host of synagogues, Jewish schools, orphanages and hospitals closed down and in 1967 all Jews were dismissed from official positions. The result was that by 1974 only 350 Jews remained of the entire population. For Iraqi Jews the story was much the same. Before the War almost a third of Baghdad's population was Jewish and the community felt itself to be thoroughly assimiliated, having lived in the country for centuries. However with the rise of the pro-Axis cabal in the army especially, it was not long before trouble erupted. Borrowing on the Palestinian experience instigated by the Mufti, anti-semitic riots broke out and culminated in a mob attack on the night of 1 June 1941 when swastikas were daubed on synagogues and Baghdad's Jewish quarter was ransacked leaving almost 200 Iraqi Jews dead in the streets. The British invasion stopped any further atrocities, but following the end of the War and Iraq's independence the nightmare began again. Jews were barred from the army, police and the civil service and prominent Jews were rounded up, tortured and executed. The 1950 Denaturalization Act revoked the citizenship of all Jews and resulted in 120,000 having to be airlifted to safety by the Israeli government and an uncertain new life in Israel. Those that were left were persecuted by the Ba'athist regime after its takeover from royal rule, until, by the end of the 1990s there were just 22 Jews left in Baghdad. The community was effectively wiped out and over a thousand years of Jewish life and culture in Mesopotamia was extinguished.

Al-Husseini – the Mufti himself

What of the ex-Mufti himself? As the Third Reich disintegrated around him and its Muslim Waffen-SS cohorts melted away, what became of the self-styled leader of the Islamic/Nazi alliance? True to form, al-Husseini declined to stay and face any accusers but sought sanctuary in flight. First he went over the border and into Switzerland, but the Swiss were embarrassed by his presence and sent him on his way. He then fled to France where, amazingly, he was given a form of asylum and allowed to live openly just outside Paris. Significant pressure was applied to France to have him extradited for his wartime record, not least following the judgement of the Nuremburg Tribunal which investigated his activities. After seeing the evidence, the International Court reported the following:

> It has been proved to us that the Mufti aimed at the implementation of the Final Solution, viz., the extermination of European Jewry, and there is no doubt that, had Hitler succeeded in conquering Palestine, the Jewish population of there as well would have been subject to total extermination, with the support of the Mufti.

Eichmann's deputy, Dieter Wisliceny, went on to speak at the Tribunal of the Mufti and his entourage:

> The Mufti was one of the initiators of the systematic extermination of European Jewry and had been a collaborator and advisor of Eichmann

and Himmler in the execution of this plan...He was one of Eichmann's best friends and had constantly incited him to accelerate the extermination measures. I heard him say, accompanied by Eichmann, he had visited incognito the gas chambers of Auschwitz.

Although loath to act for fear of stirring up trouble in the Middle East, the new French Government made it known to al-Husseini that it was time to go. But, with Arab country after country being given full independence and the continuing discoveries of vast oil wealth in the deserts, this time al-Husseini felt the safest bet was a move back to the Middle East where he could not be touched in what was now a hugely important, strategic area. The place he settled on was his old university haunt, Cairo. On the banks of the Nile he again took up his role as agitator and spoke out vehemently against Israel's creation, and then became a strong proponent of invasion by Israel's Arab neighbors. Following the utter humiliation of the Arab countries in the War of Independence in 1948 al-Husseini began to lose political clout and was never able to get it back.

The ruling Hashemite monarchy in Transjordan (and post-War rulers of East Jerusalem) were not big fans of the Palestinian leader, and succeeded in getting a rival to al-Husseini appointed as the new Mufti of East Jerusalem, thus removing the last vestige of his previous legitimacy. Recognising that his time was over, al-Husseini moved for the last time and settled in Beirut, Lebanon where he finally died on 4 July 1974.

Al-Husseini's legacy has been far-reaching. Speaking on 2 August 2002 the PLO leader, Yasser Arafat, said of his movement:

> We are the mighty people. Were they able to replace our hero Haj Amin al-Husseini? There were a number of attempts to get rid of Haj Amin, whom they considered an ally of the Nazis. But even so, he lived in Cairo, and participated in the 1948 war. I was one of his troops.

The self-styled 'Grand' Mufti's poison lives on.

As for the thousands of ordinary Muslims who donned the field-grey and fought alongside the Germans in Himmler's Black Guard, it is fair to say that whilst most were not among the finest soldiers the Wehrmacht ever put into battle there can be no denying that many fought bravely and that the standard view of them as senseless murderers is far from the whole truth. Perhaps it is best to quote from that distinguished historian of the War, Norman Davies: 'we cannot deny that particular sorts of conduct by the enemy may be judged good, even if the enemy is rightly associated with an evil cause.'

APPENDIX A

The Waffen-SS High Mountain School

As the Waffen-SS expanded out from its original establishment of motorised infantry formations into a profusion of other roles, it correspondingly began to invest in the training infrastructure needed to drive the creation and manning of armoured, cavalry and mountain units. The last of these specialist roles was to play a large part in the Waffen-SS, as 6 out of the eventual 38 divisions of Himmler's empire were mountain infantry troops. These were the 6th Nord, the 7th Prinz Eugen, the 13th Handschar, the 21st Skanderbeg, the 23rd Kama and the 24th Karstjäger. The Waffen-SS mirrored the famed Gebirgsjäger Schools for the Army divisions by setting up its own mountain warfare school, the main initial facility being the High Mountain School in the Stubai Valley in the Austrian Tyrol at Neustift on 15 September 1942. The extremely picturesque little town became the backdrop for a series of six specialist instruction courses focusing on; officer training, NCO training, assault pioneer and combat engineering training, communication training (both radio and telephone), medical training and logistics training.

Commanded from its inception by SS-Standartenführer Eberhard von Quirsfeld, the School was responsible for training the cadres and command personnel for the growing number of Waffen-SS mountain formations and large numbers of men from all of the aforementioned divisions passed through its gates. The expansion of the Waffen-SS mountain cohort in 1944 to embrace a further three divisions necessitated a corresponding growth in training facilities and the original School was augmented by three further centres, with Group III focusing on marksmanship training and Group IV dealing exclusively with officer instruction. Group II was the largest addition with a general Mountain Warfare School created in the Fleims Valley of the disputed Austrian South Tyrol (the Alto Adige region to Italians) at the town of Predazzo.

The Italian surrender in September 1943 saw the training personnel from the schools used to disarm Italian troops in their vicinity near the Reschen Pass and to secure their weapons and equipment. As the War drew nearer, the schools were then called upon to intervene directly in the fighting. Firstly, to combat the growing Italian partisan threat from the Tonale Pass in the north and as far south as the shores of Lake Como, and later to form distinct kampfgruppes to face the advancing Americans in the west and the potential for a breakthrough by the Red Army in the East. In this reaction the staff and trainees ended up exactly as did their compatriots from the other coterie of Waffen-SS training establishments across Europe. As it turned out, the War was coming to a relatively swift end and the south of the Third Reich did not become a cauldron as did the north around Berlin. The result was that the newly-formed kampf-gruppes saw little action before collectively heading west to surrender to the Americans on 3 May 1945 at Neustift.

APPENDIX B

Waffen-SS Formational Organisation

SS Gruppe (Section):
Commanded by a junior NCO such as an SS-Unterscharführer, or a senior NCO such as an SS-Scharführer.

Made up of anywhere between six and twelve men depending on casualties the section, as in all armies, was the foundation of the Waffen-SS formations. When a man first joined his unit he would be allocated to a section that would be his home and sanctuary until killed, wounded or told otherwise. If the sections did not work then nothing would. All unit cohesion and performance rested on them.

SS Zug (Platoon):
Commanded by either a junior officer such as an SS-Untersturmführer, an officer candidate such as an SS-Oberjunker or a senior NCO such as an SS-Oberscharführer.

Usually consisting of 3–4 sections depending on casualties the platoon was the most commonly used sub-unit, in panzer formations a platoon would comprise 5 tanks.

SS Kompanie (Company):
Commanded by a more senior and experienced, though still very young, officer such as an SS-Obersturmführer or an SS-Hauptsturmführer.

Usually consisting of three platoons the company was the lowest tactical unit that external attachments were made to, including artillery fire observers and forward air controllers. In panzer formations the company would comprise four tank platoons and two command and control tanks.

SS Abteilung (Battalion):
Commanded by an older and more experienced officer such as an SS-Obersturmbannführer or an SS-Sturmbannführer.

An average battalion would be made up of four companies and could have sections of specialist troops such as engineers attached as necessary for a particular operation. A battalion would be numbered with a Roman numeral in front of its parent regiments designation, such as II/ SS-Panzergrenadier Regiment 6 Theodor Eicke.

SS Standarte (Regiment):
Commanded by a senior and very experienced officer such as an SS-Oberführer or SS-Standartenführer.

Equivalent to a brigade in British Army parlance, the regiments were a division's major sub-units and as such would have their own integral staff as well as supporting elements, including a heavy gun section, an anti-aircaft defence section, a combat engineer section and its teeth arms of three infantry, armoured infantry battalions or two panzer battalions depending on its designation as an infantry, panzergrenadier or panzer regiment respectively. This was a major difference between Heer and Waffen-SS regiments with Heer formations having the same number of panzer battalions but crucially only two infantry battalions in each panzergrenadier or infantry regiment. This heavily reduced the units' combat power and meant that Heer units burned out far more rapidly in the battles of attrition prevalent on the Russian Front. It was also a major flaw in many Waffen-SS units raised later in the War including the Langemarck and the Charlemagne. The loss of two entire infantry battalions meant the units' combat effectiveness could be quickly eroded in periods of intense fighting. The regiment would be described by type, Roman numeral if it had one and then honour name if given one, for example SS-Freiwilligen Panzergrenadier Regiment 49 De Ruiter.

SS Division:
Next in the chain came the mainstay of the Waffen-SS formational system, the division.This was entirely different from the Britsh Army system, where the much smaller regimental formation is the building block of the field army and a soldier's spiritual home. A Britsh soldier would feel loyalty to the Royal Norfolks, the Cameronians or the Irish Guards but in the Waffen-SS it was to the Das Reich or the Hitlerjugend. This concept of the 'division as home' was a great help in maintaining

morale and combat effectiveness during the frequent decimations of the Waffen-SS divisions.

There were three main types of Waffen-SS division, each with its own structure: the Panzer (tank) division, the Panzergrenadier (mixed tanks and infantry) division and the non-mechanized divison (either infantry, cavalry or mountain infantry). All three types were commanded by either an SS-Gruppenführer or SS-Brigadeführer.

Just as with regiments, the division would have a structure of support units and these would typically comprise headquarters staff, military police, transport, medical support, logistics, a signals battalion, an engineer battalion, an artillery battalion and an anti-aircraft battalion (almost all entirely mechanized in panzer and panzergrenadier divisions). The teeth fighting elements of the divisions were as follows:

Panzer division:
The armoured fists of the Waffen-SS each had two panzergrenadier regiments of three battalions and a panzer regiment of two battalions. There were seven full panzer divisions in the Waffen-SS and they comprised the best of the Waffen-SS fighting strength, such as the 1st SS Panzer Division Leibstandarte SS Adolf Hitler. Of the non-German Waffen-SS formations only the famous 5th SS Wiking Division was a full panzer formation.

Panzergrenadier division
Comprising two panzergrenadier regiments of three battalions each and a single panzer battalion, these were not full panzer divisions but were still very powerful formations with their own integral armour. These formations were seen as an elite within the Waffen-SS. There were six panzergrenadier divisions including the only Waffen-SS division to fight exclusively on the Western Front, the 17th SS Panzergrenadier Division Götz von Berlichingen. Three of the non-Reichsdeutsche Waffen-SS formations attained this status, including the Nordic 11th SS Freiwilligen Panzergrenadier Division Nordland and the Hungarian volksdeutsche 18th SS Freiwilligen Panzergrenadier Division Horst Wessel.

The non-mechanized divison (either grenadier i.e. infantry, cavalry or mountain infantry):
These formations formed the bulk of the Waffen-SS order of battle during the War and indeed the vast majority of foreign formations came under this designation. As non-mechanized units they were the least well-equipped of the Waffen-SS formations and were of widely differing quality, organisation, strength and combat effectiveness. A standard grenadier division was meant to comprise two grenadier

regiments of three battalions each with supporting arms as with all the other divisions, but in practice this was chopped and changed to suit the availability, or not, of both equipment and manpower. In the French 33rd Waffen-Grenadier-Division der SS Charlemagne (französische Nr.1) for instance, there were only two grenadier battalions in each regiment (for more information see the first book in the 'Hitler's Legions' series *Hitler's Gauls*). Crucially these formations lacked any integral armour and the necessary transport to give them the mobility on the battlefield that was increasingly essential as the nature of warfare, particularly on the Eastern Front, became one characterised by a more modern mechanised concept. In total, there were some eighteen grenadier divisions including the 'twin' designation given to the 29th Waffen Grenadier Divisions der SS of Russiche Nr.1 under Bronislav Kaminski, and Italiensiche Nr.1 under Heldmann, three cavalry (Kavallerie) divisions, not including the defunct 33rd Waffen Kavallerie Division der SS (Ungarische Nr.3) as this unit was overrun before formation and its number reused for the French, and six mountain infantry (Gebirgs) divisions. A few of these formations were elites worthy of the name, including the the 27th SS Freiwilligen Grenadier Division Langemarck (the subject of the second book in the series *Hitler's Flemish Lions*) and in particular the Baltic formations, others, though not combat elites were units with good combat records such as the 6th SS Gebirgs Division Nord. The majority however were of questionable quality and many were formed as defeat loomed and were of little value at the front. Some deserve to be remembered with nothing more than horror and contempt at their records which were brutal beyond belief, the most infamous being the 36th Waffen Grenadier Division der SS under Oskar Dirlewanger. The acceptance of which into the Waffen-SS order of battle will forever stain its reputation.

SS Korps (Corps):
Commanded by either an SS-Obergruppenführer or SS-Gruppenführer.

The Corps was the next level up in organisational terms and consisted of a number of divisions, the minimum of which was two but could rise to three or even four. The Corps was a unit in its own right with a full-time staff comprising complements of headquarters staff, transport, logistics, military police, medical and signalling units of different strengths. Component divisions would then be placed under Corps command but did not belong to that Corps for anymore than the specific campaign the Corps was involved in, or even for longer than a single operation. The Wehrmachts ability to swiftly regroup formations under differing Corps commands during often complex phases of battle was one of the reasons that the German forces held out for so long. During the latter defensive stages of the Russian campaign, formations would often rapidly switch Corps control to face and close off Russian offensive threats, few armies have ever mastered this art. During the War, a total of eighteen Waffen-SS corps were formed including Felix Steiner's famous 3rd Germanisches SS Panzer Corps and the 1st and 2nd SS Panzer Corps of Kharkov, Normandy and Ardennes fame.

SS Armeegruppe (Army Group):
Commanded by either an SS-Obergruppenführer or SS-Oberstgruppenführer (only Sepp Dietrich ever achieved this rank, see Appendix C on Waffen-SS Ranks).

The largest formation ever fielded by the Waffen-SS during the War. This grouping would normally consist of several corps-sized units but was extremely unwieldy to handle even for the well trained Wehrmacht General Staff corps. During the early stages of the War the separate Waffen-SS formations were distributed between the different Wehrmacht Army Groups, such as Army Group A, B or C for the invasion of Soviet Russia, and it was only when the War was to all intents and purposes lost, that Waffen-SS formations were brought together in this way (in an interesting volte face, often with Heer formations integral to them).

APPENDIX C

Waffen-SS and comparable ranks

SS-Schütze	Private (this was the basic private rank, any speciality would be reflected in the title, e.g. Panzerschütze – tank trooper)
SS-Oberschütze	Senior Private (attained after six months' service)
SS-Sturmmann	Lance corporal
SS-Rottenführer	Corporal
SS-Unterscharführer	Lance Sergeant (this rank was above full Corporal but below Sergeant and is only used in the British Army in the Brigade of Guards)
SS-Junker	Officer candidate (acting rank only, substantive rank of SS-Unterscharführer)
SS-Scharführer	Sergeant
SS-Standartenjunker	Officer candidate (acting rank only, substantive rank of SS-Scharführer)
SS-Oberscharführer	Colour / staff Sergeant
SS-Hauptscharführer	Warrant Officer Class 2
SS-Standartenoberjunker	Officer candidate (acting rank only, substantive rank of SS-Hauptscharführer)
SS-Sturmscharführer	Warrant Officer Class 1 (after fifteen years' service)
SS-Untersturmführer	Second Lieutenant
SS-Obersturmführer	Lieutenant

SS-Hauptsturmführer	Captain
SS-Sturmbannführer	Major
SS-Obersturmbannführer	Lieutenant-Colonel
SS-Standartenführer	Colonel
SS-Oberführer	Brigadier equivalent
SS-Brigadeführer	Major-General
SS-Gruppenführer	Lieutenant-General
SS-Obergruppenführer	General
SS-Oberstgruppenführer	Colonel-General (only Sepp Dietrich ever attained this rank)

APPENDIX D

Divisional Song 13th SS Mountain Division 'Handschar' (set to the tune of Bombs on England)

'Into Battle with a Song'

A song is in the air, the entire earth is shaking,
Columns of SS men march in step,
SS men wave the sacred banners,
SS men do everything for the people.

Give me your hand, dear Ivana,
Follow God now, follow God now, follow God now,
I shall defend, I shall defend, I shall defend my beloved
Homeland, homeland

SS men are heroes in battle
Show our homeland the way
Follow the road of our glorious grandfathers
Until tyranny falls, cursed and bitter

Let love burn in our hearts
And with a song let's enter battle
To liberate our beloved homeland
For which anyone would gladly sacrifice his life.

BIBLIOGRAPHY

Books

Ailsby, Christopher, *Hell on the Eastern Front: The Waffen-SS War in Russia 1941–1945*, Spellmount, 1998

Ailsby, Christopher, *Waffen-SS The Unpublished Photographs 1923–1945*, Bookmart, 2000

Bauer, Eddy, Lt. Col, *World War II*, Orbis, 1972

Benjamin, Marina, *Last Days in Babylon: The Story of the Jews of Baghdad*, Bloomsbury, 2007

Biddiscombe, Perry, *The SS Hunter Battalions, The Hidden History of the Nazi Resistance Movement 1944–45*, Tempus, 2006

Bishop, Chris, *Hitler's Foreign Divisions, Foreign Volunteers in the Waffen-SS 1940–1945*, Amber, 2005

Bishop, Chris, *The Military Atlas of World War II*, Amber, 2005

Bishop, Chris, *The Essential Vehicle Identification Guide – Waffen-SS Divisions 1939–45*, Amber, 2007

Blood, Philip. W, *Hitler's Bandit Hunters, The SS and the Nazi Occupation of Europe*, Potomac, 2006

Butler, Rupert, *The Black Angels*, Arrow, 1989

Butler, Rupert, *Legions of Death*, Hamlyn, 1983

Butler, Rupert, *Hitler's Jackals*, Leo Cooper, 1998

Carell, Paul, *Hitler's War on Russia, Volume 2, Scorched Earth*, Corgi, 1971 (translated by Ewald Oser)

Davies, Norman, *Rising '44 The Battle for Warsaw*, Pan, 2004

Felmy, Hellmuth (General der Flieger – Luftwaffe General) and Warlimont, Walter (General der Artillerie- General of Artillery), *German Exploitation of Arab Nationalist Movements in World War II*, Hailer, 2007

Graber, G. S., *History of the SS*, Diamond, 1994

Hausser, Paul, *Wenn Alle Brüder Schweigen – Grosser Bildband über die Waffen-SS (When all our brothers are silent)*, Nation Europa, 1973

Hildinger, Erik, *Warriors of the Steppe, A military history of central Asia*, Spellmount, 1997

Kaltenegger, Roland, *Mountain Troops of the Waffen-SS 1941–1945*, Schiffer, 1995

Landwehr, Richard, *Italian Volunteers of the Waffen-SS, 24.Waffen-Gebirgs-(Karstjäger) Division der SS and 29.Waffen-Grenadier-Division der SS (italienische Nr.1)*, Siegrunen, 1987

Lepre, George, *Himmler's Bosnian Division, The Waffen-SS Handschar Division 1943–1945*, Schiffer, 1997

Littlejohn, David, *The Patriotic Traitors: A History of Collaboration in German-Occupied Europe 1940/1945*, William Heinemann, 1972

Littlejohn, David, *Foreign Legions of the Third Reich Volume 3*, R. James Bender, 1985

Littlejohn, David, *Foreign Legions of the Third Reich Volume 4*, R. James Bender, 1987

Lucas, James, *Hitler's Mountain Troops, Fighting at the Extremes*, Cassell, 1992

MacLean, French L, *The Cruel Hunters, SS-Sonderkommando Dirlewanger*, Schiffer, 1998

Paice, Edward, *Tip and Run – The Untold Tragedy of the Great War in Africa*, Weidenfeld and Nicolson, 2007

Pencz, Rudolf, *For the Homeland! The History of the 31st Waffen-SS Volunteer Grenadier Division*, Helion, 2002

Quarrie, Bruce, *Hitler's Samurai*, Patrick Stephens, 1983

Reitlinger, Gerald, *The SS: Alibi of a Nation, 1939–1945*, Heinemann, 1956

Stein, George H., *Hitler's Elite Guard at War 1939–1945*, Cornell University Press, 1966

Taylor, Brian, *Barbarossa to Berlin Volume Two: The Defeat of Germany, 19 November 1942 to 15 May 1945*, Spellmount, 2004

Ure, John, *The Cossacks*, Constable, 1999

Williamson, Gordon, *The Blood Soaked Soil*, Blitz Editions, 1997

Williamson, Gordon, *The SS: Hitler's Instrument of Terror*, Sidgwick & Jackson, 1994

Williamson, Gordon, *The Waffen-SS – 11. to 23. Divisions*, Osprey Men-at-Arms series, 2004

Williamson, Gordon, *The Waffen-SS – 24. to 38. Divisions, & Volunteer Legions*, Osprey Men-at-Arms series, 2004

Periodicals and Articles

Küntzel, Dr Matthias, 'Hitler's Legacy: Islamic anti-Semitism in the Middle East', *Jewish Political Studies Review*, 2005

Landwehr, Richard, 'The European Volunteer Movement of World War II', *Journal of Historical Review*

Landwehr, Richard, 'Siegrunen', Volume 41

Pearson, Stuart, 'The Devils Shadow – A WW II Article'

Websites

www.axis101.bizland.com
www.axishistory.com
www.ehistory.freeservers.com
www.fantompowa.net
www.feldgrau.com
www.feldpost.tv / forum
www.germanwarmachine.com
www.gutenberg-e.org
www.histclo.com
www.serbianna.com
www.srpska-mreza.com

Index